Blue Trust

The Author, the Lawyer, His Wife, and Her Money

Stevie Cameron

Research Associate
Rod Macdonell

SEAL BOOKS

BLUE TRUST
Seal Books/Published by arrangement with Macfarlane Walter & Ross
Originally published in hardcover by Macfarlane Walter & Ross in 1998
Seal Books edition November 1999
For information: Seal Books, 105 Bond Street,
Toronto, Ontario M5B 1Y3

ISBN 0-7704-2844-4

Seal Books are published by Doubleday Canada, a division of Random House of Canada Limited.
"Seal Books" and the portrayal of a seal are the property of Random House of Canada Limited,
105 Bond Street, Toronto, Ontario M5B 1Y3, Canada.

Cover photograph: Naoki Okamoto/Masterfile
Cover design: Janine Laporte

PRINTED AND BOUND IN CANADA

TRANS 10 9 8 7 6 5 4 3 2 1

Praise for Stevie Cameron:

"The finest investigative reporter in the land."
Allan Fotheringham, *Maclean's*

Critical Acclaim for *Blue Trust*:

"The whole thing is just delicious. It's the kind of story that makes you want to turn immediately to the last page, to see what happens."
Calgary Herald

"Cameron's storytelling is excellent, with characters and events introduced early on and a climax that pays off later . . . this true-life tale is thrilling and tragic."
The Gazette (Montreal)

"Cameron has produced a compelling page-turner. . . . It's titillating entertainment delivered through strong storytelling."
The Edmonton Journal

Critical Acclaim for *On the Take*:

"Remarkable and valuable . . . Conservatives who read this book will weep for their party. Other Canadians will just weep for their country."
Clark Davey, *Globe and Mail*

"A major contribution to Canadian politics and to Canadian journalism."
Richard Gwyn, *Toronto Star*

"A cornucopia of revealing information . . . a precious look at what happens behind the scenes in the corridors of power."
The Gazette (Montreal)

"Every decent citizen left in this country ought to buy or borrow this book and read it cover to cover."
Brian Fawcett, *Books in Canada*

Also by Stevie Cameron

On the Take: Crime, Corruption and Greed in the Mulroney Years

For my mother
Eleanor Robin Bone Dahl
1915–1997

Contents

Preface

In August 1994, just as my book *On the Take: Crime, Corruption and Greed in the Mulroney Years* was going to the printers, I learned something of the tragic story of Bruce Verchere. Because deadlines were long past, there wasn't time to insert more than a few last-minute details about Brian Mulroney's tax lawyer into that book, but I knew then that Verchere's story could make a book on its own.

I asked my friend Rod Macdonell, the veteran investigative reporter at the Montreal *Gazette* who helped me with *On the Take*, to come on board again. Rod not only has a law degree himself and understands the Quebec legal system, he's also bilingual. Where I would struggle through a legal file in French, he'd glance at it and point out the important nuances. This book would not have been the same without his help, his endless patience, and his wonderful sense of humour.

Blue Trust began as a story about money and politics, but over the last four years, it has evolved into something quite different: a story about life in the fast lane in the 1980s, about the kind of people who keep their money in offshore banks, about celebrity, entrepreneurship, and the law. Most of all it's a story about the marriage between Bruce Verchere, a charismatic tax lawyer, and his wife, Lynne Walters Verchere, a brilliant computer software developer.

I am deeply indebted to the many relatives, friends, and business colleagues of both Vercheres who spent countless hours with me and with Rod to make sure we got the story right. No one in this group was more important than Arthur Hailey. I want to thank him, his wife, Sheila, and their family for their indispensable help, as well as June Callwood, who introduced us. In 1997, Joan Crockatt, then managing editor of the *Calgary Herald*, invited Hailey to visit Calgary and write several guest columns; these were helpful to understanding the Haileys' background. I also wish to thank Toronto writer Jack Batten, another lawyer and the author of a 1997 official history of the Calgary-based law firm Bennett Jones Verchere, who generously shared his research with me.

Although several people spoke on condition of anonymity, only one character in the book has been disguised. Martha O'Brien is a pseudonym, and I have changed details of her whereabouts and her livelihood.

I want to thank my agent, Linda McKnight, and her team at Westwood Creative Artists for their many kindnesses. As always, my publisher, Jan Walter, and her partners, John Macfarlane and Gary Ross, were thoughtful and patient. I owe Gary a great debt of gratitude for his enthusiasm, tact, and insight. Once again, Barbara Czarnecki smoothed the manuscript with her final edit. No writer could have wiser legal counsel than I receive from Peter Jacobsen. I also want to thank the rest of the group at Macfarlane Walter & Ross, especially Paul Woods and Rosmarie Gadzovski.

At *Elm Street*, I'm grateful for the generosity and encouragement of my publisher, Lilia Lozinski, and of the president of our company, Greg Macneil. Everyone at the magazine, especially Jen Robson, Neil Morton, Dianne de Fenoyl de Gayardon, Gwen Smith, Martha Weaver, and Heather McArdle, helped in countless ways to let me finish the manuscript.

On a personal note, my daughters, Tassie and Amy, offer me unconditional support. As for David, nothing is possible without him.

Prologue

A PERFECT SATURDAY MORNING, late August in Montreal, the city waking slowly as the sun burns the dew off the carefully tended lawns. Here and there the tips of maple trees have started to turn gold, but the shady streets of Westmount are still banked by deep borders of green shrubs and mature trees. A second late bloom of roses brightens many of the deep perennial beds; dahlias and chrysanthemums and hydrangeas are in their glory. People walking their dogs in Murray Hill Park stop to rest on benches with their newspapers or to chat with neighbours. Many of the huge old houses on Montrose Avenue near the park are still empty, their owners enjoying the last summer weekend in the country. People who are at home have thrown open the windows to catch the breezes.

A young bride, preparing for her wedding at her sister's grand Montrose Avenue house, looks out the window with relief; the weather is perfect. Happily she spreads all her beautiful new things on the bed and begins to dress. Her sister, a family doctor, and her brother-in-law, a respirologist, haven't lived here long; they have just bought the house and are proud to be able to offer it for the photo session. They have opened their windows, too, and look out with pleasure. A beautiful day for a wedding, they agree, but better hurry, it's late. The cars will be arriving soon to take them to the church.

A few minutes later the respirologist, Pierre Grégoire, pauses a moment and turns to the window. What was that noise? It almost sounded like a scream. Yes! My God, someone was screaming. The dog walkers in the park across the street have heard it, too.

Grégoire waits, almost afraid to breathe; then he hears the screaming clearly, and so does his wife. It is coming from next door. Stunned, they look at one another in horror and confusion. This is Westmount. You don't intrude. Frozen in indecision, they hear faint, urgent wails that grow louder. Sirens. Then lights, flashing, as police cars and an ambulance and even a fire truck hurtle down the street and screech to a stop in front of the house next door, where anguished cries and shouts are spilling clearly out of the open windows.

As knots of anxious neighbours gather on the street, the Grégoires tell the bride that something has happened; absorbed in her preparations, she hasn't heard a thing. They explain a little of the bad history between their house and the house next door, the Vercheres' house, now crowded with policemen and ambulance attendants. The people there, they tell her, didn't get along with the former owners of our house and aren't particularly friendly, but let's pray nothing bad has happened. All the Grégoires know is that the man is an important tax lawyer and his wife a successful businesswoman. They have two nice sons in their early twenties. Could they all be in the house now? They've seen three young men living there the past few days, but they have no idea who the third one is.

For the next hour, no one knows what has happened. Preoccupied with their own activities, the Grégoires have time only to look out the windows now and then.

More policemen have arrived. By now, everything is quiet, despite the bustle of activity. By the time the wedding party leaves for the church, the street is clear enough to allow their cars to glide easily past the police vehicles. The ambulance is still parked in front of the Vercheres' house.

Looking back out the window of his car, Pierre Grégoire notices ambulance attendants leaving the house, carrying a loaded stretcher. Oh my God, he whispers to himself. Someone's dead.

ONE
Almost Paradise

April 25, 1969

Mr. Bruce Verchere
Stikeman, Elliott, Tamaki, Mercier & Robb
1155 Dorchester Blvd. W.
Montreal 102, Canada

Dear Mr. Verchere,
My friend and fellow-investor Jack Brown has, I understand, arranged for me to consult with you on May 3, an occasion I am looking forward to with much interest. Jack has asked that in advance of our meeting I send you some tax returns and financial statements . . .

ARTHUR HAILEY paused in the dictation which his secretary would transcribe and gazed out of his study window, high above the vineyards of California's wine country, the Napa Valley. This was an important letter, perhaps with implications for his family's future, and he wanted to strike just the right note. Corresponding with a stranger is different than writing to a friend or family member, and Hailey put considerable thought into how, exactly, to express himself.

Brown, at the time, was a financial advisor to Hailey, and both were investors in real estate and in a fledgling

Canadian electronics company, which subsequently failed. Brown was aware that Hailey had tax problems, which was why he had recommended Bruce Verchere.

On the face of it, life couldn't have been sweeter for Arthur Hailey in 1969. At age forty-nine, living in St. Helena, a small Napa Valley town, with his wife, Sheila, and their three children, he was earning hundreds of thousands a year as a writer. He was hot, he was in demand, the Hollywood dealmakers were calling; he could hardly believe his good fortune.

After years of writing popular television plays, then switching to novels, he had seen two of his books — *Hotel* and *Airport* — suddenly hit multimillion circulation numbers all around the world. The result was a Niagara of earnings committed to come in during the following two years. It was a fine life and, until he sat through a difficult meeting with his accountant, Hailey had every expectation it would last.

The news from Fred Howarth, Hailey's accountant, in the fall of 1969 was surprising and unpleasant: according to his calculations, Hailey could expect to earn $1 million in 1970, and to pay $700,000 of it in taxes. Hailey was stunned. How could he possibly have to pay nearly three-quarters of his income in taxes? He'd never been a feckless artist. The money had been too hard won, and from the start he'd always been prudent and businesslike. Creating a successful book was not like building a widget factory that automatically continues turning out widgets and producing profits. Hailey knew that, though fortune was smiling on him for the moment, there was no guarantee of how long it would last or if it would happen again. There was no way, he vowed to himself, he would pay the Internal Revenue Service $700,000. And once Arthur Hailey dug in his heels about something, he usually had his way. Stubborn was hardly the word for this man. Hailey had grown up poor, and his success had been the result of hard work, driving ambition, and careful planning. He didn't want to cheat the IRS or the Canadian government, he just wanted to keep his money, and keep it legally.

Born in Luton, England, in 1920, he was the son of George Hailey, a factory storekeeper, and his wife, Elsie, who had left school when she was twelve to work as a maid. She'd originally been engaged to George's brother, but Arthur was killed in the war; George, who had made it back safely from the trenches, began to court her. When he proposed she accepted him, and they named their son after her first love.

In her own 1978 autobiography, *I Married a Bestseller*, Sheila Hailey described her husband's austere childhood; his house, she wrote, "had two tiny bedrooms upstairs and two rooms and a cold water scullery downstairs, and an outside toilet in a pocket-size backyard." Just like her own childhood home. "I guess you'd call us a poor family," added Arthur, "but I never knew, through my childhood, any deprivation, and never went hungry, and was always loved, and taken care of by my parents."

In those days free education in Britain ended when children reached the age of fourteen, and to their sorrow, George and Elsie couldn't afford to send their son on to a high school after he finished elementary school. Anything past that level meant paying fees, and they didn't have the money. Keen to go on to the local grammar school, Hailey, a passionate reader who was already writing short stories and had learned typing and shorthand, tried for the one scholarship it offered; he came in second. "There have been very few sad days in my life," he recalled, "but when my schooling finished, that was one."

He found a job as an office boy. His ambition was to become a newspaper reporter, but when he asked about this he discovered, to his chagrin, that it was not possible without a high school education. Then, when he tried to join the Royal Air Force in September 1939, just before the war started and at a time when the RAF needed pilots desperately, he learned again that he didn't have the necessary level of education. "Swallowing my disappointment," Hailey later wrote in a memoir for the *Calgary Herald*, "I enlisted anyway and served on RAF ground staff, moving upward to the rank of corporal. Then, in 1941, everything changed. Suddenly, the critical need for pilots slashed the barriers. Former rejects like me were reconsidered and . . . wonder of wonders . . . I was in."

The RAF sent him to a British Commonwealth air base in Calgary to learn to fly. By 1941 Britain, which had lost hundreds of young pilots in the Battle of Britain and in its air raids over Germany, had become part of the new Commonwealth Air Training Scheme. Canada played a major role in the training program, providing bases and equipment to train air crews for the RAF and the RCAF. Both the Calgary airport and the nearby facility at De Winton became RAF bases and Hailey found himself assigned to pilot training, first in De Winton, then in Calgary, and finally in Swift Current, Saskatchewan. In De Winton he trained on small de Havilland biplanes, and soon he graduated to larger Airspeed Oxfords in Calgary. A more interesting part of his education also took place in

Calgary. It was there that he survived a severe case of mumps, an illness surrounded with scare stories which had frightened him into believing he would be not only sterile but impotent. Mumps, he was told, "could mean the end of the line for you sexually. Period." Fortunately for young Hailey, who was only twenty-two at the time, he got lucky: not long after he recovered, he had, as he described it in his seventies, his "first sexual experience on a glorious sunny afternoon in Calgary, on a grassy slope beneath a tree, and within sight of the Elbow River. To this day it remains a beautiful memory."

By the time he finished his training in Swift Current, he was a qualified pilot, and he went on to flying assignments in Nova Scotia and western Canada, even though, at the beginning of his career, he had a tendency to throw up during flights which nearly grounded him. In 1943 he was promoted to the rank of sergeant-pilot and a few months later won a commission as a pilot officer. That was another turning point in his life. "When I entered the Officer's Mess, I encountered a new world. From then on no one ever asked what my education was or where I went to school. It was assumed because I was an officer, I was an educated person." It helped to ease the sting he'd felt back in Britain in 1940 when his boss, a wing commander who was the station administration officer, was angry about a mix-up in a letter Corporal Hailey had sent out. "Yes, Hailey," he'd scolded, "you're clever, all right . . . but in *a night-school* sort of way."

In 1944, on a trip to Chicago, Hailey met Joan Fishwick, a young woman working at the British consulate there; after a few months' courtship by mail, they were married on June 23, 1944, in Prince Edward Island, where

Hailey was stationed at the time. After he served in Europe, the RAF sent him to the Middle East, where he flew Beaufighters, and then to the Far East, where he was flying transport aircraft over India.

When the war ended Hailey was transferred back to England and settled comfortably with Joan into a new house in a Surrey suburb with their first child, Roger, born in 1946. Arthur commuted by train to London to an RAF staff officer's job at the Air Ministry in Whitehall, just a few blocks, he discovered much later, from Sheila, who was working for the British publisher George G. Harrap and Co. — but they never met. During these years, Hailey, who was the founding editor of an RAF training magazine called *Air Clues*, continued writing short stories and poetry in his spare time as he had done throughout the war. During the war he'd had a short story, "Rip Cord," published in an American glossy magazine called *Courier*; now he began freelancing and was able to sell a funny piece based on real military memos to Punch. But postwar England was a grim place, despite the fact that he was doing well at work and earning a good income for those times. Hailey had liked the life he'd seen in Canada.

In 1947 he and Joan emigrated, settling in Toronto, where there were more job opportunities; after a few months selling real estate, he found work with Maclean Hunter Publishers. Although Maclean Hunter has always been best known as the publisher of such magazines as *Maclean's* and *Chatelaine*, for decades it has also published dozens of small trade magazines where many Canadian journalists have got their start. To this day when young reporters, despondent about their failures to win jobs at big city dailies such as the *Globe and Mail* and the *Toronto Star*, are encouraged to apply to these trade magazines, they are whipped on by the same promise: "After all, that's where Arthur Hailey started."

At twenty-seven, Hailey put his foot on the journalism ladder as an assistant editor on *Bus & Truck Transport*, and in almost no time, it seemed, he and Joan were raising three sons and managing a mortgage on their new four-room bungalow. By 1949 he'd been promoted to editor. But over this time, his marriage was collapsing. He and his wife, as he put it, "had just drifted apart." They separated and she returned to her family in Chicago.

"I was doing my best to get on with my life when I met Sheila," remembered Hailey. Sheila Dunlop, who had emigrated from England in 1949, was twenty-one when they met through the Maclean Hunter steno pool — Hailey wasn't important enough to rate a secretary. As Sheila transcribed his precise and clear dictation — without any direct contact with the person she was hearing — she fell in love with his voice; the reality, when she finally met the man she'd been daydreaming about, was a shock: "He was overweight and glum," she recalled. He had, she added cheerfully, "a moon face, a big mouth, and big teeth. He had a penchant for light, spivvy suits. I thought his taste was atrocious."

Despite his lack of appeal, Sheila continued to see Arthur. Both were doing well at work; she had been elevated from the steno pool and was employed as a writer on the company's lifestyle publications. She wound up as an associate editor on *Canadian Homes & Gardens* and the twice-yearly *Brides' Book*. She finally admitted she loved this man who made her laugh, who came from the same background, who had the same ambitions and passion for words. On July 28, 1951, they were married.

The next year, while automatically retaining their British citizenships, they became Canadian citizens. Hailey was hard-headed enough to know the value of a good job but still chafed at the day-to-day commitment of editing a business magazine when what he really wanted to do was write fiction full-time. He just couldn't figure out how to pay for it. Both he and Sheila freelanced at night until they were doing well enough for her to quit and start producing, as a private business, six company newsletters from their home. In 1953 he left Maclean Hunter to become the sales promotion manager for an American company that manufactured commercial trailers, but once again it was not what he yearned to do. He knew he was a storyteller and he knew he wanted to write novels and plays. He couldn't stand the idea of a lifetime writing advertising copy and company brochures.

His chance came suddenly. In 1955, he was flying home from a business trip to Vancouver on a four-engine Trans-Canada Airlines plane, a DC-4B, described by Hailey as "probably the noisiest airplane which ever flew, and impossible to go to sleep in as a passenger." Because he couldn't sleep, Hailey started wondering what would happen if the pilot and the co-pilot became ill with food poisoning, say, and weren't able to fly the plane. And what would happen if the only person who knew how to fly a plane was someone like himself, a World War II veteran, long past his prime as a pilot? This is a good idea, he thought. I'm going to try it.

Over the following ten days, writing through two weekends and five nights, he developed a play he thought could work on television and mailed it to "Script Department, Canadian Broadcasting Corp." The first important person to read it was Nathan Cohen — later to become the *Toronto Star*'s theatre critic, famous for his tough reviews — who was then script editor of CBC's *General Motors Theatre*. The only reason he paid any attention to Hailey's script, as it lay there with countless other unsolicited manuscripts, was that it stuck out like a sore thumb: it was written in three acts, for the theatre, without any of the standard directions for cameras.

Cohen liked it, authorized a fee of $600, and turned the script over to the legendary Sidney Newman, the brash, tough-talking executive producer of *GM Presents*, one of the CBC's two prestigious weekly drama series. (The other was the high-toned *CBC Festival*.) Flight into Danger was broadcast nationally on April 7, 1956, to enthusiastic reviews. Furthermore, the viewers loved it and the word got out about this exciting new writer. Soon afterwards, the play was broadcast in the United States and in Britain, and once again the response was extraordinary.

On Sheila's urging — "Let's take a chance," she said, "and do what you've always wanted!" — Hailey quit his day job, turned to freelance writing full-time, and learned the sweet art of recycling one work into a number of profitable vehicles. In 1957 Paramount hired him to rewrite *Flight into Danger* into a screenplay for a movie called *Zero Hour*. In 1958, working with two co-authors, Ronald Payne and John Garrod (who took the joint pseudonym "John Castle"), Hailey published it with London's Souvenir Press, under the original name, *Flight into Danger*. A year later Doubleday published the book in North America, under yet another title, *Runway Zero Eight*. In England, in the United States, whatever the title, it sold well, and it was eventually published in twenty-three countries and eighteen languages.

Even when he was retooling his story of the rusty and nervous World War II pilot, Hailey was busy on other projects; in 1957 he'd produced a television play, *No Deadly Medicine*, which he turned into another Doubleday novel, *The Final Diagnosis*, which was, in turn, transformed into another Hollywood movie, *The Young Doctors*, by United Artists in 1961. In the middle of these projects, he was working on an anthology of television plays, which Doubleday published in 1960 under the title *Close-up on Writing for Television*. In 1962 his play *Course for Collision* was produced for television and his newest novel, *In High Places*, was published.

Add it all up and you have a man who, between 1956 and 1962, had written twenty television dramas produced by such programs as *Westinghouse Studio One*, *Playhouse 90*, and *Kraft Theatre*, and three bestselling novels which had all been translated into several languages and were selling well around the world.

Along with the commercial success came honours from his peers; in 1956 he received the Gold Medal of the Canadian Council of Authors and Artists; in both 1957 and 1958 he won the award for best Canadian playwright, as well as an Emmy nomination in 1957 for *No Deadly Medicine*. In 1962 *In High Places* won the Doubleday Canadian Prize Novel Award. Hailey was rapidly becoming a familiar name worldwide, but what was more important to the creation of his fortune was the reputation he'd built among book publishers and movie producers for reliably delivering the kinds of stories the public wanted.

This was when he began the system of exhaustive research and notetaking that became almost as famous as the books themselves, a system he continued to apply not just to his novels but also to his personal life and his personal correspondence. Hailey's 1965 breakthrough novel, *Hotel*, was a perfect example of his writing methods.

First he developed a systematic timetable: for each novel he'd spend a full year on his research; six months reviewing his notes, planning, and writing an outline; and eighteen months actually writing the book. When he made up his mind to write *Hotel*, he read books about hotels and about New Orleans, the city that provided the locale for the book. Reading, of course, wasn't enough; he stayed at a hotel in New Orleans for several weeks, examined several other large hotels, including Toronto's Royal York, and looked at many more smaller ones. Aside from immersing himself in a business and, in the case of *Hotel*, in a city, Hailey also spent many long days interviewing people inside the business. He seldom took notes or used a tape recorder; he would either dictate notes into a tape recorder immediately after the interview or write up a meticulous summary of everything anyone said to him, and his analysis of that conversation. He kept a detailed daily diary of events, impressions of people, snatches of conversation in person or on the telephone, and meals he'd eaten — and with whom. For many years, when he was working on a novel he rarely completed more than 600 words a day, editing as he went so he wouldn't have to go back and rewrite it all. In recent years he wrote on a computer, and his production went up to about 1,000 words a day.

Hotel was a huge hit and it wasn't long before he began negotiating through an agent with producers who wanted to make it into a movie. In the meantime, he'd started the work on *Airport*. One of his research trips, in the summer of 1965, took him to Los Angeles. Doubleday's editor-in-chief, Ken McCormick, suggested he get in touch with an old friend of his, Alexis Klotz, a retired TWA pilot living near San Francisco, who might be some help. It turned out that Klotz was living in St. Helena in the Napa Valley, about 65 miles northeast of San Francisco. As soon as Hailey saw the area, he knew this was where he wanted to live. He was weary of Toronto winters, of snow and cold and slush and galoshes. He wanted to live someplace warm, and the Napa Valley was perfect.

Sheila was still in Canada, spending a vacation with the kids at their cottage at Kennisis Lake, in Haliburton, north of Toronto. On a shopping trip to the local marina's grocery store, she found a telegram waiting for her:

> NAPA VALLEY IS A FEW FEET THIS SIDE OF PARADISE. IT IS EVERYTHING WE HAVE EVER DREAMED ABOUT AND LOVE. CLIMATE SUPERB. SPRING IN FEBRUARY. ALL YEAR OUTDOOR COUNTRY LIVING COMBINED WITH CITY CLOSENESS. LOCAL SCHOOLS EXCELLENT. SAN FRANCISCO ONE HOUR DRIVE. TODAY I BOUGHT A HALF ACRE IN MEADOWWOOD DEVELOPMENT ON GLORIOUS HILLSIDE OVERLOOKING VALLEY AND MOUNTAINS. ALEXIS AND PEGGY KLOTZ EXPECTING YOU EARLY SEPTEMBER TO BEGIN PLANNING OUR FUTURE HOME.
>
> LOVE. ARTHUR

Although her first reaction was, "Oh, to hell with him!" Sheila finally went along with it. Six months later she moved down to California with the children in time for Christmas; ten months later they all moved into a brand-new house on the "glorious hillside." Although they had U.S. green cards allowing them to live and work there, the Haileys kept their Canadian citizenships, thinking they would probably be returning to Toronto before long.

In 1967 United Artists released the movie version of *Hotel*. A year after that, *Airport* was published and was, Sheila recalled, "successful beyond our wildest dreams." By 1969 it too had been made into a movie. Now the only real problem the Haileys faced was money: too much of it, all coming in at once. Hailey suspected that a tricky tax situation was looming. The meeting with his lawyer and accountant suggested it was more like a tax nightmare. When his friend Jack Brown suggested he contact a lawyer in Montreal named Bruce Verchere, a tax specialist at Stikeman Elliott, Hailey didn't hesitate. He dictated a letter to his secretary, Ruth Hunter, to be sent to Verchere right away.

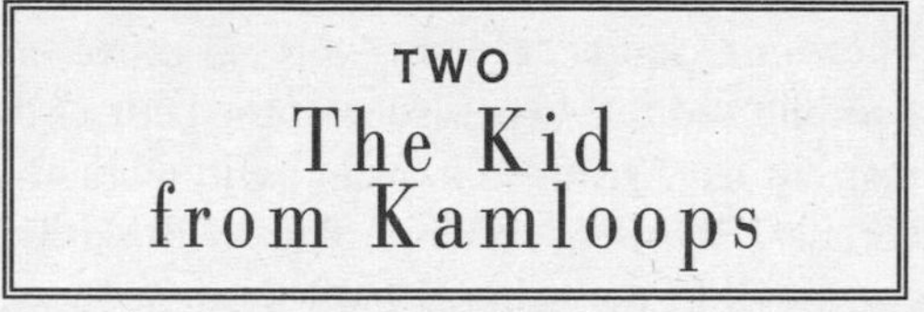

TWO
The Kid from Kamloops

WHEN BRUCE VERCHERE read Arthur Hailey's letter, he was thrilled at the prospect of landing such a high-profile client. Only thirty-three at the time, and an associate at Montreal's Stikeman, Elliott, Tamaki, Mercier & Robb, Verchere had been at the firm just two years but had already earned a reputation as a creative man to see about tax problems. Bringing in Hailey, an international celebrity, would be a coup. It wasn't that the fees Stikeman's could charge him would make a great difference to the firm, which generated most of its income from big corporate clients; it was that his celebrity status brought cachet. The senior partners, Verchere knew, men like Heward Stikeman, would take notice; the partnership he craved would be in the bag.

As solicitor and client, he imagined, he and Hailey would be a good fit. Hailey needed a smart tax lawyer, and Verchere was familiar with offshore banks and clever about setting up complicated corporate mazes to shield ownership and beneficial relationships from prying eyes — whether they belonged to government tax snoops, angry creditors, or aggrieved spouses. The more intricate his mazes, the better he liked them. "He absolutely loved doing this," said a Swiss banker who did business with him for many years. One of Verchere's former law partners made the same point. "He was very secretive, and the more complicated the structure was, the better," said the Montreal lawyer Arthur Campeau, who worked briefly with Verchere in 1983. "I came first in the income tax course at McGill Law School, and I thought I was pretty good. But Bruce was in another league altogether."

Verchere was born in Vancouver on September 22, 1936, but grew up in Kamloops, a raw little city in the B.C. interior, where his father practised law at Fulton, Rogers, Kelly, Reilly, Dohm & Hunter, a firm with strong ties to the federal Conservative Party. When he looked back on his early childhood, though, Verchere thought not of his father, David, who went off to war in 1939, but of his mother, Kitty, who brought him up while his dad was overseas. He cherished the memory of the long train trip they took, when he was four, to Halifax to visit his father, who had only a two-week leave, not enough time to get back to B.C.

After his father returned home, they became close; people often commented on how alike they were. David Verchere believed in living for the day, living well, enjoying himself; that, he taught his only child, was what life was all about. Kitty accepted his philosophy, although she was less happy-go-lucky. Still, they were among Kamloops's leading citizens and could afford to indulge themselves.

Fulton Rogers's best-known partner was the Honourable Edmund Davie Fulton, a Rhodes Scholar, the son of a provincial cabinet minister, grandson of one B.C. premier, and great-nephew of another. Fulton himself served as a cabinet minister in John Diefenbaker's Conservative government between 1957 and 1962 before becoming head of the provincial Tory party and, later, a justice of the Supreme Court of British Columbia. His was as blue as blood gets in B.C., and his firm was one of the best known in the province.

When David Verchere won a coveted appointment to the British Columbia Supreme Court, he didn't need to feel any deference towards Vancouver's private-school boys, who swaggered through the big law firms on Howe Street. And when Bruce arrived at the University of British Columbia as a freshman in 1957, everyone knew he was a judge's son. ("He behaved," said one of his friends, "like a judge's son.") There was no small-town chip on this young man's shoulder.

In those years, UBC was a big village, isolated from downtown Vancouver by its splendid perch at the end of Point Grey. Although students in the arts programs might not know many people in the professional faculties such as engineering, architecture, forestry, or music, they tended to know each other, if only vaguely. In those years there were distinct pecking orders. The athletes, the golden boys who rowed on Olympic teams, were at the top of the heap; Roger Jackson and George Hungerford, Olympic gold medallists in 1964, were two famous members of this group. Jackson became a leading figure in amateur sport, and Hungerford practised law in Vancouver. Football and rugby players also ranked highly, and Frank Iacobucci, now a justice of the Supreme Court of Canada, was one of the best football players at the university. He came to know Verchere when they were at law school together.

There was also the gang that ran the Alma Mater Society, otherwise known as the student council; the best-known member during these years was Ross

Munro, who went on to a career in journalism in Canada and the U.S. There was the student newspaper crowd, people like Allan Fotheringham and Pat Carney in the 1950s, and later Michael Valpy, now of the *Globe and Mail*, who put out the campus paper, the *Ubyssey*. There were the gold medallists, the brainy ones who would go on to compete for Rhodes Scholarships; in those days the Rhodes went only to boys, and two successful UBC candidates were Ted Chamberlin and Stuart Robson, who went on to fine careers as university professors.

Then there was the social crowd. These were the sons and daughters of Vancouver's first families, families that tended to hunker down in Shaughnessy, the old-money enclave where mock-Tudor mansions sprawled across broad velvet lawns. (Exceptions were made for some young people from wealthy families in West Vancouver, from the University Endowment Lands, and from Kerrisdale, but admittance was almost impossible for those from Kitsilano or the far side of Oak Street.) Many of the boys had gone to St. George's, or to Shawnigan Lake School on Vancouver Island; the girls, to York House or Crofton House. If they'd gone to a public school, it was Magee or Prince of Wales, West Vancouver High or University Heights School. The girls bought their cashmere sweaters and tweed skirts at Edward Chapman, and their mothers chose their own clothes at Madame Rungé. They played tennis at the Vancouver Lawn Tennis Club, they summered at Qualicum or on Pasley Island, and they married in St. John's Anglican Church on South Granville. Many belonged to the campus Tory party, the Young Progressive Conservatives, or YPCs. When they left university, the boys hoped to be invited, some day, to join the Vancouver Club while the girls yearned for a membership in the Georgian Club.

While they were at UBC — very few of them in those days, despite their wealth, ever went to university in eastern Canada — they joined fraternities. (Girls joined "women's fraternities"; at that time, the word "sorority" was considered gauche.) By the late 1960s fraternities were out of favour, and they never recovered the status they once had. But in Verchere's day, they were important and ranked according to another ferocious pecking order.

The best ones, the ones the golden boys joined, were in large modern houses on Wesbrook Crescent, the campus's fraternity row. Here, side by side, were the suburban-looking Phi Delta Theta and Beta Theta Pi houses, the boxy Phi Gamma Delta house, the modern Zeta Psi house designed by leading Vancouver architect Ned Pratt, and, at the bottom of the street, another suburban-looking box which belonged to the Alpha Delta Phis. The Zetes had a reputation as upper-class drunks who wore vests, played poker all night long, flunked out, and went on to make millions in the stock market. The Betas — nicknamed "the milk drinkers" — were viewed as nice boys who became professors or diplomats. The Fijis were the all-rounders, the handsome ones, the good athletes; they had the best parties with the prettiest girls, and their annual "Grass Skirt" Hawaiian-theme party, held in a distant hall south of the U.S. border, was an infamous boozefest. The Phi Delts and the Alpha Delts were indistinguishable; they all seemed to be headed towards careers in law or business. It barely mattered which of these fraternities you joined;

during the fall Homecoming Week, drunken boys and girls lurched up and down the street from one house to another holding sticky glasses of hot rum, knowing they were among the Chosen.

Bruce Verchere belonged to none of these elites. Although he'd played a little basketball in high school and some touch football at university, he was no athlete. Nor was he interested in student newspapers or student council activities. He was not a scholar; nor, despite his charm, was he a member of the right crowd. He longed for a secure place among the Shaughnessy set, the private-school kids who partied along Wesbrook, but could manage only, in the peculiar courtship of second-year men and women called "rushing," a bid to join Delta Upsilon. That fraternity was based in a small house in West Point Grey, the pleasant no-man's-land beyond the university gates where tenured professors bought modest stucco homes on 33-foot lots. Each of the top women's fraternities — there were four or five of these among the nine housed in a special apartment building on campus — was required by the dean of women to take at least one unpopular girl during the fall rushing season, presumably to avoid a rash of suicides. The Darwinian brutality of the men's system bowed to no such regulations. Ruthless "dinging," the word used for the fraternities' blackball system of dropping undesirables, condemned the majority of hopefuls to the cluster of small fraternities housed outside the UBC gates.

Verchere had mixed emotions about his fraternity. He had few close friends and he was lonely in Vancouver; the fraternity house became his home. Here he palled around with two young men who were to remain close to him for the rest of their lives, Patrick Dohm and Royal Smith. Dohm, now associate chief justice of British Columbia, was another Kamloops boy; his uncle was also a partner at Fulton Rogers. He'd stayed an extra year in Kamloops to complete Grade 13; that meant he could begin his studies at UBC in second year. A little older than Verchere, he was also more prudent, and he took on the thankless task of nagging his friend to study more and party less. This miserable job lasted through their undergraduate days together and right through law school. Royal Smith, a boy from the prairies who became a millionaire developer, remembered that Verchere was one of the very few DU brothers who had a car. Verchere enjoyed the parties, the hijinks, the get-togethers. He and Smith went on hunting and camping trips together; Verchere loved the outdoors and as a boy in Kamloops had learned to hunt and handle guns. And he was loyal to his university gang. But it was his nature to want the best, and Delta Upsilon was not the best fraternity — not fashionable, not smart.

In the summer of 1958 Verchere got the idea of moving to the Fiji house on Wesbrook Crescent as house manager. Each Wesbrook fraternity house had several rooms for rent during term to members; during summer holidays they were glad to rent these rooms to anyone living on campus for a summer course, and each house needed a manager to handle rents, meals, laundry, and landscaping, and to keep the bar stocked.

"Bruce was a truly engaging guy and he was very sophisticated," remembered Warren Mitchell, a Fiji who stayed on in the fraternity house over the summers. "He came from out of town but he had a sense of sophistication that knocked my socks off. His stories had a real flair."

Flair was hardly the word for it. Verchere had a different story for each girl he dated, and his housemates watched his performances with awe. "In the evening we'd all be sitting in the living room by the fire," Mitchell said. "He'd have different girls in and he'd tell each one an entirely different story. He might tell one that he had sufficient money to live on because he'd been left money by his father. The next time he'd be telling someone else he had no money at all and that he'd been turned out of his family home without a penny and made all his money by himself."

"Why do you bother?" Mitchell would ask him. "Why create such wild fictions and new personae with each new date?" "No real reason," Verchere shrugged — except a chance to live that particular life for a night. He created and polished different characters for himself, slipping in and out of these skins as effortlessly as he put on a flannel dressing gown or a dinner jacket. "He was a chameleon," said Mitchell. "He was always trying on different personalities to see which would fit. As I watched him trying out these characters, I wasn't sure that he wasn't trying to figure out just who he was."

One year Royal Smith was dating a Vancouver girl who was living with a girl from the prairies, a girl Verchere started to date. The reason was simple: Smith's girlfriend's mother loved to cook, and she particularly liked cooking for her daughter's friends. "Bruce took out the other girl because then he could eat there," recalled Smith with a smile. "Bruce loved to eat, but he never got fat."

By the time Verchere returned to the Fiji house the following summer, he'd settled down with Carol Sloan, a popular member of Delta Gamma. Royal Smith's new girlfriend, Linda Gates, was also a DG, and the four young people enjoyed hanging around together. Smith became particularly fond of the skinny, engaging lad from Kamloops who loved camping and hunting; other young men who came to know him in law school also grew to like him enormously; one was Bill Britton, a law school classmate and later a professional football player with the B.C. Lions who would eventually become his law partner. Verchere was charismatic and easygoing. (Perhaps too easygoing; the Fijis finally fired him as summer house manager because he never mastered the art of laundry. A large pile of mildewed sheets was the last straw.)

Verchere's big problem in those days was poor marks. Pat Dohm began to fear that his friend was going to flunk out if he didn't do some work. "He entered law school after I did," remembered Dohm, "but he didn't pay close enough attention to his studies. I laid the wood to him. I took him under my wing." Verchere managed to graduate — although his marks were not outstanding — and in May 1963 he was called to the bar of B.C.

Verchere stayed in Vancouver while Warren Mitchell moved to Calgary; by the fall, however, the two were thrown together again. Each of them moved to Ottawa to join the federal Department of Justice; as they hoped, they were immediately sent over to the Sussex Drive offices of what was then called the Department of National Revenue, which assigned them to the western division. This meant a kind of circuit-court life; the two travelled together as litigators for the government in tax cases in cities such as Regina, Saskatoon, and Calgary. "We'd check into our hotel," said Mitchell, "and Bruce would put on a persona. Sometimes it was the gourmet eater persona, sometimes the greasy spoon persona. After about three days I'd say, 'I can't stand it. Cut it out.' And he'd laugh and stop it and be back to his old self. He had a good sense of humour and a sense of fun."

If there was one word people used to describe Verchere, it was "charming." Like his father, he believed that life was for living. But there was a ruthlessness in him that showed up early on. He dated Carol Sloan for four years; to everyone who knew them, they seemed very much in love. Carol was the calm, wise one; Bruce, the impetuous lover. Let's get married, he urged her before he left for Ottawa in the late summer of 1963. Not now, she told him. You need to grow up a little.

Carol Sloan paid a high price for her honesty. Three weeks after she turned Verchere down, he proposed to Lynne Walters, a young woman he'd just met. They were married a few months later, on December 27, 1963, at St. Mary's, Kerrisdale, an Anglican church. Royal Smith was Bruce's best man; Lynne chose her sister, Betty Ann Walters, as maid of honour. No one in Verchere's crowd had heard of Lynne Walters, but according to the gossip flying around the DU house they had met at a Conservative Party event. She was originally from Toronto, and her father was a bank manager for the Canadian Imperial Bank of Commerce in Vancouver, but because she hadn't gone to UBC — she was a University of Manitoba graduate — she might as well have come from the moon. Although she had pledged Gamma Phi Beta at Manitoba (a very good women's fraternity by UBC standards), she wasn't even an arts grad like most of the girls, or a home economist, or a nursing science student. She had a commerce degree and a job as a computer programmer.

Computers? In 1963 people barely knew what computers were, much less knew anyone who had studied them at university. But Lynne had landed a job at IBM, and not in the sales department — where so many young university graduates were going to sell the wonderful new coloured electric typewriters — but in the engineering labs, where IBM was developing computer systems. At UBC the computers were so primitive that junior staff in different buildings had to gather up boxes of stiff punched cards at the end of each day and walk them over to the administration building for sorting and entering in the university's clunky mainframe.

Carol, of course, was heartbroken. Bruce's friends were bewildered by his impulsive change of heart. And when they met Lynne, they were taken aback. "Pretty but flinty," was the way one man remembered her. "She was very attractive and men wanted to date her, but her relationships never lasted because she had the reputation of being . . . well, cool." She was slim and blonde with blue eyes, but unsophisticated and rather shy. It was not like Bruce to choose an unsophisticated bride, not after four years with one of UBC's golden girls. But she was ambitious and bright and full of potential. "Bruce saw himself as Pygmalion to her Galatea," said one of his friends. "He was going to mould this young woman into the classy wife he needed for his career."

What few of Bruce's friends knew was that Lynne was well ahead of them in many ways. Her father had been posted to Winnipeg by the bank at the time she started university. At the University of Manitoba she'd been active in student government, becoming the president of WAKONDA, the women's association, and a member of the student council executive. In 1961, after graduating from the commerce program (freshly redesigned by its new head, the Stanford-trained economist Ralph Harris, to encourage entrepreneurship), she'd made up her mind that her future lay in computers.

In those days, IBM was the obvious place to go, even if most of the professional women there were in sales and training. That's where she started, too — as a systems instructor, "responsible for teaching and development of IBM customer and staff courses," as her curriculum vitae put it. Few women made their way into the science and technology labs, but before long the company recognized her brilliance and trained her in computer systems design. They put her through their own courses in both hardware and software, and by 1963, when she married Bruce, she was a systems engineer "responsible for design, implementation and support for IBM computer systems." When she wanted to move to Ottawa with her new husband, IBM found a job for her there. According to a later profile in the *Financial Post*, she was soon "responsible for the design of IBM installations in such mammoth organizations as Domtar Ltd. and the Civil Service Commission."

For Verchere and the other university graduates joining the federal government in the early 1960s, life was great fun; the work was interesting and the opportunities, for anyone with ambition, seemed limitless. Verchere knew that a few years of slogging in the government tax offices would give him an advantage over his peers once he went into private practice. He was one of four young tax lawyers who joined the federal government that spring. The only one from Ontario was Bob Lindsay of Toronto, a

Dalhousie law graduate, who stayed in Ottawa — with a new tax analysis group set up by the federal government — long enough to become the main legislative draftsman of the massive 1971 changes in federal tax legislation. Lindsay went on to join the Toronto firm Osler Hoskin & Harcourt, where, in 1972, he began to build a group of tax lawyers that became the pre-eminent tax group in Canada. Warren Mitchell was the third; he later joined Pat Thorsteinsson, whose growing Vancouver firm became the only law firm in Canada to practise tax law exclusively. The fourth man in this group was Les Little, a Maritimer who also moved to Vancouver to practise with Thorsteinsson's firm and eventually became a director of the Canadian Tax Foundation and a director of the Bank of Canada. For the rest of their lives, their careers were to intersect.

Ottawa was something of a small town in those days; people got to know one another quickly. Best of all, this was a city where talent and hard work were what counted; money and pedigree and connections mattered less than they did in places like Vancouver. The high flyers in government seemed to be a bunch of brainy guys from small towns who'd gone to places like Queen's and the University of Manitoba and the University of Saskatchewan. With no night life to speak of and few cultural opportunities, people entertained in their homes and formed lifetime friendships.

Most young couples started out renting small walk-up apartments in old houses in the Glebe or Sandy Hill, but the Vercheres were different; they rented a handsome four-bedroom house in the Gatineau Hills, just north of the village of Larrimac. "They had nice furniture," recalled one friend, "and their china matched." They decorated their rented home in the style of the times — thick yellow shag rugs and white walls — and entertained elegantly. "This was all Bruce's plan for a perfect life," explained Warren Mitchell. "Now we're living in the Gatineau, now we'll do gourmet cooking, now we'll entertain."

The only time anyone got a hint that everything wasn't perfect in the Verchere household came when Verchere was out of town on a tax case. He didn't like the idea of his wife being alone in the country, so he taught her how to use a gun. Even then he was uneasy about leaving her, so he dreamed up a new way to keep her safe. To get ahead in Ottawa you had to speak French, and Verchere decided Lynne should learn it, too. Across the street from Revenue Canada's offices on Sussex Drive was a dormitory for young women run by the Grey Nuns, the French Catholic order that had supervised the education system for proper young French-Canadian girls in Ottawa for generations. While he was away, he thought, it would be the perfect place for Lynne to stay — so she could study French. Meekly, Lynne submitted to his scheme, but the night after he left she turned up at Warren and Doreen Mitchell's place, her clothes in her arms. "I can't stand it," she told them tearfully. "Let me stay with you until Bruce gets back."

Verchere's real problem about leaving his wife alone, said another friend, was that he was fiercely jealous. "Lynne and I were friends at the University of Manitoba," said the man, now a senior government bureaucrat. "We served on the students' council together. And when I ran into her in Ottawa I invited her to lunch. It was just to get caught up, but when Bruce found out, he was beside himself." The message was clear: tête-à-tête lunches with men — even old friends — were out.

Verchere discovered that he had a real gift for tax work, and after three years in Ottawa he felt he had enough experience to be valuable to a big law firm. In 1967 he accepted an offer from Stikeman Elliott in Montreal. For both Vercheres, leaving Ottawa was a nerve-racking adventure. It wasn't that they were sorry to leave; his time in government had been part of their career plan, one being followed by most of Verchere's colleagues at Revenue Canada. But all of them knew they were leaving the gentlemanly precincts of the civil service (as they were in those days) for corporate bear pits. With such good training from Revenue Canada, they felt confident, and all went on to careers at the top of their profession. "Well, there were the three of us — Mitchell, Little, and Verchere," Mitchell said. "And then there was Lindsay." And what he meant by this was simply that while the others were all Revenue Canada alumni who had done well, Lindsay had left Revenue Canada to become the country's leading tax lawyer. Many law firms courted the four young lawyers and, not surprisingly, Stikeman's was among them. But both Mitchell and Little wanted to go to Vancouver, while Lindsay found the team of lawyers at Osler's, in his home town, the most talented and congenial group he'd met, and he cast his lot in with them. The only one who finally decided to accept a position with Stikeman Elliott was Verchere. He was actually lucky to get the offer; of the four, Verchere would have had the most difficult time landing a good job simply because of his so-so marks at university, but he was able to overcome this handicap with his engaging personality.

LYNNE HAD HER OWN career concerns. In 1968 she and Bruce had a baby, David, and most lawyers' wives in those days were staying home, at least while the children were small. She and Bruce were about five years too old to catch the hippie, drop-out, smoke-up wave of the late 1960s; and the feminist revolution urged on by activists such as Betty Friedan and Germaine Greer was still in its infancy in Canada. Consciousness-raising women's groups in middle-class communities across the country were just beginning to meet in the late 1960s and didn't really become a movement until the 1970s, when *Chatelaine* editor Doris Anderson led the way with rousing "You can do it!" editorials promoting women's equality. Lynne was ahead of the trend, a Canadian pioneer in her field. There was never any doubt in her mind that she'd work, or that she'd succeed brilliantly. But that didn't mean she lacked the same desires as most women of her generation and background: she wanted a successful husband, she wanted a family, and she wanted to live graciously, in a big old house with Canadian art on the walls and fine furniture. A devout Anglican, she also wanted to make regular church-going a part of their lives. She loved her husband and wanted to be the kind of wife who helped his career. She also had her own interests and aspirations. She would just have to do it all at the same time.

It couldn't have been easy for them at first in Montreal — a young man from Kamloops, a town Montrealers had barely heard of, and his sweet-faced wife, a computer expert who'd done her degree at Manitoba. Once again, Verchere found himself an outsider in an old-guard community of bluebloods, only this time it was Westmount, not Shaughnessy. His last name seemed French, but as far as people could tell, he wasn't French. Who was he? No one had heard of his father, and few Montrealers knew or cared that Davie Fulton had been part of his father's firm.

In the late 1960s, even though French-Canadian nationalists were visible and active, Montreal was still fat and prosperous and run by the Westmount Anglos. Their sense of superiority was unassailable. Instead of summer places at Qualicum and Pasley Island, the Vercheres heard about family compounds in Murray Bay, Métis-sur-mer, and the Eastern Townships; instead of the Vancouver Lawn, Montreal's establishment played tennis at the Hillside; instead of St. George's and Shawnigan Lake, boys went to Selwyn House or Bishop's College School. The girls attended the Study or Miss Edgar's and Miss Cramp's instead of Crofton House or York House. Despite their social handicap, Bruce and Lynne were young, ambitious, and anxious to make a good impression. They might not have had the family connections, but they had talent and dreams and they were willing to work. They were a team, and nothing was going to stop them.

Stikeman Elliott was a good place to start. The firm was — and remains — one of Montreal's legal powerhouses. Founded by Heward Stikeman and his close friend Fraser Elliott in 1952, Stikeman's wasn't a big firm at the time, but it had attracted talented newcomers who were already making names for themselves; one was another UBC graduate, John Turner, who read law at Oxford as a Rhodes Scholar and joined Stikeman's in

1953. (He left a few years later when he was elected as a Liberal member of Parliament.) Another was Stanley Hartt, who was to become a major player in Toronto's business community in the 1990s after a stint as chief of staff in Prime Minister Brian Mulroney's office in Ottawa. There was also Sonny Gordon, who was close to the Bronfmans, and David Angus, another Mulroney friend, soon to become his chief fundraiser and later a senator.

Fraser Elliott, one of the firm's founding partners, was a man Verchere envied and admired. In 1917 Elliott's father had been appointed the first deputy minister of the new Department of National Revenue in Ottawa, so it was no accident that Stikeman Elliott had always kept an eye out for talented alumni from the department. After an education that included Queen's University, Osgoode Hall Law School, and a Harvard MBA, Elliott moved to Montreal in the 1950s to practise law, specializing in mergers and acquisitions. Business interested him as much as law, and with his senior role in the firm, he became involved with the high-tech conglomerate CAE Industries, eventually becoming its largest shareholder and chairman. Elliott also had interests outside law and business. One of them was art; among his closest friends in Montreal was the art dealer Walter Klinkhoff, who helped him put together a fine collection of Canadian art.

There was only one man at the firm Verchere truly revered, however, one man he patterned himself after, and that was Heward Stikeman. A Montrealer and McGill graduate, he too had started at Revenue Canada to learn more about tax law before moving into a Montreal firm as a tax specialist and then setting up his own shop. To Verchere, Stikeman wasn't just a successful tax lawyer, he was an intriguing gentleman with passions Verchere shared: he was a keen fisherman, he skied, he loved to cook and to eat well. He was a skilled pilot and used to fly his own Cessna to meetings; often he took Verchere with him. Under Stikeman's tutelage, Verchere became as keen a pilot as his mentor. He told friends how much he looked forward to the day when he too could afford his own plane.

Montreal in those days was irresistible. No city in Canada was more exciting. As host of the 1967 World's Fair, the city had created an international reputation as a sexy, vibrant place with a dynamic cultural community, a powerful business core, and a fascinating political scene. From its restaurants — the best in the country — to its cobblestoned streets and historic buildings, its shops and literary salons, it made most other Canadian cities feel like small towns. For Verchere, it was perfect; he had the Ottawa know-how, a beautiful wife, a good salary, and even a French name (although it was at least another twenty years before an *accent grave* appeared over the second e).

The city was also full of interesting, ambitious young men, and Verchere became good friends with another young lawyer on the rise — a labour lawyer named Brian Mulroney. They had in common a relationship to Davie Fulton, Verchere through his father's Kamloops law firm and Mulroney through federal politics. In December 1956, when Mulroney was only seventeen and an undergraduate at St. Francis Xavier University in Nova Scotia, he'd been in Ottawa as a youth delegate for the federal Conservatives' leadership convention. He'd made up his mind to support Fulton, rather than the Toronto corporate lawyer Donald Fleming, who seemed a dull fellow indeed, or John Diefenbaker, a charismatic criminal lawyer from Prince Albert, Saskatchewan. Just a few hours after he arrived in Ottawa, Mulroney saw which way the winds were blowing; Diefenbaker had captured the imagination of the delegates, so the teenage pol quickly hopped over to his camp. Once Diefenbaker had won the leadership, gone on to a massive election victory, and appointed Fulton the minister of justice, Mulroney made it his business to become Fulton's close friend and ally.

By the 1967 party leadership, when disillusioned Tories were meeting to dump Diefenbaker and choose a new leader, Mulroney was back in the Fulton fold. This time he stuck with his choice even when Robert Stanfield, former premier of Nova Scotia, entered the field at the last minute and won the leadership. Later Mulroney raised money to help Fulton pay off his campaign debts.

Mulroney and Verchere crossed paths in Montreal after Verchere started at Stikeman Elliott. Two years younger than Verchere, Mulroney was working for Howard, Cate, Ogilvy, one of the city's largest and most important firms, where he'd been since graduating from Laval Law School in 1964. (Now called Ogilvy Renault, the firm is once again home to Mulroney.) At Stikeman's, meanwhile, Verchere discovered that his colleague David Angus was one of Mulroney's closest friends and political allies. In 1976 Angus would set up a fund to raise money for Mulroney's run at the Conservative Party leadership. It was only natural that Verchere and Mulroney would get along. Not only were they lonely Conservatives in a town full of Grits, they were both small-town boys raised far from the boulevards of Westmount, sharp young lawyers who wanted to make good and liked to live well.

It didn't take Mulroney long to see that Verchere could be useful to him, and eventually he retained him as his personal tax lawyer.

More and more clients were hearing about Verchere's cleverness, and even as a junior he was gaining a reputation as a rainmaker, someone adept at drawing business to the firm. He intended to solidify that reputation when, on May 3, 1969, Arthur Hailey came to see him.

THREE

A Failed Coup

BY THE TIME the two men met in Montreal, Verchere had carefully studied the financial statements of earnings, expenses, taxes, and cash flow for 1968 and 1969 that Hailey had sent him. Hailey had also been putting in long hours with his Toronto accountant to make sure he was up to date on his present cash and tax positions.

Verchere wasted no time laying out his new client's situation; he told Hailey he was going to have to move. "I shall never forget his words," remembered Hailey. "'If you want any of those earnings left for your family and old age, get out of North America fast, and move to a tax haven.' Bruce named several places, including Malta, Sierra Leone, I believe, the Isle of Man, Bermuda, the Caymans, and the Bahamas." Hailey shook his head sadly. "Can't do it, I'm afraid," he told the engaging, well-dressed young lawyer. "It would be asking too much of my family. They love where we live. And there's the children's education."

Shaken and depressed, Hailey flew back to the Napa Valley to talk it over with his family. He dreaded the conversation. He adored his wife and was devoted to their children. During their dinner that evening, Diane, who was only eleven, knew that her father was troubled. "Out of the blue," Sheila recalled, "Diane suddenly said to Arthur, 'Dad, how are your tax problems?' And he put his head into his hands and said, 'Not good.' We didn't pursue it then, at the table, but after the children left I said, 'Tell me the news.' And he brought figures out and together we mulled over them and it was then that I said, 'This is outrageous. I will not let this happen to you. We should take Verchere's advice and leave.'"

Show me that list of places, she told Hailey. A few minutes later, she said simply, "We will go." While concerned about the children — all three were in school in the Napa Valley — she remembered the time she was evacuated from London to Cornwall during the early years of World War II and knew her kids would be resilient enough to handle any upheaval.

They decided to try the Bahamas for two years, save their money, then move somewhere else. "My thinking was that Arthur had been struggling ever since he left school at fourteen to be a successful writer and now, when he was forty-nine, I felt it wasn't fair that he should have to give up three-quarters of his earnings — which, in any other business, would have been regarded as capital for future projects."

Within days both Arthur and Sheila Hailey were back in Toronto for another meeting about his finances; then, on November 18, 1969, armed with first-class tickets, they boarded a flight for Nassau. They were introduced to a fellow passenger, E.P. Taylor, and it wasn't long before they were deep in conversation. "E.P." normally flew in his own private plane, but on this day it was in a hangar for repairs and he'd been forced to take a commercial flight. When he learned that the Haileys were hunting for a new home, his reaction was instant. "You must come and live in Lyford

Cay!" he exclaimed. "Come to my house for lunch on Sunday. I'll show you around."

The Haileys had never heard of Lyford Cay. Taylor, the multimillionaire Toronto businessman and horse breeder, enthusiastically told them all about it. Taylor had built Don Mills, in Toronto, and many other suburban subdivisions in Canada. He owned the fabled Windfield Farm stables, home of the Kentucky Derby winner and legendary sire Northern Dancer. He was also the man who had created Lyford Cay. In 1954 he'd bought 1,100 acres of mangrove swamp from Sir Harold Christie, a Bahamian property developer, and within a few years he'd turned it into one of the world's most exclusive residential communities. Taylor had also planned and built the Lyford Cay Club as a social hub, but in 1969 owning a home in Lyford Cay did not guarantee membership in the club, nor does it today. It's not easy to get in; applications are carefully vetted. There are 1,240 members now, two-thirds of them from Canada and the United States, most of the others from Europe and South America. When the club opened in 1960, it cost $250 to join; today, for non-residents of the Bahamas, it costs $50,000 (U.S.), for residents it's $60,000, and there's a waiting list.

Immediately, the Haileys fell in love with Lyford Cay. They chose a lot with nearly an acre of land, on a wide canal where they could dock the 155-horsepower boat they'd just bought in California, and started building their new home. They began, in 1970, with Arthur's study, a six-sided writing room, with picture windows overlooking the garden, the swimming pool, and the canal. Sheila Hailey described the cathedral ceiling as "a masterpiece of carpentry in pickled fir." They lined the remaining walls with bookcases built to contain all the different editions and translations of all Hailey's books, including the ones in Serbo-Croatian and Bengali. Part of this space enclosed a bathroom and a storeroom full of office supplies and equipment, and Hailey moved in to work here before the main house was finished. Connected to his study by a covered walkway, the new house was not vast in scale; it contained a large living room, dining room, three bedrooms and bathrooms, a big kitchen, and a two-car garage. It wasn't until 1978 that they bought an additional parcel of land next door, also just under an acre, and built a large guest cottage with a comfortable living room, another good kitchen, a generous bedroom with its own bathroom, a well-equipped study, and a second bathroom. They wanted Arthur's sons to be able to visit often with their families, and they hoped friends would come to stay, but they also wanted to make sure they weren't tripping over their visitors and that Arthur had the privacy he needed to get his work done.

The dock at the canal was big enough to hold the Mako speedboat they'd brought from California for waterskiing, snorkelling, and picnics; later they bought a new 28-foot Bertram flybridge cruiser that they used for fishing and for trips to the outer islands.

Was there a down side to this new life in the Bahamas? Not as far as the Haileys could see. Jane was ready to go to university and Steven was about to start high school at a private school in Pennsylvania. They would stay with friends in California until their school year was finished. Only Diane would be moving with them, and they found her a place at St. Andrew's, a good private school in Nassau. Six months after the first meeting with his new client, Verchere had set up Seaway Authors Limited, a holding company for the Haileys, with its registered office in Saint John, New Brunswick. The three directors were Arthur and Sheila Hailey and Verchere himself. Because the Haileys were both canny businesspeople experienced at running their own small kitchen-table company from their days in Toronto, they remained completely involved with his work on their behalf.

Hailey made Verchere understand that every transaction had to be clear and completely above board. He worried lest anyone think of him as a tax cheat. "Nothing that Sheila and I did then or have done since," he said, "is in any way illegal. We each have two nationalities, British and Canadian, and neither of those countries imposes taxes on its citizens who are domiciled beyond their borders, nor do they require the filing of a tax return."

WHILE THE HAILEYS were getting settled in the Bahamas, and Verchere was basking in the glow of having landed a celebrity client for Stikeman's, Lynne Verchere was quietly establishing herself in Montreal's business circles. With her background at IBM, she found a job at the Royal Bank as a planning analyst; as her curriculum vitae put it, she "was responsible for long range planning and conceptual design of a customer information system for branch office customer data." Her goals went beyond branch banking systems, however, and she decided she needed more education. In 1970, just before their second son, Michael, was born, she began the master's of business administration program at Sir George Williams University (later Concordia University). She also started working as a consultant to Micrographics, a Montreal firm specializing in computers and microfiches, a business closer to her own interests than banking. Today micrographics, which basically means computerized information storage and retrieval, is big business, especially for law firms, because it allows them to store hundreds of thousands of pages of documents easily and cheaply. In 1970, however, the technology was still creaky; documents were photographed and shrunk onto microfiche. Today they are scanned directly into computer hard drives and easily read with inexpensive and fast optical character recognition technology.

Over the next few years, as her husband developed his tax law practice, Lynne laboured over her MBA and taught classes in the Quantitative Methods Department in the Commerce Faculty at Concordia. Her courses were not for the faint of heart: statistics, computer languages, computer systems design, computer auditing, computer applications. In 1971 she published an academic paper titled "Data Processing Problems for Students of Commerce and Administration," and in 1972 she published a second paper, "Application of a Computer to Law Office Management," which not only grew into her MBA thesis but also pointed the way to her own career in business. It took four years, but she finally completed her MBA in 1974.

One unexpected windfall dropped into the Vercheres' laps in 1972. Arthur Hailey, grateful for Verchere's good advice, paid $15,000 to buy a membership in the Lyford Cay Club for him and Lynne. "Bruce did not ask for it," said Hailey. "I simply offered it as a gesture of appreciation." From this time on, the Vercheres made regular use of the club, and for young associates around the law firm who knew Verchere was only thirty-six, the membership became a touchstone of success.

Verchere had come aboard as Heward Stikeman's tax wunderkind, a junior associate spoken about as a future managing partner. By 1973 he'd solidified his reputation as a rainmaker. A former articling student also remembered him as a superb mentor. "Bruce worked terribly hard, but he always took the time to explain things to me. He was really nice, really kind. When I stepped out of bounds, he would say so, but not in a way that makes you feel diminished."

He was just as pleasant with his clients. "He had a wonderful bedside manner," agreed Dick Pound, who joined Stikeman Elliott as a partner in 1972 and worked on several files with Verchere; later he became vice-president of the International Olympic Committee. Pound had not forgotten how Verchere operated. "Bruce always left clients feeling very confident. He was very effective in the care and feeding of clients. He was pretty good on his feet in court, not the best, but certainly very competent."

As Verchere's reputation grew, however, as his client list lengthened, as his billings doubled and then doubled again, he became increasingly restless. He wanted the very best for himself and his young family and it just wasn't happening fast enough. "His lust for money was very obvious in the way he managed his affairs," said a former partner. "He liked luxury." Verchere was close to one or two of the firm's partners, especially James Grant, who eventually became chairman; but he was impatient with many others among the old guard, especially "Stike," who had brought him in and treated him like a favoured son. "Stikeman thought he was the future of the firm," said another partner. In 1973, Heward Stikeman was sixty and still in his prime, but Verchere viewed him and another senior partner, George Tamaki, as old men in his way. He preferred to forget that it was Tamaki, an infinitely more experienced tax specialist, who had actually prepared the Hailey tax plan and then stepped aside to allow Verchere to take the credit.

The firm's other partners began to get wind of Verchere's opinions — according to Pound, one of Verchere's special talents was, as he put it, "fomenting discontent." Verchere's fatal mistake was to imagine he could outgun Stikeman and Tamaki. What he did seems incautious beyond belief: he went to Dick Pound and Fraser Elliott with a plan for a swift and brutal putsch to remove Stikeman and Tamaki and take over the firm. Elliott and Pound listened carefully, unable to believe what they were hearing. Sensing their discomfort, Verchere put forward another option: if they didn't want to push Stikeman and Tamaki out, what about leaving as a group and starting their own firm?

"I thanked him for the compliment and told him I was quite happy where I was," said Pound, who contemptuously dismissed the notion that Verchere was the successor. "Bruce was certainly a good addition to the team, but we had Stanley Hartt in that age group, and Sonny Gordon, Jim Grant, David Angus — all of them were major players, so it was not a question of some heir apparent having arrived on the scene and taking over the world." Even if Verchere had tried, added Pound, it wouldn't have been easy. "It's very difficult in an environment like Stikeman Elliott, because it is filled with Type A personalities who are not going to be taken over."

When Stikeman got wind of what was happening, he didn't hesitate, although he knew he would have to get Tamaki on side before he acted. "Tamaki was in Bruce's thrall," explained one partner, "because Bruce was doing all of George's difficult jobs, ostensibly very well, and George was a brilliant guy and a very innocent guy." To convince Tamaki that Verchere's plot was real, Stikeman brought the two men into his office and asked Verchere what his plan had been. Without hesitating, Verchere repeated his earlier admission that he wanted to take over the firm. "We weren't good any more," the partner recalled. "The future was with him and Fraser. Fraser had the commercial clients and he would produce the tax work."

Tamaki didn't need to hear any more. Stikeman ordered his protégé to clear out his desk and be gone by the next morning. Verchere left shaken and humiliated, his future, he feared, in ruins. What Stikeman didn't do, however, perhaps out of compassion for Lynne and the children, was make Verchere's disgrace public. Even inside the firm not everyone knew what had happened. Jim Grant knew the story, and was upset by it, but was too junior to stick his neck out and defend his friend. When Grant confided in another of the juniors, the man walked down the hall to Verchere's office and found him apparently relaxed and confident, stuffing books and files into his bags. "I want you to know I'm going off to start my own firm," he told the young man. The face-saving story Verchere was able to get out was that Stikeman's was sorry to lose him and wished him well, but that he couldn't pass up the chance to run his own boutique firm, one that would handle only tax matters. Given that Stikeman himself, many years earlier, had left his first law firm to start his own practice, it seemed perfectly plausible. And Stikeman was too much the gentleman to go for blood.

Because of the spin put on Verchere's departure from Stikeman's, the rest of Montreal's legal community was happy to send clients Verchere's way. "Most lawyers don't dabble in tax," explained Arthur Campeau. "If they do, they are not really doing their clients any service. When Bruce left to start his own firm, he wisely decided he was going to limit his practice to tax. In that way, other firms would not hesitate to refer files to him."

One client he was able to keep was Arthur Hailey. "When Bruce left Stikeman Elliott I had no idea whatever that it was anything but a normal departure," says Hailey. "Bruce simply told me that he had decided to leave and set up his own business, and it was assumed by both of us that I would go with him as a client. This, because he had already set up Seaway Authors Limited, which was working and entirely legal, and by that time we were used to each other, and it would have seemed foolish to do otherwise."

Stikeman Elliott made no effort to hang on to Hailey, even though, by that time, the Haileys had become personal friends of Stikeman himself and his wife, Mary, and also of Fraser and Betty-Ann Elliott. They were all members of the Lyford Cay Club, and the couples would meet occasionally for dinner at the Haileys' house. The subject of Hailey staying with the firm or moving with Bruce Verchere just never came up.

Verchere might have been able to fool outsiders, but his miscalculation had scarred him. Lynne was also upset, especially as he'd successfully sold her his version of events, in which he cast himself as the innocent victim of an office power play. About a year after he left the firm, the Vercheres attended a large garden party in Westmount. "There must have been about a hundred people there," said one of Verchere's former partners. "Lynne sees Jimmie Grant in the garden and she walks up to him with this big smile on her face. 'You're the worst of all of them,' she says to him. 'You're the worst because you were his friend. You didn't stand up for him.' And then she turned away."

To the outside world, the Vercheres' message was that everything was peachy. Bruce's reputation was growing, and so was his clientele. "From a professional point of view Bruce was one of the best tax lawyers in North America," said Arthur Campeau, who had reason to dislike Verchere. "His knowledge of the tax treaties between Canada and other countries and of the Tax Act itself was just stupendous. I thought — and I would bet you that everyone else thought — that Stikeman would have done anything to hold on to him."

In his mid-eighties, Stikeman still guarded his firm's secrets tenaciously. All he would say was that he indeed threw Verchere out. Why? "He had," said Stikeman, with lofty contempt and brevity, "feet of clay."

There were other lingering embarrassments from the years at Stikeman Elliott that Verchere had to deal with. When he left, he'd taken some of his clients with him, and stories began filtering out that he had pushed the envelope too far with tax schemes for a few of them. Some clients wound up returning to Stikeman's, asking the firm to clean up the mess Verchere had made. One client, for example, paid Verchere $35,000 for a legal opinion which turned out to be in direct contradiction to an earlier Supreme Court decision. Dick Pound said the stories were true.

"I myself acted on a case where that happened," he said. "I think he was very definitely on the blacklist of the Department of Justice." Why Justice instead of Revenue? Because Verchere was often before the federal tax courts on cases. "If they do not believe you or trust you, or think you are a liar or think you tried to trick them," said Pound, "then things get nasty."

Because he couldn't afford to be seen working from anything but the best address, Verchere rented a two-room suite on the sixteenth floor of Place Ville Marie, the forty-two-storey cruciform tower built eleven years earlier, the tower in which Howard, Cate, Ogilvy also rented offices. Ever since it was built, Place Ville Marie has been a Montreal landmark. TrizecHahn, the company that now owns it, has always been able to get a premium for rents, a company vice-president explained to a *Globe and Mail* reporter, "because of who we are and what we are and who lives here." When you rent in Place Ville Marie, he boasted, it says to everyone, "Wow, I've finally made it." This was certainly the message Verchere had in mind when he leased the offices.

It wasn't long before he discovered that the sting of being fired was soothed by the pleasure of being his own boss — even though he could afford to bring in only a second-year McGill law student, Sydney Sweibel, to help. And there was another plus; freed from the constraints of a big legal factory, he was able to bring his wife into the firm, a move that would change their fortunes. For Lynne, this was a terrific opportunity — the chance to put her MBA thesis to the test. They agreed that she would come in as the firm's manager, running the premises and handling all the administrative and financial work. Shrewdly, she decided she should join not as an employee but as a consultant on contract. Verchere wasn't the only one who wanted to run his own company; besides, it made sense for tax reasons for a law firm to have a separate management company. The new tax laws which had come into force in 1971 gave excellent tax breaks to law firms that set up their own separate management companies. These companies could also offer interest-free loans to allow partners to, say, make a large downpayment on a house.

On December 7, 1973, Lynne incorporated Mancor, her own management company, but what made her new venture so different from the norm was that she alone owned it. One of the conditions Verchere placed on new partners in his firm was that they would have no share in the management company, an arrangement that would eventually lead to friction.

While he was still working alone in one office, with only Lynne and Sweibel, who shared the second office, to help, Verchere worked like a madman to build up his business. By himself he generated enough work to keep two shifts of secretaries busy. One day his little team was shocked when he arrived at work sick and yellowed with jaundice; he refused to go home because he had to set the pace for the rest of the office. He was also teaching a tax course at McGill, and while the prestige was pleasant it didn't generate more than beer money. "He was driven, focused, and ambitious," said one former colleague. "He was determined to build a big partnership of tax specialists."

The first person he hired was André Primeau, a former Revenue Quebec lawyer, and the firm became Verchere & Primeau; the next new partner was André Gauthier, who had worked at Revenue Canada, and the letterhead changed to Verchere, Primeau & Gauthier. The partners paid Lynne's management company to run their firm. Primeau soon left, however, and the letterhead morphed into Verchere & Gauthier; soon it expanded once more to Verchere, Gauthier, Sweibel, Noël & Eddy when Verchere made Sweibel a partner and brought in Marc Noël and Ross Eddy. Shortly after being made a partner, Sweibel accepted an offer from an accounting firm, and then Gauthier disappeared. Three other bright young lawyers, Robert Reiche, Nathan Boidman, and Jack Bernstein, all left as well. Losing Boidman was a real disaster; he was considered a technical genius. "I always thought there was someone behind Bruce who was doing the thinking," mused Warren Mitchell. That someone, for a long time, was Boidman.

By 1976 the letterhead had shrunk to Verchere, Noël & Eddy. Oddly, Lynne's curriculum vitae made no mention of the new law firm that Bruce and his various partners kept going for three years under a string of different names. Instead, it stated that she started working for Verchere, Noël & Eddy in 1973 and stayed there until 1976 — although Verchere did not even found Verchere, Noël & Eddy until 1976. Perhaps it was just simpler. Or perhaps she wanted to obliterate all reference to partnerships that did not work out.

Lawyers who joined the firm during these years couldn't resist Verchere's charm and promises. "Bruce created a great environment for building a practice," said one. "He was able to seek out the top tax people in Toronto and Montreal. He was friendly and jovial, he paid well, and he competed with the top firms. But it wasn't a great environment for lawyers. He couldn't hang on to his core group." Why did they leave? Most objected to the way he ran the financial side of the firm. He didn't know how to cut corners, only how to spend. If he had to get to the airport, he'd insist on the same driver each time and a Mercedes to get him there. And he ran the firm on a line of credit.

"Bruce's draw was being financed by a line of credit instead of by his receivables," said one partner. "His style was to say, 'How much credit do we have left?' and to live on that."

This kind of high-wire act appalled some of the partners. They also didn't like what they saw in the backrooms, especially during billing meetings. "It was the way bills were generated," said one. "He would add what he thought was a respectable premium. If he felt the client could afford it, he'd add it. He'd start rationalizing. Say the time on a file was $10,000. He'd sit at the meeting and say something like, 'When you think of what we've achieved, it should be $17,500.' And it was always Bruce who made the call." By 1975 the legal practice was finally doing well enough that Verchere declared a taxable income of $135,000 — not bad for the times, though far from the millions he hungered for.

Lynne was doing well with Mancor, and on February 6, 1975, she took possession of her dream home, an imposing twenty-room brick house built in the 1920s on Montrose Avenue in Westmount. The owner, a widow named Muriel Mary Thompson, agreed to sell it to the

Vercheres for $150,000, a bargain even then. This was the year before René Lévesque's Parti Québécois won the provincial election; Montreal house prices had not yet started to sag under the fear of a separatist government. To cover the price, Lynne borrowed $100,000 from her management company and Mrs. Thompson agreed to take back $10,000 a year for five years. No one could fail to be impressed by the house, and the location — even by lofty Westmount standards — was better yet. The property was on the corner of the block at the end of the street, across from Murray Hill Park, where the city's Anglo grandees took the air. Some of Montreal's wealthiest citizens were neighbours. Just across the street, for example, was the impressive brick home of financier Stephen Jarislowsky. Moving into their fabulous home, imagining how they might furnish it and restore it to its original grandeur, Bruce and Lynne felt as if they had finally arrived.

Though the Vercheres were excited about the new house and about their businesses, which were flourishing, life at times was almost unbearably stressful. The city had changed since their arrival in 1967, the year Expo had given the city a shining self-confidence. After the October Crisis in 1970, when terrorist members of the Front de libération du Québec kidnapped James Cross, the British trade commissioner in Montreal, holding him hostage for weeks, the divisions between French and English became angry and fierce. Lévesque's separatist party, campaigning hard for the upcoming provincial election, frightened business groups and some English-speaking Quebeckers; many of them were thinking about leaving the province for good. Because the separatist movement was becoming more popular, even more respectable, the early 1970s were an uneasy period for the business community as well as for Westmount Anglos like Bruce and Lynne. Even the Olympic Games, scheduled for 1976 in Montreal, were failing to reawaken the euphoria of Expo 67; rumours of contract kickbacks, overspending, and widespread corruption were already staining the city's reputation.

Bruce was concerned about the possible effects on his firm's client base; Lynne had more pressing issues to worry about. Her commitment to her developing company was wholehearted, but so was her commitment to her sons. Although the Vercheres had a rule that one of them would always be home to tuck David and Michael into bed, the responsibility usually fell to Lynne; Bruce was out of town on business more than she ever bargained for. Even a live-in maid and a nanny couldn't make up for his long absences. In 1975, as the Vercheres organized their schedules for the summer holidays, they tried to think of someone who could help with the boys. Lynne was swamped with work and the demands of two young kids.

Over the years their relationship with the Haileys had evolved into a deep-seated friendship, and it occurred to the Vercheres that the Haileys' youngest child, Diane, who was sixteen and a student at the Emma Willard School in Troy, New York, south of Montreal, might be willing to come up and help for a few weeks. The Haileys and the Vercheres had seen each other in Lyford Cay over the Christmas holidays, and Diane had got along well with David and Michael. When they proposed the nanny idea, it seemed like a good plan all round. Lynne would have some relief, and the Haileys, who believed in the virtues of hard work, liked the idea of their youngest child being given responsibility in a family they liked and trusted. This would be her first summer job, and her first big stay away from home beyond school.

On February 13, as a courtesy from one parent to another, Verchere sent Hailey copies of letters between himself and Diane making the arrangements. Diane's letter, painstakingly written on Emma Willard writing paper in the prim, round hand of an expensively schooled teenager, was proper and polite as she sorted out the dates. "I'm writing to thank you for the job opportunity this summer," she said. "I'm very grateful." She told Bruce she was free all summer, would like to start on July 1, and looked forward to living with him and his family. "Be sure to tell the boys I don't carry my golf cart where ever I go," she added. "My love to Lynn [sic] & the boys. I appreciate what you've done for me. Thank you. Diane."

Verchere's reply was formal. July 1 would not be convenient, he wrote, "the reason being that we will be using you as a relief person for various members of the staff who will be commencing holidays on July 1. If you wanted to stay on beyond 16 August, it would be fine but that is entirely up to you."

An odd exchange in some ways: Diane may have been only sixteen and was indeed grateful for a summer job, but she was not exactly a supplicant. She was the daughter of one of the most famous writers in the world and a student at one of the more exclusive and well-endowed private schools in the United States. The Emma Willard School, founded in 1814, takes up 92 acres of prime Hudson Valley real estate and runs an annual budget of $9.3 million. With a strong emphasis on academic achievement, sports, and the arts, it trains girls from wealthy and powerful families — Jane Fonda is one of the best-known graduates — to become independent, well-rounded leaders.

Verchere's coolness seems surprising, but what was stranger was the implication that he and Lynne had a large domestic staff to manage and that Diane was rotating through various vacation schedules. In fact, he and Lynne had a nanny and a maid. Was his well-hidden insecurity showing through? Was he seeking to impress a sixteen-year-old? Or was he seeking, by extension, to impress her parents, whose stature and affluence grew by the year as Arthur turned out one international bestseller after another? In any case, Diane spent a pleasant couple of months with the Vercheres and enjoyed getting to know the boys. The Haileys were pleased and grateful, and the experience deepened the already sturdy bond between the two families. Bruce was often away that summer; Lynne had the most contact with Diane.

"When I was a teenager she was warm and friendly," remembered Diane, "but she was also very hard to get to know. Very reserved. After that summer I didn't see them again for sixteen years."

FOUR
The Blue Trust

BY THE TIME Diane Hailey spent the summer with the Vercheres, Bruce had watched her father build a beautiful new house on an acre of land on a canal in Lyford Cay, dock his yacht just steps from his front door, and enjoy a comfortable, tax-free life among the international community of multimillionaires at Lyford Cay, a place the Vercheres visited regularly as the Haileys' guests. By now the rarefied community included many of Eddie Taylor's chums, Canadians with old money as well as Americans and Europeans who preferred to live discreetly, people like Toronto cable millionaire Ted Rogers — whose wife, Loretta (the daughter of a former governor of Bermuda, Lord Martonmere), had lived on the island — and John Bassett, another Toronto millionaire in the media business. Arthur Hailey was enjoying the kind of life Bruce Verchere wanted for himself.

Verchere knew he'd been fortunate that his failed coup attempt at Stikeman Elliott had been hushed up; such an ill-considered act could have seriously damaged his career. He was less fortunate to find himself at war with Revenue Quebec. He had become interested in the movie business, perhaps because the Haileys had built their place with the proceeds of *Hotel* and *Airport*, both of which not only had enjoyed huge book sales but also had been made into successful movies. In 1971 Hailey had published another blockbuster, *Wheels*, about Detroit's automobile industry. By this time, his novels were selling like hotcakes in dozens of languages around the world. He published *The Moneychangers*, about banks and bankers, in 1975, and that book was turned into a television mini-series.

Hailey had become a literary alchemist, a storyteller who was able to spin his tales into movie gold mines. Still, it was the books that had made them financially independent. "Most outsiders think we made our money from the movies," said Sheila Hailey. "But it was royalties from book sales that were the bulk of our income. Movie rights were sold for a flat sum with no extras, and prices paid then were not in the same league as those earned by top writers today. Books continued to earn royalties — in Arthur's case particularly — when they were published in foreign languages."

At about this time Verchere learned that Revenue Canada had designed an interesting new tax shelter for investors in Canada's movie industry, then taking baby steps into feature films and television production. Verchere had a little insider knowledge about the business, and this looked like a sure bet. He acquired a $90,000 interest in three video productions with the firm Inter-Video Inc., as well as an interest in episodes of another video production called *City Lights*.

At first the investment was fun. People didn't pretend they really wanted to support Canadian culture or promote Canadian talent. This was about money and taxes, and everybody was into it. John Turner, for instance, who resigned his cabinet portfolio in 1975 and left federal politics for the next eight years, became chairman and a major shareholder in an Ottawa company called CFI Investments Inc. CFI sold units in movie projects to investors who could claim tax writeoffs. Turner's name, which still resonated at Stikeman Elliott because of his years there, attracted such investors as Charles Bronfman, then vice-president of Seagram's in Montreal, Bernard Ostry, a former top federal civil servant, and his wife, Sylvia Ostry, federal deputy minister of international trade. A *Globe and Mail* story on CFI listed several others: "Oil magnate William Siebens, president of Candor Investments Ltd. of Calgary; A. Davidson Dunton, director of Carleton University and Shell Canada Ltd., a former chairman of the Ontario Press Council and former president of the Canadian Broadcasting Corp.; Hartland MacDougall, founding chairman of Heritage Canada and vice-chairman of the Bank of Montreal; H. J. Robichaud, Lieutenant-Governor of New Brunswick, and James Gairdner, president of Security Trading Ltd. of Toronto."

Almost all of these investors lost money. Movies made as tax shelters invariably bombed at the box office; by 1980 CFI was moribund and three years later it went bankrupt. After a nasty public court battle, Turner and a few other film partners were forced to pay $1 million to their angry investors.

Verchere's flyer in the entertainment business fared no better than Turner's. In 1976 Quebec's Revenue Department refused his claim for a capital cost deduction of the $90,000 he'd put into the movie units; just for good measure, it also denied his claim of another business loss for $25,000 he'd invested in oil and gas exploration. Verchere fought back and the case went to court.

The fight with Revenue Quebec was a setback for Verchere, an embarrassing one, and, as it turned out, only the first of a number of unpleasant clashes he had with tax officials.

By September 1976, for example, he was already well into a battle royal with Revenue Canada over an insurance company called Richards Melling & Company Ltd. When a British firm, Hogg Robinson Corp., invested $3 million in Richards Melling to help it open new offices across Canada, Verchere came up with an unorthodox and complex way to avoid paying tax on the investment. Revenue Canada balked and the fight was on. Even Hogg Robinson had reservations. In a letter to Fred Melling on September 18, 1976, Verchere complained about one of the investor's lawyers being too thick to appreciate the clever structure he'd built. "Mr. Brown is obviously going to be difficult," Verchere explained to Melling, "as he would seem to be the type of lawyer who sees a problem behind every phrase and is also somewhat offended by the novel nature of the transaction."

With the exception of the Melling case and despite his own tax mess, Verchere's law practice was doing well. He nonetheless began to see that if he and Lynne were ever going to become rich, it would probably happen through her business acumen. The life he craved — sailing in Maine, hunting in Georgian Bay, skiing in Switzerland, flying his own plane, enjoying fine food and wine with the kind of people he met in Lyford Cay — would take more money that he could ever earn practising law. He also knew that he was, in some ways, a lazy man, quite unlike his friend Pat Dohm, for instance, who had nagged and bullied and cajoled Verchere through law school and who kept on working hard even after he'd achieved his goals. Verchere liked tax law for its mysteries and puzzles, for the satisfaction of bringing in business, and for the challenge of legally hiding money. There was a subtle pleasure in exerting power over much wealthier clients, and a vicarious kick in knowing every detail of their wealth. But he didn't like it enough to want to do it indefinitely, and billing by the hour — even at very handsome rates — was not how the residents of Lyford Cay got wealthy. By 1976 he was already thinking about the day he could retire and have fun, and he knew he was lucky to have married a ferociously smart and capable woman who was single-minded in her pursuit of success.

Lynne was equally impatient. Running a law firm like Bruce's, with its paper-driven accounting, billing, and filing systems — perfectly modern for the times — seemed to her like something out of the horse-and-buggy era. "She said, 'Wait a second. Why is all this stuff being done manually? What the hell is going on?'" recalled Bryce Liberty, a young computer expert she hired in 1976. The more she thought about it, the more she was convinced she could design software for Bruce's firm that would run it smoothly, with fewer errors. It would be faster and more efficient. And she knew where to find the expertise she needed.

After her years at IBM she had good contacts there, and because she was prepared to make a deal with IBM to use its hardware, IBM was interested in talking to her. Still, making a deal with IBM in 1976 was not simple. Despite her excellent reputation, the corporation had to get past the fact that she was a woman. And it was not interested in helping her develop a product for a three-man law firm.

She had to convince IBM she'd set her sights higher. "So she went back to IBM," Liberty explained, "and said, 'Listen, there has to be some kind of hardware that small law firms can afford.'" Once they all agreed to define small law firms as those with about twenty lawyers, the IBM people showed her the kind of hardware they believed could do the job. The next step was up to her — develop the software. They knew she was a good designer; what she needed now was a technical expert, someone who could write the code and work with her to develop the programs. IBM had suggested Liberty because he was working with the corporation on other projects. The match was ideal.

As soon as he met Lynne, they clicked. Liberty listened to her ideas and understood immediately that she had the intellect, the imagination, and the drive to develop a good product. Usually IBM charged a premium to anyone doing a deal with it, but it made an exception in Lynne's case. "There was no fee charged," explained Liberty, "because IBM hoped she would develop a product that would sell IBM hardware — which, eventually, she did."

On September 23, 1976, Lynne set up a new company, Lexis Computer Systems Ltd., to develop the legal software. Although she had a $50,000 line of credit from the bank, she was determined not to use it except in emergencies; she invested $10,000 of her own money to hire staff, lease a computer, and rent office space on the floor below Bruce's office in Place Ville Marie so that she could run upstairs as often as needed to keep his office running smoothly. "I worked with small business at IBM and am very aware of their failure rate," she told Margaret Laws, a *Financial Post* reporter who interviewed her as an example of a woman entrepreneur. "I don't plan to become another statistic."

In later months Lynne changed the company's name a few times; eventually she settled on Manac Systems International Ltd., registered with the federal Consumer and Corporate Affairs Department as 159409 Canada Inc. Manac's incorporation documents show that Lynne owned 80 percent of the company in Class A voting shares; the other 20 percent, made up of Class B non-voting shares, was to be put aside in a trust for David and Michael. Liberty had no shares in the company, nor did he expect any: "Lynne was just one of my clients, and she paid me well for my consulting help." Today Liberty runs his own consulting firm with about 150 clients in Montreal; the company he helped Lynne develop, now called Manac Solutions, is one of them.

By this time the ownership of Manac, and of Lynne's management company, Mancor, had become an issue with some of Verchere's law partners. As far as they were concerned, Mancor should have belonged to the partnership. If a firm had, say, ten partners, each would own 10 percent of the firm. Usually each owned 10 percent of the management company as well. The management company never made much money because its only client was the firm; it was merely a way to do some income-splitting for tax reasons. "So the way it works," explained a former partner of Verchere's, "is that for each dollar the firm earns, the partner gets 75 cents and the management company gets 25 cents. The partners should then split the 25 cents earned by the management company. That's the way it should work. After all, the partners are paying a fee to an in-house management company. Why should the partners pay her to run the firm and not have some share of this income?"

That's not the way the Vercheres saw it, and Bruce brooked no interference. Mancor was out of reach for anyone but himself and Lynne. "The firm poured at least $100,000 into software development," said another former partner. "She and Bruce built a software company on the back of the law firm. If I'd still been there, I wouldn't have liked it." But, he acknowledged, Bruce made this condition clear before you joined his firm, and you had to agree to it. One of the reasons it rankled Verchere's partners was that it was possible, under the Income Tax Act, for shareholders of any company to borrow money interest-free from their companies. Such a perk was denied lawyers at Verchere, Noël & Eddy, and more than one of them gulped when Lynne herself took the $100,000 interest-free loan from Mancor to finance her new house in Westmount.

As Lynne and Bryce Liberty worked on their software project, their goals were ambitious and unusual. First of all, the new computer system had to record a lawyer's billable hours. The simplest way was to have the lawyers, when they were in their offices, press a switch of some kind each time they dealt with a client over the phone or in person, or when they worked on a client's files. But Manac had to do more. Lynne and Liberty also designed a system to record, sort, and process time, expenditures, and related financial information. It would handle all the normal accounting and payroll duties; it would also record all the firm's escrow accounts and legal diary reporting.

In thinking through the next set of computer chores, Lynne drew on her experience at Micrographics. Manac, she decided, should also be able to run a research classification and retrieval system, allowing busy lawyers and their staff quick computer access to the firm's internal research and to their store of legal precedents. Although other software systems on the market could do much of what she designed into Manac, this document retrieval service was what made her company unique in North America.

Lynne was rather hurt and frustrated that her husband didn't appear to share her vision of the company. To him, it seemed, Manac was nothing but the "family charity" — in fact, she told friends, he sometimes called it "Lynne's hobby." Perhaps this patronizing attitude was the result of his own insecurities; perhaps he was jealous. In any case, he drew up proper ownership and incorporation documents for the company, and, even though he and Lynne were still not earning big incomes, decided it was time to set up a family trust to shield their future income, both from tax inspectors and from importuning creditors. Should Manac go under, he wanted to make sure that neither he nor Lynne would be liable personally; should it do well, he wanted to make sure they would hang on to as much of the profit as legally possible.

Family trusts, of course, were nothing new for Verchere; by this time he was routinely setting them up for his clients. Now it was time for Verchere to create one for himself, with Lynne and the boys as beneficiaries. It would be called the Blue Trust, and he turned it over in his mind at length, designing it, polishing it, reviewing every contingency. The trust he finally crafted was to become his masterpiece, a legal firewall that could not be breached. Prosaically, the trust's stated purpose was to create a patrimony for his sons, Michael and David, but the real objective was tax planning:

to organize what Hailey called tax avoidance, which is legal, as opposed to tax evasion, which is not.

Verchere needed to find someone willing to become a "settlor" to start the process; the word refers to the donor who contributes the property to the trust. Often tax lawyers act as settlors for their wealthy clients; Verchere did this for Arthur Hailey when Hailey moved to the Bahamas. This time, Verchere asked if Hailey, in turn, would become the settlor for the Verchere family trust, one Bruce also intended to keep headquartered offshore. Hailey good-naturedly agreed, though he frankly admitted later that he did not understand the legal ramifications but trusted Verchere, figuring it was the least he could do for the man to whom he owed so much. Article I, Clause vii, of their twenty-page agreement states: "Settlor shall mean Arthur Hailey being the individual who has transferred property to the Trust for the purpose of creating a trust." The Vercheres were staying in Lyford Cay at the end of December 1976, when the papers were signed and Hailey wrote a cheque for $1,000 to settle on the trust, assuming Verchere would reimburse him later.

FIVE
The Sweet Life

BY THE EARLY 1980s, Lynne's "family charity," owned 80 percent by herself and 20 percent by the Blue Trust, had turned into a full-fledged success. More and more law firms were signing up for her software, and the support service package was proving to be almost as profitable. Mancor, the little consulting firm she'd created to run her husband's law firm, was still making money, and by February 14, 1980, it had generated enough profits to allow her to repay the $100,000 she'd borrowed from it to buy their home on Montrose Avenue. They now owned the house outright; they'd also just finished paying Mrs. Thompson the annual $10,000 they owed her on the purchase price. This gave Lynne a tremendous feeling of security and relief. Whatever else happened, they now owned their lovely home.

Verchere, Noël & Eddy was also doing well. Bruce had landed an important new account, the Swiss Bank Corporation, which had its Canadian head offices in Toronto. It became his highest-paying and most important client, and the Swiss Bank president, Louis ("Sam") Wiedmer, who had come to Canada to run Swiss Bank's Montreal office, was a believer. He told his friends that Verchere was "the most brilliant lawyer he'd met in Canada." As evidence of Verchere's adroitness, Wiedmer liked to tell about the time Swiss Bank's Montreal office had a visit from Revenue Canada officials who demanded the names of the bank's private clients. "The guy in charge of operations immediately called Bruce and said, 'We have a problem. These guys want to see our secret files.' Bruce said, 'No, wait. Don't do anything. I'll be right there.' When Bruce arrived he said to them, 'You need a search warrant or a judge's order to do this; you're not allowed to come in here and go on a fishing expedition.'" Chastened, the officials slunk away and did not come back.

The Swiss Bank work was a plum and Verchere wasn't shy about letting people around town know he had landed it. It wasn't just the cachet; it was the fat retainer. The Vercheres' way of life was becoming increasingly self-indulgent and costly. Meanwhile, the boys were getting older and eating up after-tax income. David, who was twelve in 1980, and Michael, who was ten, both went to Selwyn House, one of the best and most expensive private English-language schools in the city.

The family's growing affluence was allowing them to enjoy life in new ways. Bob Fasken, a Toronto mining promoter and, at the time, chairman of Camflo Mines, became a friend of Verchere's and eventually made him a member of Camflo's board of directors. Fasken discovered that Verchere was a keen hunter and fisherman, as he himself was; before long he invited Verchere to join the Griffith Island Club, an exclusive hunting and fishing club on a 3,000-acre resort in Georgian Bay, north of Owen Sound. Founded by a small group of men including Fasken, a well-known Liberal, and former Ontario Conservative premier John Robarts, it was a private retreat for some of the wealthiest sportsmen in Ontario to hunt white-tail deer, pheasants, and other game birds.

The guides had to know how to handle the club's sixteen flushing dogs and eight pointers; they also had to be experienced with all types of shotguns and rifles. Although there are twenty-seven recognized game preserves in Ontario, Griffith Island is one of the most difficult to get into, and one of the most expensive; membership fees, when Verchere joined, were $25,000 a year. Because of Robarts's roots in London, Ontario, many of the members came from there; one was David Weldon, the former chairman of Midland Doherty and former president of the Royal Agricultural Winter Fair. Others included John Pallett, a Port Credit lawyer and a former Tory MP; Toronto lawyer Douglas Gibson, a partner in the law firm known as Fasken & Calvin in those days; and Toronto Tory Joe Barnicke, one of the most powerful real estate magnates in the country.

Verchere loved the Griffith Island Club and enjoyed taking his sons there and teaching them to hunt and fish; sometimes, on "ladies' weekends," he took Lynne. Often he led the boys on long tramps through the countryside to look at the wildlife, rather than joining the guides on hunting outings. The camp staff liked Verchere; they found him friendly and full of "quick and sensible opinions," as one person put it. It was about this time that he decided to get his pilot's licence — he wanted to be able to fly into Griffith Island.

Learning how to fly was something he'd wanted to do since Heward Stikeman had taken him on business trips in his Cessna. During these years, he would go back to British Columbia, to a small flying school on Vancouver Island near Sidney Harbour, stay at a local bed-and-breakfast, and take a few days of lessons. The school was called Juan Air; his teacher was John Addison, an Australian pilot who now flies out of Luxembourg for Korean Airlines. Partly because Verchere was totally relaxed back in B.C. and partly because he was a naturally gifted pilot, the two became close and stayed in touch for years. "Bruce was a good pilot," confirmed Bruce Gorle, Juan Air's owner, who remembered him well. "He got his pilot's licence here."

Once he had the licence, Verchere tried to think of a way he could marry his love of flying to a business opportunity or, at the very least, to a tax break. His answer was Niskair, another new company he started in 1977. (Niska was a name he would use again; it came from a Northwest B.C. Indian people, the Nisga'a.) In theory, Verchere's plan was a good idea: what he wanted to do was set up a charter aircraft service which would allow him to fly as often as he had the time or whenever he had a business trip which could pay for his costs, and at the same time rent planes out for charter runs. This way he could write off the costs of his new hobby as a business expense. In practice, it never worked out as a moneymaker, but Verchere didn't really care; for him, it was great to be able to get the tax writeoff.

On December 19, 1977, Verchere set up Niskair, initially under the registered name of 85525 Canada Ltd., "to operate," the documents stated, "as a commercial air service." As soon as he could afford to, he bought a float plane, which he kept in a private hangar at Dorval Airport; he used this plane for hunting and fishing trips, mostly to Griffith Island, and to take friends and business associates for sightseeing jaunts over the Eastern Townships and through the Laurentians. Shortly after buying the float plane, he also purchased a small single-engine Cessna which could land at any airport. And by April 1979 he had structured Niskair's ownership so that he was the sole owner; Lynne had no role in the company at all. For Lynne, what her husband did with Niskair and the two planes was of little interest at the time; later she would complain that the little charter airline he'd babied along was an expensive self-indulgence they could ill afford.

But collecting Canadian art became a hobby they both enjoyed. When they had spare time in Montreal, the Vercheres visited the city's leading private galleries to look at traditional Canadian landscapes and still lifes; slowly they began to acquire a fine collection of paintings, the kind Walter Klinkhoff carried in his gallery, the kind Heward Stikeman would have appreciated. Over the next few years they bought works by a handful of leading Canadian artists, a collection they carefully catalogued for their personal files.

When they found an artist they liked, they often bought more than one work. Molly Lamb Bobak was a special favourite; they owned four of her watercolours of flowers. There were a couple of Quebec landscapes in oil by Robert Pilot, two still lifes in oil by Goodridge Roberts, and one or two surprises — jarring notes in rooms of safe traditionalists — including an oil of a Cape Dorset sunset by William Kurelek.

As part of his estate planning for his family, Verchere moved the ownership of their paintings to Mancor, Lynne's management company. (A former colleague of Verchere's described this action as imprudent — he said it could cause "horrific tax problems with shareholder benefits" and most tax lawyers rarely do it.)

Restoring their Westmount house to its original 1920s elegance, decorating it, and furnishing it beautifully with antiques had become important to them, and as they could afford it they undertook the complex renovation. "It was pristine," said a close friend. "It was elegant, but almost felt unlived-in. It was all Norman-Rockwell-esque, but I don't remember any family pictures anywhere. The boys were extraordinarily well behaved and they were really nice kids." Lynne rarely had time to cook, but she made sure the meals prepared by their maid were excellent. Bruce, a developing oenophile, chose the wines, and they were always memorable.

Socially, the Vercheres were slower to make their mark. By this time they were well entrenched in Westmount, but many of their neighbours found Lynne cool and standoffish. Bruce, who seemed to be away on business most of the time, was taciturn and sometimes ready to pick a fight when he was in town. His legendary charm seemed to disappear when he wasn't trying to make an impression. The image people in the neighbourhood had of him, when he made his cameo appearances on his front porch in summer, was of a solitary man, sipping a glass of one of the white Burgundies he loved, gazing down the grassy slope of his front lawn at the people strolling by on their way to Murray Hill Park.

"The Vercheres stuck to themselves in Westmount," said the tax lawyer Norman Tobias, who lived nearby on Forden Crescent at the time and who later took a job with Verchere, Noël & Eddy as an associate. "I remember my sister was walking my dog by their house and it urinated on their lawn. Lynne yelled out a window, 'Get your bloody dog off my lawn!'"

People understood that the Vercheres were stressed; it wasn't easy maintaining and renovating a large house, raising two children, and working at incredibly demanding jobs. Lynne travelled almost as much as Bruce did, and whatever free time she did have she devoted to David and Michael. When Bruce was home, he went to watch his sons play hockey at school; other fathers came to know him slightly there. But community participation was clearly not a high priority for the Vercheres, and few people went out of their way to get to know them.

On Sunday mornings, if they were in town, Bruce and Lynne sometimes walked hand in hand, carrying their prayer books, to morning church services. The church was an important part of Lynne's life; as the years went on she became a member of the Social Outreach Steering Committee of the Anglican Church of Canada as well as a director of the Canadian Bible Society. Verchere became an enthusiastic convert; not only did he serve as a church warden at his local parish church, St. Matthias, on Churchill Avenue, just around the corner from his house, but he was also, at one time, legal counsel to the Anglican Diocese of Montreal. When Warren Mitchell heard that his old law school classmate had changed churches, he burst out laughing. "Bruce would!" chortled Mitchell. "When I knew him he was United Church, but of course he became an Anglican!"

Along with their interest in the church, the Vercheres began circulating in the city's cultural community. Lynne was especially interested in Montreal's Museum of Fine Arts — she later became a member of the President's Circle there — but she also got involved with the Montreal Symphony Orchestra, the Opera Guild, and even an avant-garde theatre group called Bulldog Productions Theatre.

They left behind their ties in British Columbia. Lynne stopped going west except on business; Bruce went back only once or twice a year to visit his parents. More often, his relatives would come east to see them. Gradually he also drifted away from his old friends Pat Dohm and Royal Smith. They were realistic about what had happened. Lynne, said Dohm, "was a very brilliant person. I only met her once prior to their getting married, and then Bruce kind of dropped out of B.C. for the next twenty-five years." Dohm was fond of Bruce's mother, Kitty, though, and they became close friends. After Kitty's death, Dohm stayed in touch with Justice Verchere; when he remarried, his new wife, Fanta, also became close to Dohm. But Bruce saw his old friends infrequently, and Dohm and Smith both put it down to Lynne. She didn't seem to care for her husband's fraternity brothers and didn't try to hide her disdain.

As their fortunes in Montreal improved, Lynne become more extravagant with her clothes. She could easily justify the expense; as a businesswoman in what was still very much a man's world, she knew the importance of looking successful. Montreal women pride themselves on being chic; they follow fashion trends with more enthusiasm and attention than women in most other parts of Canada, and these were the days when even Eaton's had a special category of clothes for its Montreal clients and lower-end styles for customers elsewhere. (In the 1960s, Eaton's ranked its main store in Montreal as its number one fashion centre; Toronto came second, Vancouver and Ottawa tied for third.) Holt Renfrew led the way for the well-heeled, fashion-conscious Montreal woman, and Lynne started to look there for her clothes. Encouraged by the wives of some of Bruce's friends, she even started to shop at Serge et Réal, the expensive Montreal couturiers favoured by Jeanne Sauvé, Jackie Desmarais, and Mila Mulroney. Lynne's model-thin figure made it easy for her to dress elegantly, though she was not what Montrealers would describe as chic; she limited her choices to crisp silk blouses and neat business suits, with the skirts hemmed to skim her knee. Anything revealing or trendy she avoided.

Bruce was delighted to see her spend money on herself. He spent a fortune on his own clothes and wanted his wife to look just as smart and expensively turned out as any other corporate wife in Montreal; he loved being with a woman who turned other men's heads, and he loved spending money. Whatever he bought had to be the best. Cars were important to him. Before Jeeps became fashionable, he bought two of them; later he started buying Range Rovers, among the most expensive four-wheel-drive vehicles available.

Another of his indulgences was less expensive. He loved good books; he sometimes prowled through Montreal's better English-language bookstores, particularly the Double Hook on Greene Avenue in Westmount and Paragraph Books on Mansfield, looking for the latest hot fiction, anything that had been well reviewed in the *New York Times* or the *Globe and Mail*. "He liked American fiction, accessible fiction, like the novels of Anne Tyler," said a close friend. "And he liked biography. One he bought me, one of his favourites, was Susan Cheever's biography of her father, the novelist John Cheever."

Another friend who vacationed with him in New England remembered him making his way through novels, books about politics, even books on Greek philosophy.

When Verchere went out for dinner, it had to be at a fine restaurant. He studied the wine list until he found a vintage that interested him; price was not a consideration. Hard liquor held no appeal, nor was he a smoker, but he became a connoisseur of fine wines and indulged his passion to the hilt. He thought nothing of spending $600 on dinner for two, though he actually preferred fairly plain fare; a thick steak with a baked potato was his idea of a perfect main course.

He billed back the cost of dining out to his law firm. Some of his dinners for two were legitimate business expenses, but some were intimate evenings with women he saw privately, women he was attracted to. If Lynne were to go through his credit card receipts at home, she might ask awkward questions. Theoretically, she could have done the same at work, given that she had established the administrative systems of the firm, but she would not have demeaned herself in front of Bruce's staff by checking his expense accounts. Furthermore, by 1980 she had stepped away from the day-to-day management of Verchere, Noël & Eddy to put all her time into Manac; even though she was working in the same building, she wasn't around Bruce's office much. The women in Verchere's life — and there were a few of them, usually much younger — dealt with his confidential secretary, Sandy Wardrope. They never called the house. "He was discreet outside the office," said a former partner. "Inside . . . well, he wasn't so discreet."

One woman with whom he often travelled took a week of sailing lessons with him in Newport, Rhode Island, and spent another week with him in Florida. They visited Nashville to see the Grand Old Opry; he didn't like country music but liked the idea that they'd been there. Every once in a while they spent a weekend at her cottage, where he did the cooking — breakfast, lunch, and dinner — and the dishes while she did chores around the property. "I remember the time he was the most pleased with me," she said. "He'd brought back all this venison and pheasant, from Griffith Island, and I did a pheasant consommé. I didn't particularly know what I was doing, and unwittingly I put it on low. It turned out to be this clear, perfectly strong consommé. Bruce was so happy."

At his age, Verchere was required to take regular flight tests. He took his girlfriend with him to Kansas. Before taking the test at the Cessna Center in Wichita, he always took a refresher course. There wasn't much else to do in Wichita while she waited for him, so she took flying lessons, too, and eventually got her pilot's licence. Because he was the prudent tax lawyer, and because flying lessons were considered education and therefore tax-deductible, "he paid for it," she chuckled, "and I got the deduction."

Through all this Lynne kept a dignified silence. "She knew he was a womanizer," said one of her closest friends. "She used to say, 'He'll come to his senses.' She was very open about it; she would just say, 'Bruce makes mistakes.' She figured he'd had affairs during the years she spent building up her business." Perhaps not surprisingly, Verchere maintained a double standard. He would not have put up with Lynne having affairs. He was suspicious of her and jealous. In Montreal, he got rid of an employee he suspected of having an affair with her, though the very idea was preposterous to the employee. Bruce didn't care. Goodbye.

Verchere's fondness for sexual adventure outside his marriage was not altogether surprising. He'd become engaged to Lynne just three weeks after meeting her, and just after breaking up with his university sweetheart. For himself, Bruce thought, life had been one long haul of keeping his nose to the grindstone. His true nature was warm and effusive. He loved to hug people and to please them. He loved to play. It galled him that Arthur and Sheila, older role models, people who were almost like parents to him, were having more fun than he was.

By this time Hailey had published eight novels in thirty-one languages. He underwent a quadruple heart bypass in Dallas in the summer of 1980, just after he'd announced his retirement, but recovered so quickly that he agreed to write a screenplay of his most recent novel, *Overload*, and soon afterwards decided he was feeling well enough to tackle another big novel, his ninth. *Strong Medicine*, an inside story of the drug industry, was published in 1984, and as Verchere discovered, Doubleday gave Hailey one of the highest advances ever paid to a novelist: $1,750,000. "What Hailey has found," wrote Victor Paddy in a *Globe and Mail* profile in 1982, "is obviously more than a formula for creative success and more than the financial means to charter private jets or secure his 1,000-bottle wine cellar — Hailey has rediscovered life after near death."

"There were two points in my life," Hailey told Paddy. "One was after the Second World War. Many of my contemporaries didn't come out on the far side. I realized I was very fortunate. Life was a bonus. In the same way, I remember thinking when I reached 40 and then 50 and particularly 60, I've won. No one can take this away from me. Now I've come out of this heart surgery, and in a way every day since has been a bonus, a privilege, something to be thankful for. I don't believe in God, I have no religion, but I think I've always had this feeling about life."

It was precisely this feeling Verchere so clearly lacked and so desperately wanted. He wanted all the toys his celebrated client had, sure, but he also longed for the joyousness that was a fundamental part of both Arthur and Sheila. It was this joie de vivre that linked them — they were both realists but optimists; they were prudent, open-hearted, frank. They were not impressed by important people or money or power; their best friends were the same friends they had in the 1950s. These were all qualities Verchere admired and envied but could not share. It wasn't in his nature. He might have been living the sweet life, but he did not embrace the notion — as the Haileys did — that life itself is sweet. And he may have become a devout Anglican while Hailey proclaimed a stout atheism, but there was no question which man felt more fulfilled, or which had the richer spiritual life.

SIX

Manac Energy

WHEN IT CAME to running her business, Lynne Verchere left nothing to chance. If an important letter was going out, she'd get a ruler and measure the margins to be sure it looked flawless. The message was clear to everyone who worked for her: each task, no matter how small, had to be done perfectly. This attention to detail caused tension in the Manac offices. People bent over their desks would suddenly hear heels clicking on the floor and "out of nowhere," said one, "she'd appear in front of an employee to ask questions about a particular subject, showing that she knew more about the file than the employee did."

The reason she knew more was that she put in seventy- and eighty-hour weeks building Manac's client list and ensuring that the software and the services they were selling were better than anything her competitors could offer. The talented young employees she liked to hire feared her because she was so demanding, but they also respected her. She paid them well and got results. "I never had a problem negotiating with Lynne," said Bryce Liberty. "A lot of people were scared to deal with her. I was independent enough to be able to say, 'Lynne, this is how it is.' Even if she got bigger than me, she always kept me around as an insurance policy. With her and me together there was never anybody who could hold her up for ransom. There would never be a senior employee who would say, 'You know what, Lynne? I'm going to do this or that or I'm leaving.' She knew that with her steady control of sales and marketing and with me on the technical side, if anybody stepped out of line we could tell them to go to hell."

To build the sort of business that Manac became, Liberty added, was not easy for a woman in the 1980s. "You might expect it from an entrepreneur, but not from a woman entrepreneur, because there were not that many women entrepreneurs in the 1980s." It was one thing, Liberty believed, to have a nice office in Place Ville Marie — "You can go downstairs and go shopping or go over to Crescent Street, you are right in the action downtown" — but quite another to understand that the woman you were working for was going to pressure you to produce. When her employees were unproductive, they were out.

At Manac, Lynne used a trick law firms often use to keep employees hard at work at their desks: she generously stocked the company fridge. Each week she spent as much as $1,000 on cheese, cooked meats, yogurt, fruit, soft drinks, and other treats, stuffing the fridge and the cupboards in Manac's company kitchen. "But you know what?" Liberty said. "A thousand dollars a week is $50,000 a year. And do you know how many people decided they were not going to go for lunch and would have cheese and crackers and a soft drink and be back at their desk in fifteen minutes? Or it's five o'clock and you get hunger pangs and go have a yogurt and you end up working until seven. She had fifty people. If she got an hour out of every person a week, that's fifty hours, which is an employee's salary, and I guarantee you she was getting a hell of a lot more than an hour a person. I thought it was a brilliant idea."

Another former employee admired her as much as Liberty did. "She was very bright," he said. "She was a whirlwind. She had charisma." Still, he admitted, her employees never had any sense of who she really was. You could sit beside her all day, day after day, working on a project, solving problems, and never get past the invisible wall she put up around herself. No one got close to her.

If Lynne didn't trust anyone at Manac with her secrets, she also didn't want to share authority or delegate. Her mania for micromanaging was so all-encompassing that she even prepared a detailed manual for her housekeeper, setting out all the tasks she wanted done at home. Sometimes she took effective time management too far; on one occasion she sent a Manac employee to Montrose Avenue to fire a maid because she believed it would take too much of her time to deal with the woman herself. It's not that she avoided confrontation; far from it. Her employees all found her a much tougher negotiator than her husband. It's just that she didn't think such tasks required her presence. And when she was angry in the office, she never shouted. What her employees found far more frightening was that she would drop her voice a notch and hiss, "I'm not happy." Maybe it was because Bryce Liberty wasn't an employee but rather a consultant that he had a different view of Lynne.

As Lynne's list of law firms grew, said Liberty, "she killed them with service." Although computers were starting to replace electric typewriters in some offices in the early 1980s, many law firms still resisted them, considering them frills or fads. Manac's software ran on IBM System 34 or System 36 mini-computers, large, noisy mainframes that could support up to five "seats," as the salesmen called them; this meant that up to five administrative support staff could work on individual terminals hooked up to the computer. The lawyers were not connected; in those years it never occurred to most of them that they'd ever touch a keyboard. (By 1983 Lynne had added new PC/AT and PC/XT micro-computers to the systems.) Any law firm willing to sign on, she knew, would need plenty of technical support. "Lynne would say that anyone who thought they could do it on their own is going to be a disgruntled Manac client," Liberty recalled. "She said, 'The hell with them.'" To their faces, of course, that was a message they would never hear from Lynne Verchere. When she put her mind to it, she could outcharm and outsell anyone, said Peter Tolnai, who joined Manac in 1980 after a few months of working on freelance projects for Bruce.

Dark and handsome and preppy, with an irrepressible sense of humour and a quick mind, Peter Tolnai was a Queen's University economics graduate who'd completed his MBA at Harvard in 1977. While trying to raise money for a new venture capital company, he'd met Verchere through mutual business friends. This was a man, Tolnai had been told, who had good financial connections and international tax experience and could be useful to him.

Verchere, for his part, liked Tolnai immediately and saw the twenty-seven-year-old whiz kid as a potential employee; it was just a matter of where to put him. It wasn't a lawyer-client relationship they had, Tolnai said, but a mentorship. "Bruce took me under his wing. If I can quote him, 'You're a young, aggressive, apparently intelligent fellow and I'd like to help you in your efforts.'" Tolnai was just one of the many talented young men Verchere spotted as they were beginning their careers; to them he was a mentor who understood their insecurities and knew how to boost their confidence. He not only taught them business skills, introduced them to valuable contacts, and brought them into his deals, he looked to their broader development and educated them about wine, food, and books. He advised them on their clothes and on their personal lives. It was as if he had a need to shape young people into perfect beings, just as he had done when he'd met the shy, unsophisticated, immensely promising Lynne Walters in 1963.

By April 1980 Verchere thought he had just the job for Tolnai: developing Niskair into a profitable charter airplane company in return for 30 percent of the company. At the time, Niskair had only the two small planes in a hangar at Dorval Airport in Montreal; one was the float plane Verchere was using for his trips to the Griffith Island Club and to camps in Northern Quebec and Labrador; the second was the little single-engine Cessna he'd bought to fly to business meetings in Toronto and Ottawa.

"They were toys," said Tolnai, adding that Verchere never seriously expected to make a business out of them but for tax reasons wanted Niskair to look like a business. The best Verchere hoped for was to break even; if, by some miracle, Tolnai could develop a marketing strategy and make some money, then Verchere was willing to turn over 30 percent of the company to him. It was a tempting carrot and Tolnai agreed to work on the plan on a freelance consulting basis, living in Toronto and commuting to Montreal from time to time. Using money drawn from a personal joint account he shared with Lynne, Verchere paid Tolnai $250 a day plus expenses to develop the Niskair business plan; the Vercheres deducted the costs from their personal income tax as investment advisor fees. In early July 1980 Tolnai received an advance of $5,000 and started to work.

"One day, I was in Montreal working with Bruce on Niskair," said Tolnai, "and he said, 'I want you to meet my wife, Lynne, who has a very interesting software company.'" Verchere took Tolnai up to the Manac suite, now on the thirty-fourth floor; almost immediately he and Lynne found they were kindred spirits. Oblivious to Bruce, they talked the talk of recent MBAs: personnel, marketing, growth. Manac looked like a wonderful company to Tolnai, and he seized his chance.

On July 9 he met Lynne in Toronto for lunch at the Toronto-Dominion Centre and showed her an informal agenda he'd drawn up; on it he listed, as he put it, "my views on how she could grow the company." Impressed, Lynne said she'd think about his ideas.

Then Bruce called again; would Tolnai be willing to write a speech he had to deliver to the executives of Hoechst Canada, a subsidiary of a large West German chemical company? Verchere wanted its legal business, which came with an annual retainer of $30,000. No problem, said Tolnai, who by now was beguiled by the couple and the wonderful future they were holding out to him. In September Verchere delivered Tolnai's barn-burner to Hoechst's managers — all about the investment opportunities waiting for them in Canada — and won the company's legal business.

On July 23 Verchere called Tolnai, suggesting that the three of them meet for dinner in a couple of days at the Ritz-Carlton in Montreal to discuss an idea. Intrigued, Tolnai agreed. Once they'd settled down to their meal, the Vercheres made their pitch. We like your ideas, they told him, we like the way you think, you've got the right sort of training. What about moving to Montreal to work with Manac full-time as vice-president of marketing? Tolnai listened carefully. It was one thing to like people, he knew, quite another to work for them; as a young Harvard MBA, he had other offers by this time, and he enjoyed living in Toronto, where there were all kinds of business opportunities. Why move to Montreal to work for an unknown software company?

Bruce outlined an offer he hoped Tolnai would be unable to refuse. The compensation package would include modest cash compensation, but the real upside was 25 percent of the issued and outstanding common shares of Manac Systems. They didn't bring with them that evening the Manac financial statements, but Tolnai had already seen them during a meeting with Lynne back in June, when Lynne had been showing him where their revenues came from. The earnings weren't exciting, but he believed the company had real promise. Think about it over the weekend, the Vercheres urged, and give us an answer Sunday night or Monday.

Tolnai spent the weekend with his parents in Ottawa mulling over the offer. In truth, he didn't need more persuading; Sunday evening he phoned and accepted. Delighted, Bruce welcomed him into the company. The next step, he said, would be to draw up preliminary papers as the basis of the shareholders' agreement they would negotiate. Verchere said he'd do this at once and get a copy to Tolnai.

A few days later Tolnai arrived in Montreal to start the negotiations and begin work. The Vercheres could not have been friendlier. Come to the house, they said. We'll talk over a glass of wine. It was a lovely August evening, and the three of them sat outside on the porch, pondering their wonderful futures together. Bruce would draw up the legal contract between them, giving Tolnai 25 percent of Manac, when he got back into his office at Verchere, Noël & Eddy. They settled on a base salary; Tolnai would receive an after-tax income of $27,500 a year. As a tax lawyer, Bruce said, his advice would be to accept a lower base salary and opt for perks worth about $7,500 a year through an expense account, extras that would include a car allowance, French lessons, and a tennis club membership.

Lynne would be the technical leader. She was the one who understood the software and worked with Bryce Liberty to improve and expand the systems. Tolnai's job would be to market the product. He'd be in charge of corporate development, sales, and marketing. One of his first tasks would be to hire a new sales force. Pretty heady stuff at twenty-seven, regardless of the Harvard degree, and Tolnai was thrilled. Within days he was established in the office at Place Ville Marie. While he was looking for an apartment, the Vercheres insisted he stay with them. Life on Montrose Avenue was well-ordered and pleasant. David and Michael were delightful boys, and Tolnai enjoyed being around them; Bruce and Lynne were gracious hosts and made him feel welcome during the weeks it took to find his own place. But the real kick was getting into work and devising a strategy to convince clients that Manac offered the best solution for law firms.

Tolnai was disturbed when he learned that Manac was carrying $180,000 in debt and had only $20,000 remaining in its line of credit. "We had to start selling," he said, "or we'd be in trouble." The situation became even more tense when Bruce had to tell Lynne that Revenue Quebec had become aggressive over the film tax credits he'd tried to claim and was now demanding about $91,000 in taxes. To stave them off while he fought the case in court, Bruce had to ask her if she would allow the province to put a $91,000 mortgage on their house. She had no choice but to agree, though it wasn't pleasant remembering how wonderful it had been, just seven months earlier, to have paid off the mortgage in full.

The good news was that by the end of 1980, Manac had sold eight systems in thirteen weeks, sales that would keep the company comfortably afloat until mid-1981. By the end of January 1981, the bank loan had been reduced to less than $50,000, and everyone breathed a sigh of relief.

During these months, Tolnai got used to the Vercheres' idiosyncratic management style. Although Lynne no longer had a hands-on role at Verchere, Noël & Eddy, she and her husband kept in close touch about their separate businesses. Bruce's assistant, Sylvia Power, worked as an administrator for both Manac and Niskair and issued Tolnai's paycheques, even though she worked out of offices in the law firm.

In idle moments Tolnai could not help but wonder about the Vercheres' marriage. "I would say their relationship was a business relationship. They wanted to be successful, to have prestige in society, and they marched ahead together." He especially liked working with Lynne. "She was the driving force in a lot of ways. Bruce and Lynne were just like Governor Jack Stanton and his wife, Susan, in that movie *Primary Colors.*" Like Stanton's, Verchere's charm was cosy and irresistible: "He could make you feel like a million dollars." And like Susan Stanton, Lynne was tough, more remote. "She was not hard-edged," Tolnai explained. "In fact, she was cute in a wholesome sort of way. But there was no sense of warmth."

It was, for a young, ambitious man, marvellous excitement. The two of them spent long days travelling together to pitch their software to the executive committees at law firms across Canada and the United States. They flew first-class, stayed in good hotels, and talked strategy even during down times. Lynne was always reserved. "She was aloof. Remote." What they mostly talked about was how to overcome the biggest problem they faced — educating lawyers about what Manac's new computer software could do. Lawyers were a hard sell, especially because most of them mentally checked out at the mere word "computer." The word "software" was even worse.

In the elevator, on the way to a meeting, Lynne would be quiet and withdrawn, staring at her shoes; Tolnai learned not to push her into conversation. She was focusing her thoughts. Once the elevator door opened, she put on a big smile, her eyes lit up, and there was a bounce in her step. "As soon as we got in to work the room, she was brilliant," Tolnai said. "She remembered names. She knew the names of people's kids. She was wonderful. Charming."

When it came time to strut their stuff, they were an engaging tag team; he the attractive young businessman with a great rattle of information; she the sharp, winsome blonde with the big blue eyes, trim figure, and wholesome friendliness. It was clear to everyone that they were having fun together, though the lawyers they met soon understood they were dealing with a pair of steel-trap minds. The lawyers tended to sit back and enjoy the show. One of Tolnai's strategies was to sell Manac's products in bite-sized pieces. Tolnai and Lynne would ease into the pitch with a demonstration of the basic package, the client accounting software which started at $16,500 and, depending on the type of computer the firm used, could run up to $22,500. "It was the old razor-blade strategy," remembers Tolnai. The "razor" — the basic accounting software — was relatively inexpensive; the company made its money on the "blades," or the Manac extras. Once the lawyers understood what the accounting software could do, they'd ask what else was available. "So we'd show them how they could add modules, which cost $5,000 each."

The modules included software to handle the law firm library, research and precedents, statutory dates (a sophisticated bring-forward system), patents and trademarks, and litigation support. Not only could the software manage databases and use keywords and directories to retrieve documents, it could update work summaries and case notes. Tolnai's marketing strategy was to sell the lawyers on the razor and then entice them to add on the modules — the blades — though his approach sometimes led to arguments with Lynne. She believed they ought to try to sell the whole package for a possible $45,000 each time out; his approach was to coax, softly, softly, the clients into adding the bite-sized pieces. On top of all this, of course, was the annual $5,000 technical support contract.

One way to make clients feel in touch was to send them a monthly newsletter keeping them up to date on Manac and on new developments with the software. "She had what she called 'the Manac network,' and she made people proud to be a member," Tolnai explained. It wasn't always easy. At first some of the firms that bought software packages worth up to $45,000 balked at signing on for Manac's $5,000 annual service contracts; if they persisted in refusing the service contract, she'd cancel the sale. The network, she said, was her support group, and if they didn't want to be in it, the sale wasn't worth it. The network, she promised, guaranteed that her systems would never be obsolete. What clients received for their $5,000, she believed, was worth every penny; it included training, technical support, and regular servicing for the software.

In the spring of 1981, Tolnai hired a senior sales executive to help him sell the systems. The person he chose was Larry Smith, a handsome, personable lawyer who had been a star football player at Bishop's University in Lennoxville, Quebec, where he'd set Canadian college football rushing records. After his 1972 graduation, he'd gone on to a successful professional career with the Montreal Alouettes in the Canadian Football League; at the same time, he'd taken a law degree at McGill.

Smith was a high-profile catch and his $55,000 annual salary reflected it; it was higher than anyone else's at Manac. Around this time, Lynne hired three other employees and gave three raises — one of them to herself, so that her new salary was about $31,000 a year. And more Manac money — between $16,000 and $20,000 a year — went as dividends into the Blue Trust, ostensibly to pay the boys' expenses. The company also purchased better computer equipment. The result of this increase in payroll and capital costs, said Tolnai, was that Manac's bank debt shot up, this time to about $250,000.

Even when firms signed up for the full package, though, and the money was pouring in, there were anxious moments about the company's financial state because sales had levelled off to about one system every six weeks. Alarmed at the way money was rolling out without profits rolling in, Tolnai told Lynne in the spring of 1981 that he thought it was time to look for some venture capital money. "You can't be a player in the software industry without outside investment," he told her. "We have to have more cash in this place." This was not what she wanted to hear. Opening Manac's books to outsiders, especially given Bruce's careful arrangements with the Blue Trust and his other tax avoidance plans, was anathema to her.

Tolnai had another concern. He wanted Lynne to stop talking to the people at Wang Computers about converting the Manac software to its computers from IBM's System 36 computers. "You're going to piss off the guys at IBM," he warned. "We've got a good thing going with them, and converting to Wang will ruin it."

The problem was that the IBM computers they were using to run Manac software in 1981 did not support letter-quality printers. This drove a perfectionist like Lynne crazy. Her clients wanted neat, letter-quality documents, and it made complete sense to her to make a deal with Wang, whose printers produced smooth and slick documents. "Stick with IBM," Tolnai pleaded. "It's just not worth changing and IBM will have its act together on printers soon." He knew that on a purely technical basis, she was right. "But from a business point of view it wasn't sensible. We had sixteen IBM guys recommending Manac software; if they knew that we were working with Wang, they would have been outraged. They would have stopped recommending us immediately, and our sales would have gone to zero."

At the time that Tolnai was arguing this issue with Lynne, IBM was under investigation by the United States Justice Department in a massive anti-trust lawsuit, because it had 75 percent of the American computer business. While the lawsuit was on, IBM wasn't allowed — formally — to recommend any particular software. This meant that IBM was forced to recommend three suppliers of legal software, not just Manac's, even though Lynne and Bryce Liberty had designed their system with IBM help and IBM computers. The Justice Department's lawsuit raged all through 1981. Tolnai was confident it would be settled, however, and when it was, he told Lynne, Manac would become IBM's sole-source-recommended legal software. Why jeopardize the relationship with IBM now?

Tolnai also couldn't understand why Lynne was being so pig-headed about venture capital. Worry began to overtake his optimism. As he sat in his apartment at night, he began to fret about his contract with the Vercheres, too. They'd all been so busy and so happy together that he hadn't pressed Bruce to draw up his deal. Besides, said Tolnai, "I trusted him. I'd never met a more charming, seemingly trustworthy, likeable guy. I am from a very professionally accomplished but modest family, my parents are both doctors but we are immigrants, and then I found myself with the Vercheres in Westmount where he has people filling up his car for him because he never went to the gas station. A woman named Nicole was like a personal concierge. She was a gofer at the law firm. I'd go to Westmount and sit out with Bruce and Lynne and have these fantastic white wines on his porch, and it was a magical thing for a guy like me who was maybe smart, but quite inexperienced. During the fall and winter, asking for my shares and the shareholders' agreement seemed irrelevant."

As time went on, said Tolnai, he started to become nervous. "I realized it's not coming around and I started to get desperate. I said things to sort of encourage them and make sure that they did it and finally realized they had no intention of doing it. I was stupid because I trusted them."

Each time Tolnai broached the subject of his shares, Bruce would say he'd have to talk to his wife. "They had a fantastic ability to play off each other. Bruce made me the promises and I'd go to Lynne, who was my president, and she'd say, 'Well, Bruce is doing the papers.' I'd go to Bruce and he'd say, 'I have to check with Lynne.' That kind of routine, and they'd never let themselves get in the same room at the same time. That was the whole gig: the oral contract."

By mid-July, Lynne found another reason to delay making commitments in writing to Tolnai. She discovered that he had hired Norm Steinberg, a lawyer at Ogilvy Renault, to draw up his understanding of the agreement.

Furious, Lynne told Tolnai that her husband wouldn't cooperate with Steinberg. And, she added tartly, he should know that she'd just promoted Larry Smith, who was now reporting directly to her; the two of them would market Manac Systems in eastern Canada, a territory that included Toronto; from now on Tolnai would work in western Canada. Smith was clearly the new favourite and he took advantage of the chance to learn from Lynne. "The experience was very interesting," he recalled, "because I had never worked with an entrepreneur before in a young startup-to-growing business like she had." Smith had at least two major advantages over Tolnai: his legal education, which let him talk to lawyers as one of their own, and his fame as a football hero, a big plus in a male world of law firms and software companies, where a female CEO might be viewed with surprise and misgivings. "I had a bit of a name," Smith said modestly, "and a bit of energy, and my job was to solicit people to get them to use Lynne's software."

For Tolnai, the reorganization was a turning point. He stopped trusting Lynne and their relationship turned sour; soon they avoided talking to each other altogether. A week later Tolnai met Bruce for a drink at the Beaver Club in the Queen Elizabeth Hotel and poured out his frustrations. "I'd like to get back on track," he told Verchere, "but part of the problem is that we never finalized my deal. It's been ten months now." Verchere was sympathetic. "I'll talk to Lynne," he soothed. "I'll get back to you." Typical, thought Tolnai.

Verchere was good at good conversations; bad conversations he simply avoided.

Two days later, at 9 a.m. on July 27, Lynne walked into Tolnai's office and shut the door. Without looking at him, she read out a statement telling him what was wrong with his performance at Manac. Shocked and furious, Tolnai left the office and went home. The first thing he did was call Bruce. "He wouldn't take my call. It was very clear where this was going."

The more Tolnai thought about the way he'd been treated, the angrier he got. He'd worked like a dog and he'd trusted them, and what hurt the most was that he'd fallen for them. He felt betrayed, professionally and personally. He couldn't do anything about the personal grief, but he thought he'd better recoup his professional losses and decided to sue them. Easier said than done, as it turned out. He tried to retain a lawyer and at least eight Montreal law firms said no. "Nobody was going to fight Bruce; it was an establishment thing. Bruce was an up-and-coming guy and Mulroney's tax lawyer and nobody would take the file."

Finally he got a yes from James Woods, who had turned him down earlier when he was still at Stikeman Elliott; now Woods was opening his own firm, and he called Tolnai the week he left Stikeman's, drumming up business. Tolnai sued for two sets of damages: $165,000 in lost wages under the five-year contract he'd negotiated, and $500,000 as his share of Manac (he believed the company was worth $2,000,000 and he was entitled to 25 percent). His problem was that the contract was verbal, and the Vercheres fiercely resisted his claims in their statement of defence. Their response was a litany of complaints about his performance at Manac; they said he was "entirely unable to do the kind of work that he was supposed to have been qualified to do." They blamed him for such things as poor morale in the office, losing deals, being unable to accept advice, poor writing skills, and a last-minute approach to his assignments.

Tolnai still flushed in anger years later as he scanned Manac's statement of defence again. "I got screwed," he said. "I'm not the kind of guy who sues people and it was the only lawsuit I have ever been in, ever, ever. It was one of the weirdest things that ever happened to me. But I wanted to put it behind me." In a 1982 out-of-court settlement, the Vercheres paid him about $100,000.

When Larry Smith thought back on the dispute, he was unwilling to take sides, saying he had sympathy for both Tolnai and Lynne. But he pointed out that she was the one in charge. "Peter was a young Harvard graduate and he had certain ideas about how things should be done," said Smith. "He was a very assertive young guy and she was a very assertive owner, and the difference is that the person who writes the cheques makes the final decision." Part of the problem, Smith thought, was that Tolnai was young and not used to working with a tough boss. It's not that much different, he said, than being a professional athlete. "There is no question that she was demanding and tough," said Smith. "A lot of the coaches I've had have been demanding and tough so I'm used to working in that environment, and you look at it in a different way. She was just as tough as those people. At the end of the day it was her business, her life, her money."

Smith left Manac a year after he joined the company. His memories, he said, were positive — especially of Lynne. She taught him how to be a manager. "I thought she was very direct, enthusiastic, assertive. She had good leadership skills and it taught me a lot that I used later in my career. What I learned from Lynne were the types of skills you need for survival and to build something from scratch. What I learned was intestinal fortitude and drive, which were her greatest strengths."

Smith left, he said, not because he was unhappy but because he'd learned what he could and wanted to run his own show. "Lynne was a very demanding person, and that's what she had to be because she was trying to build her business. I just decided that it was probably best. I am a fairly assertive person myself, and I could see myself not necessarily lasting long-term in that sort of environment. So it was better for me to go somewhere else." He did not, he said, have any problem with the way she ran Manac or dealt with her employees. To him, she seemed a very private person with a big heart and a sense of humour that flashed all too seldom. She was proud, he said, and protective of her family and her husband. But more than anything, she was driven.

SEVEN
Special Risks

ZENA CHERRY, the *Globe and Mail's* society columnist, was usually blasé about even the most exclusive parties, covering them with a kind of weary friendliness. But when the Swiss Bank Corporation's Canadian branch threw a thirtieth-anniversary party at the Royal York Hotel in Toronto on September 17, 1981, her prose went into overdrive. "The most lavish of evenings," she gushed, describing the "nine-course dinner with Landson Champagne Brut, four vintage wines, a floor show with Shirley Jones, dancing to Howard Cable's orchestra and the final dessert served about 12:55 a.m. with liqueurs. Even the sherbet was made with Dom Perignon champagne." The chef said to Cherry, "'I told my staff to do their proud best, because this power group could have chosen any one of many places, but it chose to come here.' As for going-home gifts, every man received a brass desk clock and the women were given silver brooches. Gorgeous."

If Zena Cherry was impressed, it's easy to imagine how Bruce Verchere felt. After slogging in the trenches as the bank's lawyer for five years, the evening was a personal celebration for him; the next day, he knew, Sam Wiedmer would be making the formal announcement that Verchere had been elected to the bank's board of directors; that delicious news would also appear in the *Globe and Mail*. Except for the lingering unpleasantness of Peter Tolnai's lawsuit, the fall of 1981 had been sweet. Although the Swiss Bank Corporation (Switzerland's second-largest bank at the time) had been active in Canada for nearly thirty years and had offices in Toronto, Montreal, and Vancouver, it didn't receive a Canadian bank charter until July 1981. As the bank's lawyer, Bruce had worked hard on this file, and the directorship was, he believed, a richly deserved bonus. What made it an even better night was that two old friends had also joined him on the board: Bob Fasken, the Toronto mining promoter who had put him up for membership at the Griffith Island Club, and Vancouver businessman David Helliwell, an old classmate from UBC, by then the chairman of British Columbia Resources Investment Corporation.

As Cherry circulated through the crowd, taking note of such bank luminaries as its Swiss chairman, Hans Strasser, from Basel, and the general manager in Canada, Franz Luetoff, she also ran into many of Canada's business elite. Fredrik Eaton, the chairman of his family's department store chain, was there; so were Trevor Eyton from Brascan, Thomas Bata, the founder of the Bata shoe empire, Cedric Ritchie from the Bank of Nova Scotia, and Kurt Aach, chairman of Hoechst Canada. Many of Verchere's business cronies were invited: Klaus Brose, for example, from Wild Leitz Canada Limited (later Leica), on whose board Verchere sat, and Fritz Henning Baehre, who also served on two or three boards with him.

Cherry jotted down the names and positions of all the important people in the crowd (all there, in the vernacular of the times, "with their wives"), struggling to understand what they had in common. "Present were some people known as the big money movers," she wrote in her column. "I was told, 'They spend their days placing millions upon millions of temporarily surplus funds around the globe in short-term investments; and, for major projects, raise funds in various financial centers of the world. The moving of very large blocks of money is a sophisticated operation."

Indeed it is, and Verchere's work for the Swiss Bank Corporation was giving him the experience he needed to master the art. As the years went by, he spent more and more time flying to Toronto Island Airport for meetings with Sam Wiedmer and Franz Luetoff at the bank's headquarters at the renovated warehouse called Queen's Quay Terminal, an unusual location for an international bank in Toronto; most banks bunched themselves in skyscrapers around King and Bay. Bank officials at first had thought the location, nestled beside a small marina on the waterfront and looking over at the Toronto Islands, was trendy and smart; Wiedmer and his wife moved into one of the condominium apartments above the offices. But "QQT," as Swiss Bank officials called their offices, turned out to be a little too smart; tourists crowded into the shops and restaurants in the building and wandered up and down the sidewalks outside. "Riff-raff," bank officials sniffed. They longed for the more convenient towers of Bay Street, but the bank had too much money invested in its quirky space to move.

For Verchere, the location was perfect; his Cessna sat waiting for him at the Island Airport, just a few blocks further west off Queen's Quay. The bank was his biggest client and he was dealing with many different issues there; one was the federal government's insistence that foreign banks limit their growth in Canada to prevent them from dominating the country's financial system. Foreign banks could carry assets of up to only twenty times their deemed capital; the Swiss Bank's deemed capital was estimated to be $15 million, for total assets of $300 million. Not surprisingly, foreign banks were opposed to such limits, and Verchere kept a watching brief for the Swiss Bank Corporation on this issue. His other clients included wealthy individuals such as Hailey and others who planned to become wealthy, such as Brian Mulroney, all of whom he advised on financial issues. He was also looking after some other large corporate accounts, including Alcan.

Verchere enjoyed having big-name clients and though he was discreet about their files, he didn't hesitate to drop their names, especially to juniors in his firm and at Manac. Even the juniors knew, in those years, that Mulroney was the man to watch in the Conservative Party, an almost sure bet to replace the hapless Joe Clark as party leader. Knowing that Verchere was his trusted financial advisor, a member of the inner circle around the man already being touted as the saviour of the Tory party and the next prime minister, gave lustre to everyone in the firm. Unfortunately, not all his clients were as impressed with Verchere as he'd have liked. Some felt that he was — to use the euphemism tax lawyers like — "too aggressive" with his tax planning. There were also rumours floating around Montreal that he'd put together tax shelters that had fallen apart. "I don't know if these problems were negligence or sheer silliness," mused one senior Stikeman's partner. "He did do things that had no legal basis whatsoever and charge immense amounts of money for them. The stark fact of the thing was that he did not have any moral fibre and that appears in his actions vis-à-vis his clients."

Still one of Verchere's nastiest files was the Richards Melling case, known around Montreal as "Special Risks." The wise old taxmen use it as a horrible example to warn impressionable articling students of what can happen if you get too clever. Back in 1976, when Verchere took on the mid-size Montreal-based family insurance firm Richards Melling, it was run by Fred Melling, the son of the founder. Richards Melling was owned by Melling's personal company, Special Risks Holdings Inc. After Melling accepted the $3-million investment from Hogg Robinson, Verchere's job was to figure out how to pay the least tax on the $3 million and keep Fred Melling in control.

Verchere had structured a new ownership agreement, giving Hogg Robinson 49 percent of the company and Richards Melling 51 percent. Eleven days later he rejigged the ownership to give each side 50 percent. Fred Melling and Verchere enjoyed a rapport that was at first a strictly client-lawyer relationship, but that with time grew into a friendship as well. Melling put him on the board of his insurance firm. The bond he developed with Verchere may have blinded Melling to the reality that Verchere's tax work, which at first blush looked quite reasonable, was in fact a time bomb.

Back in 1976, about six months before the Parti Québécois came to power, Melling had been toying with the notion of pulling some value out of the family-owned insurance business. Still, he wished to retain control of Richards Melling; after all, it had been passed on to him by his father. Melling hoped Verchere would be able to come up with a clever way of selling off a big chunk of the firm without triggering a tax liability. As Melling later testified, "I had been spending some time with our tax advisors, specifically Bruce Verchere of Verchere Gauthier, to put together a scheme or a plan . . . Bruce had come up and suggested to me there was a way to do this through preferred shares." Verchere's solution was simple, but it was wrapped in a sufficient swirl of transactions to make it appear far more complex.

It was always understood that Melling, through Special Risks Holdings, was to retain a 51 percent interest in Richards Melling Company and to keep control of it. However, Melling would obtain a significant tax advantage if, immediately after Special Risks exchanged its voting shares of the capital stock of Richards Melling for non-voting shares of Richards Melling, it could argue successfully that Special Risks did not control Richards Melling. Thus, for that short period of time, Special Risks and Hogg each appeared to control and own 50 percent of Richards Melling, through a holding company they called Melling, Hogg, Robinson Ltd. Hogg then transferred one share of Melling, Hogg, Robinson to Melling's company, Special Risks Holdings, even though it was under no obligation to do so. This strategy reinforced the conclusion that Melling and Hogg Robinson had never intended that Melling give up control of Richards Melling even though, for tax purposes, it was made to appear as if he had done so.

Years later, Madame Justice Barbara Reed of the Federal Court of Canada described the way Verchere had assembled this complicated deal:

On December 1, 1976 Melling owned 2,500 class "A" shares and 2,300 class "B" shares of Richards Melling Company Limited (RMC). All shares carried voting rights and the plaintiff's [Melling's] holdings clearly constituted ownership of a majority of the issued shares of the company. On December 17, 1976, Richards, Melling's authorized capital was increased by 100,000 common shares (of a par value of $1.00 each). On the same date a new corporation, Melling, Hogg, Robinson Limited was incorporated under the laws of Canada. On December 20, 1976, 50,000 common shares of Melling, Hogg, Robinson were purchased by the Hogg Robinson Group Limited, and 50,000 common shares were purchased by the plaintiff. On the same date Melling, Hogg, Robinson purchased 100,000 common shares (voting) of Richards Melling (RMC) thereby acquiring control in terms of share ownership of RMC. On December 23, 1976, Richards, Melling's (RMC's) authorized capital was modified and new classes of preferred and common shares were issued and the plaintiff exchanged its old class "A" and "B" shares in Richards, Melling for new class "A", "B" and "C" shares all of which were non-voting. On December 31, 1976, the Hogg Robinson Group sold 1,000 of its shares in Melling, Hogg, Robinson to the plaintiff; the plaintiff thereby acquired 51% of the shares of that corporation.

That was the way it stood for two years. Then Revenue Canada's auditors gave it a close look, and it did not pass what Heward Stikeman had always called "the smell test." This test, famous in Stikeman Elliott lore, was simple: a deal will not pass, explained one Stikeman partner, if it is legal "but if you also know it will fly for only a limited time — and if it does fly, it will be attacked and the client will not thank you for his becoming the butt of public denigration." Not only did the auditors not like its odour, they disallowed the tax claims. Melling went running to Verchere to set them straight and the Special Risks battle was on — a fight with Revenue Canada that was to last seventeen years.

There were other problems brewing at Verchere, Noël & Eddy as well; the firm was getting a reputation as a difficult place for some of the tax lawyers it hired. André Gauthier, who had started with Verchere in 1973, had finally had enough by 1979 and left. Several other young hotshots brought in by Verchere's charm and promises were quickly disillusioned. Norman Tobias, the tax lawyer whose sister found Lynne yelling at her to get her dog off the Vercheres' lawn, was one of them. "Bruce always struck me as having that number of seconds or minutes for you that was directly proportional to how important you were," said Tobias. "The sum total of my interaction with Bruce? It wasn't much. I just worked at Verchere, Noël & Eddy for three months. It's been a revolving door for most lawyers." (Tobias moved to Toronto in 1984 and now runs his own successful tax practice on Bay Street.) All this was unfortunate for the firm because Verchere's partners, Marc Noël and Ross Eddy, had excellent reputations.

The unhappiest former Verchere, Noël & Eddy alumnus was Arthur Campeau (later appointed by Brian Mulroney as Canada's ambassador for the environment). Nearly six feet tall and handsome — he looked so much like the hockey star Jean Béliveau that he was always being mistaken for him — Campeau had been practising law at Ogilvy Renault with close friends like Mulroney and Bernard Roy. Although he loved working at Ogilvy Renault, in 1983 Campeau was dreaming the dream of so many prosperous lawyers who toil in the big legal factories: Wouldn't it be nice to run my own firm? A boutique, specializing in litigation or entertainment or communications or the energy sector. A place where I could have just a few hand-picked guys around, whose practices would dovetail with mine.

Campeau had some good clients he could count on; one of the best was Bell Canada, for whom he'd worked as a high-profile lawyer on the creation of Bell Canada Enterprises. Finally, in 1983, when Campeau landed an extraordinary file, one which could virtually finance a new law firm, he decided this was his chance. Before he made the move, however, he decided to retain Verchere as expert tax counsel on the new file, and they met to discuss it. Not only did Campeau respect Verchere's opinions, but he'd retained him before on tax matters. This new file was more complicated than most.

As soon as Verchere heard about Campeau's extraordinary clients and understood that Campeau now had the ability to start his own firm, Verchere offered him a partnership. "Sure, I understand the desire to start your own firm," he reassured Campeau. "That's the dream I had, too, and I did it. But look: Verchere,

Noël & Eddy only has tax lawyers and we know we have to set up a litigation department. This would be just the place for you."

Verchere poured on the charm, showed Campeau healthy statements of accounts receivable and cash flow, and made him feel as if he was destined to be part of the firm. It wasn't easy for Campeau to relinquish what he called Plan A to go with Plan B and join Verchere. Finally, though, feeling comfortable and wanted, he surrendered. "I thought to myself, 'What the hell, he's already found the location, the space, the office is here, it's sound financially, he has good banking relations, a good reputation.'" Campeau, of course, had no idea that his new partner had been turfed from Stikeman's.

When Campeau agreed to come on board, bringing his splendid file as a dowry, he was starstruck. "Bruce was warm. Kind. Just a generally nice guy." Campeau himself was always an impressive man, gregarious and funny and very frank. He and Verchere had always gotten on well and had plenty in common; their sons were at Selwyn House together, and the two dads sometimes saw each other at the school's hockey games. Both men also had pilot's licences and a deep enthusiasm for flying. And Campeau believed his new partner to be one of the best tax lawyers in North America. Verchere could spread his wonderful optimism to cloak the most stressful situation. "He gave the impression of someone who was very comfortable at making a lot of money and of really enjoying himself in the process," said Campeau. Even with the most complex files weighing on his mind, Verchere presented a happy-go-lucky front. "He always seemed to be relaxed and enjoying life to the fullest."

Within two months, however, Campeau knew, with a sick feeling in his gut, that he'd made a big mistake. It was a realization Peter Tolnai could have predicted almost to the minute. Instead of drafting a legal agreement before he started, Campeau and Verchere merely shook hands on a gentlemen's agreement, Verchere promising to produce a contract quickly. Once he'd hooked Campeau, however, he stalled on the contract. In the meantime, even though he was becoming increasingly anxious, Campeau was too preoccupied with his new file to find the time to argue. The file, the one that had prompted Verchere to press so eagerly for Campeau to join him, was not simply a cash cow, it was a unique, intriguing, and historic case; even the small part of it that Campeau had snagged made him the envy of many of his peers. Quite simply, it involved the most sensational banking scandal in Europe in generations, a scandal whose many tentacles stretched into Canada.

EIGHT

The Calvi File

ARTHUR CAMPEAU had been retained to act for the widow and the son of Roberto Calvi, the man known around the world as "God's Banker" because of his close ties to the Vatican. Until August 1982, Calvi had been chairman of the Milan-based Banco Ambrosiano, Italy's largest private banking group, which crashed in a $1.4-billion (U.S.) bankruptcy earlier that year. Three of the bank's Latin American subsidiaries had loaned at least $1.24 billion to ten Panamanian shell companies owned by the Vatican Bank, which was set up in 1942 and is known as the Istituto per le Opere di Religione, or IOR. The money quickly melted away through a clever and massive fraud perpetrated, it was widely believed, by Calvi himself.

When the scandal broke in 1981, Calvi was arrested on charges of illegally exporting currency. After being released on bail, he disappeared; in June 1982 his body, with stones weighing down his pockets, was found hanging by a rope under Blackfriars Bridge in London. Although early reports called his death a suicide, a London coroner's jury later reversed that decision, ruling that it could have been murder. Perhaps their failure to reach a suicide verdict was influenced by the fact that the same week Calvi's body was found, his secretary tumbled to her death from her fourth-floor office window in Milan. Perhaps it was because the jury was well informed about Calvi's ruthless colleagues, who would think nothing of having him silenced before he could cut a deal with the authorities.

In the worldwide publicity about the scandal, most eyes were on the Vatican and on Italian businessman Licio Gelli; it was not widely known that the money trail led to Canada and that Arthur Campeau was helping Calvi's widow, Clara, and their son, Carlo, stave off creditors and international investigators. How a Montreal lawyer came to be involved is rather mysterious. Along with the stones, and money of various currencies, the London police found Campeau's business card (among several others) in Roberto Calvi's pockets. "How it got into his pocket," Campeau mused, "I have absolutely no idea." Campeau had once acted for First National Bank in Boston and the Royal Bank, both of which were investigating Michele Sindona, another crooked Italian banker who had once been Calvi's mentor and who had moved huge amounts of money out of Italy. Some of that money was said to have come into Montreal in the form of real estate investment; one example, said Campeau, was the Port Royal apartment building, the first condominium apartment complex built in Quebec, on Sherbrooke Street near the Ritz-Carlton Hotel.

"We were going after Sindona," said Campeau, "trying to unravel his empire and get at money that we were convinced he had, which the First National Bank of Boston wanted." Perhaps because Campeau's name was floating around in this proceeding, Roberto Calvi heard about him. That's why, Campeau figured, when Calvi's widow and son needed a Canadian lawyer, they fished out the card found in Calvi's pocket. It didn't matter to them that he'd acted against Sindona; as far as they were concerned, if he did a good job, he was the lawyer they wanted. Campeau believed they probably even checked him out with Sindona.

The Calvis didn't just depend on a piece of paper and Sindona's say-so. Before they hired Campeau, they ran a thorough check on him. Carlo read through newspaper clippings, tracing Campeau's work on behalf of two former RCMP officers, Donald McCleery and Gilles Brunet, who had been charged with dirty tricks and other offences connected to RCMP investigations into suspected French-Canadian terrorists in the early 1970s. Campeau had appeared before two royal commissions looking at RCMP wrongdoing, and clearly Carlo was impressed by his performance; he also knew that Campeau had become a close friend of both officers. Soon nothing could shake Carlo's conviction that Campeau himself was a member of Canada's security services.

"I was in a huge shopping mall in Calgary with Carlo Calvi," remembered Campeau. "Part of it is like an amusement park, and there was a shooting gallery where little animals go by on a track. You have a rifle with a laser beam on it, and if you hit the target you get points. I was having one of those days that I just could not miss. I discovered that Carlo had been staring at me while I was doing this. Given what had happened to his father and his father's secretary, it's not surprising he was paranoid."

After the collapse of Banco Ambrosiano, international investigators swarmed through the bank's offices and files looking for the money; senior bank officials were arrested and charged; others, including some of the Vatican's most high-ranking priests, were implicated. It wasn't long before it was discovered that at least $300 million of the money had wound up in the hands of Propaganda Due, P-2, the illegal and ultra-secret 900-member Italian Freemasons lodge organized by Gelli, an unapologetic fascist. Gelli was an arms dealer, a veteran of the pro-Franco forces in Spain during the Spanish Civil War, an interrogator for Mussolini's forces during World War II. He had even worked as an advisor to the Argentine dictator Juan Perón. He was also P-2's grand master, overseeing the politicians, military officers, intelligence officers, businessmen, judges, and senior journalists who made up the lodge membership, a membership later described by a parliamentary committee as Italy's "hidden power structure," and a group that worked closely with ultra-right political groups involved in arms trafficking. Gelli worked hand-in-glove with Roberto Calvi, P-2's paymaster. According to investigators, the $300 million that Calvi funnelled through the Panamanian shells to the Freemasons went to pay for bribery and influence-peddling to support right-wing political groups in other countries.

In Italy, P-2 was connected to right-wing terrorist bombings — including the 1980 bombing of the Bologna train station in which eighty people died — as well as kidnappings and assassinations. It was suspected, for example, of plotting the 1978 kidnapping and murder of P-2's most serious enemy, Italian prime minister Aldo Moro. During these years the United States was still preoccupied with Cold War politics and the Communist threat. Italy had a strong Communist Party and the United States would have reacted negatively if Italy had come under a Communist government. The repercussions for the defence of Europe and in NATO would have been enormous.

"If Italy had become Communist," Campeau said, "you had a whole different geopolitical map to deal with. U.S. interests might have required that the Americans hold their noses and work with the ultra-right forces financed by Banco Ambrosiano cash. I never had any doubt that it involved money from the proceeds of crime or drug money, that sort of stuff. I never had any doubt at all."

Investigators looking into the collapse of Banco Ambrosiano eventually discovered that Gelli and his second-in-command, Umberto Ortolani, had accounts with the Bank of Montreal in Montreal. They found that Calvi also had several Canadian connections. An affidavit later sworn by a Touche Ross investigator stated that Calvi moved millions of dollars through the shell companies for his own use and that of friends, and that the paper trail led to two safes held by a trust account at the RoyWest Trust Corporation in the Bahamas. (RoyWest was a Royal Bank of Canada subsidiary.) Further tracing found that the largest part of the Bahamian money wound up in a New York branch of the Royal Bank. When the investigators finally obtained access to these hidden accounts, they discovered cash, jewellery, and information about three other secret accounts with assets of $9.5 million, along with details of the deals that Calvi had done with Gelli, Ortolani, and Michele Sindona.

This was not Calvi's only link to Canada. Touche Ross investigators later claimed that he funnelled other sums of the missing money from Swiss banks into Alberta in the 1970s. In 1974, for example, Calvi bought the Rocky Mountain Plaza in Calgary for $7.6 million. He sold it in 1982 for $24.9 million. Also in 1974 he paid $830,823 for the 2,000-hectare Dunkeld Ranch west of Edmonton, buying it from businessman Donald Cormie, who founded the Principal Group financial empire, which collapsed in 1987. Carlo Calvi later told *Globe and Mail* reporter Christopher Donville that his father had applied for landed immigrant status in 1974 and hoped to retire to Alberta. He also insisted that his father had bought the Alberta property with money he'd earned legitimately as the well-paid chairman of Banco Ambrosiano. Investigators did not share Carlo's view and as early as 1982 were chasing his father's money in Canada and looking in particular at Calvi assets held in Montreal. But the financing of the Alberta properties, especially the Dunkeld Ranch, was so complex, so carefully run through secretive Swiss banks, that its source could not be traced.

Campeau's belief was that Calvi intended to invest in Cormie's Principal Group of financial companies. "I don't know the full extent of the financial transactions that may have taken place between Calvi and the Principal Group," he said. "It may have been that Calvi intended to invest in the Principal Group building. I think it was the beginnings of a growing relationship between Calvi and Cormie."

Campeau had no trouble getting Bruce Verchere's attention when he outlined his work for the family of God's Banker; without disclosing his client's confidential affairs, he gave Verchere a whiff of the elements he loved so much: offshore banks, Panamanian trusts, Bahamian and Swiss accounts, shell companies. An added fillip was that Calvi's family was now living in a place Verchere knew well, Lyford Cay. The Calvi house was just a block away from the Haileys'.

Calvi had been a big shooter and a wily plotter, someone eminently worthy of Verchere's attention; Verchere was naturally delighted to think his firm would get a piece of this action. It promised to be a long and unusually profitable undertaking, and it also promised to be exciting. Did Verchere want Campeau on board simply because Campeau owned this file? Campeau thought not. "I think he did genuinely want to start a litigation department or expand beyond simply the tax practice and thought that with the clients that would follow me from Ogilvy Renault, financially it would be a good proposition and would enhance his reputation. I don't think he made me the offer he did with a view to trying to get the Calvi file. It had to be in his mind, but I think it was secondary. Of course, I may be dead wrong."

When Campeau tried to bring Verchere in to help with the Calvi file, the mother and son were suspicious. On one occasion, when the two lawyers flew to Nassau together to meet with them, the Calvis refused to talk to Verchere. Persisting, Campeau took his partner to a dinner meeting. The Calvis wouldn't sit with him; Verchere had to move to a table across the room and eat by himself while Campeau talked business with Carlo and Clara. The Calvis' cool treatment didn't stop Verchere from confiding to Arthur Hailey that he was now acting for the family of God's Banker.

Because his clients were so demanding, the file so complex, and the sums of money so vast, Campeau was consumed with the Calvi case and kept postponing a showdown with Verchere over his contract. "I teamed up with Bruce in roughly August 1983, and by the end of September or October I realized I had made a horrendous mistake," Campeau said. "I was travelling a lot and the stuff I was working on was too complicated. I just could not afford even a two-week or three-week interruption to pack my stuff, disentangle whatever my financial relations were at that time with the Verchere firm, and do all the stuff you need to do to start up a practice."

The trouble really started when Verchere finally had to give Campeau a statement of the firm's accounts receivable and cash flow. He had grossly exaggerated the law firm's income, said Campeau, and because of this, Verchere's bank, the Canadian Imperial Bank of Commerce, was unwilling to grant the firm its usual discount against receivables. A law firm's bank will usually advance between 70 and 80 percent of the firm's accounts receivable for cash flow, but the CIBC would advance the money only if the receivables were due in less than ninety days. The bank simply didn't count money due after ninety days. "In Bruce's case a lot of them would come awful close or fall off that ninety-day table," Campeau said, "and then he would negotiate a deal with the client whereby the client would pay, but not the amount of the account that Bruce had rendered."

Campeau suspected that Verchere was gouging his clients, then settling for less when they squawked or refused to pay. "Bruce purposely padded bills, sent bills to clients that were way out of whack, far higher than the client ever expected, and then would get on the phone and try to negotiate a fee that was more acceptable to the client. His bills were very high. The Commerce was squeezing him hard because his receivables were turning sour. They were turning sour because he was overbilling. Shortly after I arrived, I realized that he was overextended at the bank because of the number of receivables that had gone past ninety days. I recall he and Marc Noël were on the phone to a whole slew of clients trying to collect the outstanding receivables."

Noël, today a Federal Court judge, made no apologies for their cash flow crunch. In big silk-stocking firms like Ogilvy Renault, conceded Noël, the partners certainly would not have chased deadbeat clients. But a new firm, a smaller outfit, had no choice but to call and ask for the money. "We were not as established. Things were not quite as easy as they would have been in a major law firm."

Campeau didn't accept Noël's explanation. Yes, he said, even in large firms senior partners pick up the phone and ask clients if they have a problem with their bill and if that's why they haven't paid. But that wasn't the point, Campeau argued. The point was not whether in a smaller firm it was the actual partners who got on the phone. The point was that, as Campeau put it, "Bruce's bills were exorbitant." In the early 1980s, he said, Verchere charged at least $400 an hour, perhaps the highest rate in Montreal. "If you added the total number of hours, let's say ten hours, then that's $4,000. But if you get a bill for $25,000 — hey, whoa, just a minute."

One client who had no problem with Verchere's bills was Arthur Hailey. "They always seemed reasonable in view of what Bruce and his organization did for me," he said. "For a while his bills included details of expenses apart from legal fees and I remember scribbling on one bill something like: 'Bruce — in future please don't bother me w/all this detail. Don't need it. Just show total amount only. I trust you. Arthur.' From them on, he did just that and the amounts still seemed to me entirely reasonable."

Whether or not Verchere was overbilling, the cash wasn't coming in fast enough to suit him, and Verchere was angry about the recalcitrant attitude of the CIBC. He asked Campeau to talk to the Royal Bank to see if they would be interested in Verchere, Noël & Eddy's business. Campeau agreed, but as soon as the Royal had a confidential chat with the CIBC, the answer that came back was no thanks.

Campeau, too, was getting angrier by the day. He felt betrayed and embarrassed and stupid. "I realized I had not been astute enough to ask the right questions." The problems came to a head when Campeau realized he was not going to earn the large monthly draw Verchere had promised him. Verchere, he said, deliberately misled him. "Bruce knew damn well," Campeau said. "Every partner of a law firm receives a draw every month, and that draw is based on the projected income of the firm for the year, and that is based on past financial experience of the firm. If you project that you are going to make x million dollars net, you know just about how much money is going to be shared among the partners. The draw is always going to add up to less than the actual total in order to be conservative. And so at certain times during the year, or at the end of the year, depending on the practice of the firm, there is a further distribution of profits because it looks like you are on target with your budget or you are going to go over. You release more money to the partners."

That didn't happen. Campeau heard one excuse after another from Verchere. When he thought about the attitude of the CIBC, the problem with receivables, his own failure to demand a written contract, he blamed only himself: "It was a stupid, stupid thing for me to have done. It was not that Bruce had miscalculated. It was that Bruce knew damn well what the financial situation of the firm was and withheld that information from me."

What Campeau was going through was not new around the firm; it was the reason other lawyers had left before. In the 1970s, Verchere could perhaps have excused his payment practices by saying the firm was new and underfinanced; by now, however, it was well established and prosperous. Verchere seemed to be more comfortable handling money this way, but he paid a high price in senior staff turnover. Though still swamped by the Calvi file, Campeau finally lost patience. Not only had Verchere airily reneged on his promises, it didn't seem to bother him. That, more than anything else, was what made Campeau's blood boil. Campeau even began to suspect that Verchere was stealing from his own firm. "I figured if I was to probe long and hard enough, I would find that Bruce was siphoning profits away from the Montreal partners into some other arrangement so that the Montreal partners would end up getting less and Bruce would end up getting more. At that point I was just fed up. I remembered the old adage that a lawyer acting for himself has a fool for a client, and I retained Peter Blaikie."

Blaikie, a partner at Heenan Blaikie, where Pierre Trudeau went after he retired from politics in 1984, began preparations to sue Verchere; Verchere, in turn, hired Jim Woods, the lawyer who had gone after him on behalf of Peter Tolnai. (Perhaps Verchere had been impressed by Woods's work for Tolnai.) When Campeau heard about Woods, he was stunned. "I'd had lunch with Ross Clarkson, Woods's partner, only about a month earlier, and I had talked to him quite candidly about the situation

I found myself in with Verchere. I was hesitating about what I was going to do and I was really talking to Clarkson to determine whether to retain Clarkson to go after him." Because Campeau knew he would definitely be starting his own firm now, he had talked to Clarkson about the possibility of inviting Clarkson's firm to join him.

"And then, to my great surprise, it's Clarkson's partner who ends up representing Verchere after I had very detailed discussions with Clarkson about my side of the case. I almost went to the bar association with it. It's a conflict of interest, no question about that. It may well have figured into the conversations Peter Blaikie had with Woods about the settlement. At that point I wanted to put the whole goddamn experience behind me, and although the settlement was for much less than I thought was due, I took it just to get on with my life and get away from Bruce. I just did not want to have anything further to do with him."

The lawyers quickly worked out a settlement without messy litigation, something everyone was anxious to avoid that spring. The Tories around Brian Mulroney, who had become the party leader in 1983, were planning for the federal election expected for the fall — and Montreal was a small town. Verchere would be Mulroney's financial trustee for the blind trust he would be obligated to set up if he became prime minister; Blaikie was the national president of the Tory party; not only were Campeau and his former wife, Cathy, friends of the Mulroneys, but Campeau had also been Mulroney's law partner at Ogilvy Renault. It was all just too sweaty. No one wanted any simmering disagreements among Mulroney insiders at such a delicate point, not when they all expected a Conservative majority and a big patronage pie of legal work to cut up afterwards.

There was another reality Campeau had to face. If he went after Verchere publicly, there could be a backlash from clients who would question his judgment. "So other than taking out a front-page ad in the newspaper to explain what was going on, or holding a press conference, which of course was unthinkable, I was at the mercy of scuttlebutt at that time." Even many years later, however, the settlement rankled Campeau. "I know a number of the guys who were with him when I was there have since left the firm, and I don't think they would have charitable things to say about Bruce. They share the same view of, 'You too, eh?'"

Marc Noël dismissed Campeau's complaints with the assertion that Verchere's partners always did well from their association with him, but some became jealous. Once your firm becomes successful and starts to make money, he said, there will always be an issue of how to divide the money equably. Should one person make more than another? "And then you get into typical human conflicts about one's own perceptions about one's worth versus someone else's," he said. "Bruce was basically the client-getter. How much was that worth? As against, for instance, a Nat Boidman, who was obviously the intellectual conceptualizer of brilliant tax plans. Who should get the reward? The person who has the ability to bring the client in? Or the brilliant conceptualizer who works behind closed doors to satisfy their needs? Those are the debates that arose and they are normal. At the end of the day, when people don't understand one another, what do they do? They part company."

Noël added that Campeau was wrong to accuse Verchere of gouging. What went on in the firm, he said, was fair and ethical, and Bruce deserved the money he earned. Furthermore, every law firm has to chase clients for money. "I don't know of any firm that does not ask its lawyers to do that."

In the spring of 1984, soon after settling his lawsuit against Verchere, Noël & Eddy, Campeau finally set up his own firm. He left the Calvi file behind him. He wasn't sorry to part with it. It was a file, he laughed nervously, in which people tended to die in mysterious circumstances. Frankly, he said, he was afraid. There was just too much money involved, and too many powerful people with powerful interests who would prefer that there be no one walking around who knew how all the pieces fit together. "There came a point when there was too much cloak-and-dagger stuff," Campeau admitted, "and I did not know what the hell I was involved in — whether this was a struggle between the CIA and the Communists or God knows what. If you continued to probe and get those answers, then you knew too much."

Campeau believed that the CIA and other security forces were pulling strings in the affair. "They had to be. It just made complete sense to me that they would be. There was just too much money. So I did not know whose bloody side I was on in all of this, as I realized it wasn't the Calvis who were controlling all this money. Somebody else was. I did not know who, and I did not want to know."

After Campeau left Verchere, Noël & Eddy, the file stayed with the firm. Verchere no doubt discussed the case with the Calvis' lawyers in Nassau. "This is the kind of file that to Bruce would have represented a private pension plan," said Campeau acidly. "This could have gone on for years and years and years." But Ross Eddy wound up with it and looked after it until the late 1980s, perhaps because by then Verchere had started to pull out of the practice.

"At about the point that I withdrew from the file," said Campeau, "my discontent with Bruce had reached such a level that I was in a depression and close to breakdown, and I was punishing myself for my stupidity in making a handshake deal with a guy who turned out to be one of the biggest crooks walking the streets of Montreal. I still feel that way. I have nothing kind or generous to say about Bruce Verchere. Nothing."

NINE

All the Prime Minister's Men

THE EARLY 1980S were fruitful and lucrative for the Vercheres; the contretemps with Peter Tolnai and Arthur Campeau were minor blips in their steady upward progress. Verchere, Noël & Eddy was doing so well and developing such a national profile that the partners decided to open an office in Toronto. Manac was doing even better. By 1984 Lynne had forty-two law firms signed up for software modules and technical support packages.

Selling the software grew easier every month, but there was more to her success than convincing lawyers she had the best system; she also had to keep IBM happy so that the company would continue touting Manac as its licensed legal software. When it was important to put on a show for important IBM executives from out of town, Lynne would recruit Bruce's help in arranging a dinner, usually at the Ritz-Carlton. She and Bruce were, as one of Lynne's staff admiringly put it, "an unbeatable negotiating team." Bruce usually met the clients for drinks at the end of the day in the Maritime Bar; Lynne, he would explain, had been held up at the office. Subjected to Bruce's focused charm, the visitors relaxed right away; within minutes they'd be clinking glasses, throwing back hors d'oeuvres, and exchanging the latest business gossip. By the time Lynne arrived, they'd be ready to make a night of it. Lynne would come in, trim and neat in an expensive suit, just as the group was going in for dinner, and impress them with her smile and warm interest. She and Bruce usually saved serious business discussions for the next day. Cognac and other liqueurs would follow the dinner; often a nightcap would end the evening, and the visitors would roll off to bed, happy and tipsy.

In the morning, the group would gather again, the visitors usually a little under the weather. Lynne, fresh and brisk, was in complete command of the agenda. She'd present a carefully drafted plan for the group's meeting, one that highlighted Manac's strength. "That was when Lynne was at her best," remembered one employee. Almost always the executives would agree with her analysis and go back to their headquarters happy about a productive session after a pleasant evening. They had no idea how carefully and skillfully they'd been handled.

On one occasion, in September 1982, Lynne invited representatives from several Montreal law firms to a symposium in Montreal to show off the software; one of the firms was Lapointe Schacter Champagne & Talbot. The two famous partners were the legendary criminal lawyers Gabriel Lapointe and Raphael Schacter. Lapointe was well known in Quebec for his successful defence in the murder trial of a Montreal lawyer, Claire Lortie, nicknamed "Chainsaw Lortie" by crime reporters because she had used a chainsaw to cut her dead lover into pieces and stuff them in a freezer. (Lapointe was later to become famous for defending Conservative member of Parliament Michel Gravel on bribery and influence-peddling charges during the Mulroney years. He was brilliant at delaying the charges and sentencing for years, but Gravel finally pleaded guilty and went to jail.)

Raphael Schacter also defended high-profile clients; among those in the 1990s were Prime Minister Jean Chrétien's son Michel, in a sexual assault case; Tory senator Michel Cogger, found guilty in 1998 on charges of influence-peddling; and a former chief of defence staff, General Jean Boyle, over his role in the Somalia scandal. Both Lapointe and Schacter have long been considered deans of the defence bar in Montreal. Back in 1982, when Lapointe and Schacter first saw the Manac software, they were impressed and signed a contract to buy it. Two months after they'd started to use it, however, their staff ran into serious problems; they told Lynne that despite the promises made by Manac's salespeople, the software did not handle French text as well as expected. After many complaints, Manac asked for another $14,000 to fix the problems. Infuriated, Lapointe slapped a lawsuit on the company.

Part of Manac's defence was that Lapointe's people were not used to running sophisticated computer systems. Lapointe quickly dismissed that argument. His firm had been among the first in Montreal to computerize its operations, he said; his problems began when Manac recommended a particular IBM computer to run his office, one that was simply not powerful enough to run the software properly. "A normal computer response time to a keystroke is a fraction of a second," Lapointe said, "but if I remember clearly, the response time was twenty-four seconds. IBM recognized that it was an inadequate machine and withdrew it from the market not much later." The IBM-Manac system, he added sourly, created havoc at his office. "We had to hire additional employees to make the system work twenty-four hours a day. People came in to work at night and on the weekends to do entries, and the system worked all night and we arrived in the morning to see how far it had advanced." When IBM realized the flaws in its computer, he said, it reimbursed his firm right away and took back its computer. Manac was not so agreeable. To get a refund, he and Schacter had to pursue Lynne through the courts, suing her for $50,588; eventually Lapointe Schacter won a substantial out-of-court settlement.

Arthur Campeau remembered Verchere, before their falling-out, asking him to defend Manac on occasion when the company was threatened with lawsuits by unhappy clients. Although he never had to do more than offer advice, Campeau said that Lynne's response was always that the customers simply didn't take the time to understand what they'd bought. "It's not the software," Bruce Verchere would say in exasperation when they'd meet to look at claims from angry clients. "It's just that they don't know how to use the goddamn software." Given that law-firm software was still newfangled in the early 1980s, and given that few firms had computer experts who knew how to deal with software glitches, Verchere probably had a point.

Even with Luddites as clients, Manac prospered. Verchere could see the firm was going to become increasingly valuable, so he turned his attention again to estate planning for himself and his family. In July 1982, when IBM finally chose to license Manac as its official legal software, he began thinking through the way their assets were held, everything from their house and the paintings which adorned their walls to the ownership of Manac, Niskair, and Mancor. Prudently, he also made sure he had a carefully wrought will. On Christmas Eve in 1982, he signed the will, which essentially left everything to Lynne and the boys. Marc Noël and Lynne's sister, Betty Ann Dungate, were named as executors; his confidential secretary, Sandy Wardrope, witnessed the document.

Gradually Verchere started moving shares of the family companies and family assets under his own control. That was fine with Lynne. Bruce was the expert, after all, he'd set up the Blue Trust, he knew how to avoid taxes better than anyone else. She had every confidence in his judgment, and she trusted him. She was so busy with Manac and the boys that she didn't want to deal with estate planning. And because they were doing so well financially, she also didn't worry about her husband's personal extravagances. It wasn't cheap to belong to the Griffith Island Club, for example, and in 1983, during a club fundraising drive, he arranged for Mancor to buy four $5,000 debentures, a total of $20,000. He didn't use personal income from the law firm to pay for the debentures; he directed Lynne's small management company, Mancor, to pay instead. Lynne didn't know they were held in Bruce's name alone. By this time, Bruce had turned Mancor into a kind of family holding company under the umbrella of the Blue Trust.

By the end of December 1983, he was looking for a way to reduce his taxes. Even though his movie venture had proved disastrous, he couldn't resist using the same scheme — trying to get a tax break by claiming research and development costs as tax credits. He started this manoeuvre by reorganizing the ownership of Manac; company documents describe it as "correcting" an error in the official description of the share ownership. The "correction" gave Lynne full ownership of 4,000 Class A shares of the company. Once that was tidied up, Verchere borrowed $300,000 as a personal loan from the Dorchester Street branch of the CIBC, where he banked, to buy 600 Class A Manac shares for himself. At this time in December 1983, Manac's balance sheets were healthy. Although the company had a bank loan and overdraft which totalled $307,511 as well as further liabilities of $168,846, unaudited financial statements showed assets of $524,370 and working capital of $48,013. The statements did not show Manac's income flow and profit. Sales of software systems brought in $783,998; technical support earned $558,770; and the sales of forms made another $257,493. Total 1983 revenue was $1,600,261; after-tax profits were $64,508.

By the beginning of 1984, Verchere had realized that the upward trend of Manac's profits pointed the way to his own future. Not that he was interested in software and computers; he wasn't. But he was losing interest in the law and his practice. What he really wanted to do, he thought dreamily, was retire. He wanted enough money to be able to do the many things he enjoyed more than practising law. Flying had become his passion. He wanted to spend time with his sons. He liked cooking and having discreet dinners with interesting women. Maybe he'd even do something in politics. He didn't want to go into elected politics; not at all. His forte, he knew, was the backroom stuff, the dealmaking, the structuring of money, the sort of thing he did for clients and friends like Arthur Hailey and Brian Mulroney. A patronage appointment from Brian, something not too time-consuming, would be nice. To win complete freedom, though, he'd need money, real money. Again and again, he went through Manac's receivables and looked at the profit lines. Keep it up, he knew, and they'd be able to sell this company. This was the golden goose. This was where the money was going to come from.

In February 1982 Verchere went back to the CIBC and took a personal loan for another $300,000 to buy 600 more shares of Manac. The company didn't need the $600,000 he invested; it was done only to finance a research and development tax shelter.

Although Verchere recognized Manac as the earner, his law firm was still thriving and his own reputation was still excellent. One happy client was the Montreal-based Morgan group of companies, a conglomerate originally built from the Morgan stores, which served the city's upper crust.

The Morgans themselves were one of Montreal's blueblood families, and as their fortunes grew they had begun a trust company, Morgan Trust. Montreal businessman Leo Goldfarb, then the executive vice-president of Steinberg's, was on the Morgan Trust board, which was looking around for a tax expert in the 1970s to deal with the federal government. Verchere had been recommended by Goldfarb's own people at Phillips & Vineberg, so Goldfarb and Morgan Trust chief executive officer Aubrey Goodman, unaware of the circumstances of Verchere's hasty exit from Stikeman Elliott, brought him in and liked what they saw. Very shortly Verchere became a board member himself. "He knew his stuff as a lawyer," said Goldfarb, "but he was no pussycat. He was tough." Goodman agreed. "He was invited to join the board because he provided us with absolutely first-class service and some very fine advice. He was not a low-fee lawyer, but I don't think there is a really good lawyer who charges modest fees. He was in the league of Stikeman Elliott."

Not only did the senior executives admire Verchere's shrewd advice, they also developed a healthy respect for the service provided by his partners, especially Marc Noël, Ross Eddy, and Geoff Lawson. By 1984 the Vercheres and the Goodmans often had dinner together, and Goodman developed a great affection for Lynne. "A very, very smart lady," he recalled. "She was a very attractive woman, interesting and a good conversationalist." (Morgan Trust was sold to the late Toronto businessman Gerry Pencer in the mid-1980s and Verchere's work for the company ended.)

During this period, Verchere's attention was diverted, to an annoying extent, by his dispute with Arthur Campeau; that file wasn't settled until the spring. To make matters worse, two more unhappy partners, Mario Ménard and Guy Dubé, left the firm in 1984. What soothed the sting of his poisonous relationships with ex-partners was the certainty of Mulroney's coming political triumph; Verchere spent long and happy hours contemplating the victory. Mulroney was, by this time, a member of Parliament from Central Nova, Elmer MacKay's old riding in Nova Scotia, and the team around him in Montreal met day after day in the Mount Royal Club or the Ritz-Carlton Hotel or in one another's living rooms to plan election strategy and the government after the victory. Many of them were lawyers, men Verchere had come to know well during his years in Montreal. The lawyers in the inner circle included David

Angus, Verchere's old law partner at Stikeman's; Bernard Roy, who was at Ogilvy Renault; Michel Cogger, a lawyer at Lapointe Rosenstein; Jean Bazin, who was at Byers Casgrain; and Fred von Veh, who worked at Stikeman's Toronto office.

Besides the lawyers, there were a handful of businessmen: insurance executive Guy Charbonneau, a Tory senator appointed (at Mulroney's request) by Joe Clark in 1979; lobbyist and former Newfoundland premier Frank Moores; Ritz-Carlton manager Fernand Roberge; Regina businessman Ken Waschuk; and advertising and public relations advisor Rod Pageau. Verchere knew them all, but he was not in their group. He was outside, almost invisible, which was fine with him. It was one thing to drop names at Lynne's company or in his law firm, but in public his role was to remain unobtrusive, not to become one of the boys. As Mulroney's tax lawyer, the lower his profile the better. Among the inner circle, the only Mulroney cronies he really became friendly with were Fred Doucet and Frank Moores. Moores, especially, enjoyed his company, and Verchere would fly his float plane to the remote fishing camp in Labrador where Moores hosted marathon drinking, fishing, and political strategy weekends.

This political period in Montreal had a strange, unreal quality to it. A legendary Liberal prime minister had finally retired; Pierre Trudeau had bought a historic Art Deco house on the crest of the hill along Pine Avenue in Westmount, moved in with his three sons, established them all in good private schools, and started his own law practice at Heenan Blaikie. A new prime minister was in power in Ottawa, but this one, John Turner, had a strong

Liberal network back in Montreal; not only were some of his old Stikeman Elliott colleagues still loyal, but his sister, Brenda Norris, was working hard to bring together a coalition to work for him in the coming election. And finally, there was the Conservative prime minister in waiting, Mulroney, the MP for Central Nova.

Because of the election work and because he was preoccupied with Manac's finances, Verchere did not pursue an enticing personal opportunity that came his way in the spring. He was in Toronto to meet with Arthur Hailey, whose newest novel, *Strong Medicine*, was in the final stages of editing for fall publication. As Verchere often did in Toronto, he went to lunch one day at Winston's on Adelaide Street, then the place where many of Toronto's top lawyers and power brokers gathered every noon hour to swap gossip and do business under the watchful eye of owner John Arena. During this particular lunch, Verchere was introduced to Martha O'Brien, a young television producer whose quick wit and sparkling eyes appealed to him. He was tempted, but there wasn't time to pursue her.

By September it was clear that Mulroney was going to win a massive majority, though no one could predict he would bring in the largest majority in a federal election in the country's history. The Tories swept 211 of the 282 seats in the House of Commons. Jubilant, Mulroney's friends thronged to Ottawa with him to celebrate.

Once the cheering and back-slapping died down, Verchere's job was to understand what it meant to run a blind trust for the prime minister of Canada. The theory was that cabinet ministers and the prime minister would put their holdings into a trust run by a trustee empowered to make decisions about how the assets were managed. The trustee was not supposed to tell the politician what was happening to the assets, nor was he allowed to take any instruction from his client about what to do with the assets. Once a year, when the politician had to prepare a tax return, the trustee could pay a visit to disclose what financial returns had come in from the trust over the year. That was the theory, anyway. At that time few people much cared about blind trusts or understood what they meant; everyone was assumed to be honourable. Unfortunately, during the first Mulroney mandate, from 1984 to 1988, some of his cabinet ministers were sloppy about their trusts. Two got caught. The most famous case was that of Industry Minister Sinclair Stevens, forced to resign from the cabinet in 1986 after he was found to have kept up an active role in managing his own finances. "A seeing-eye trust," opposition MPs called it. A royal commission called to look into the allegations swirling around Stevens concluded he had been guilty of breaking the rules of his blind trust and had been involved in literally dozens of extreme violations of the government's conflict-of-interest guidelines.

The second cabinet minister to get into trouble was Halifax lawyer Stewart McInnes, then minister of public works; leaks to opposition MP Sheila Copps showed he had been receiving regular statements from his stockbroker back home. That scandal blew over in a few days. No one was charged in either the Stevens or the McInnes case because violating the spirit of a blind trust was not a criminal offence, though in Stevens's case the affair ruined his career. Politicians were sobered by the sight of two cabinet ministers in trouble over blind trusts, and the public servant responsible for overseeing the trust, the assistant deputy registrar general, had to draw up new guidelines making the rules even clearer.

Verchere was proud of his role as Mulroney's chosen trustee but was always discreet about what he did for the prime minister. What gave him the most pleasure was ordering the limousine on his annual summer excursion to the prime minister's residence to deliver the statement of income. "Take me to the prime minister's residence at Harrington Lake," he would say, sitting back in delight. Telling the driver where he was going, he once said to a close friend, made him feel more important than anything else he ever did.

Aside from the blind trust, Verchere met the prime minister for lunch every so often and did favours for Mulroney. One small example was the time he ordered office stationery for Verchere, Noël & Eddy from a Montreal printer. Included in the work was an order for business cards for the prime minister's brother, Gary, a Montreal schoolteacher who had agreed to become administrative chief for Mulroney's Manicouagan riding headquarters. The printer sent the invoice for the business cards to Verchere at the law firm.

As trustee for the prime minister's blind trust, Verchere was not the only person who made decisions about Mulroney's money. Verchere was a tax lawyer, not an investment advisor. He knew how to organize family trusts and shell companies and foreign bank accounts, he understood writeoffs and tax credits and deferred payments. Beyond Verchere, Mulroney needed someone to supervise his investments and skillfully manage his money. The person who'd been doing this in the early

1980s was Montreal stockbroker Jonathan Deitcher, a partner at Dominion Securities, who managed a special office created for him in Westmount where he supervised a few top-notch brokers. Deitcher says he didn't handle Mulroney's investments while he was prime minister; it is not known who did.

In the fall of 1984, during the euphoria surrounding Mulroney's triumph, Verchere had more on his mind than politics. Two days after the election, he got a nasty shock from the Federal Court of Canada when a judge ruled that his client Fred Melling owed Revenue Canada $1.2 million for the Hogg Robinson injection of capital. The defeat was crushing because it again exposed the badly flawed tax structure he'd set up for the company. Understandably, Fred Melling was frightened and angry. Verchere calmed him with soothing reassurances about reversing the decision in the appeal court. Outwardly, Verchere appeared serene, but the ruling weighed on him. Increasingly he was finding the practice of law a sad and sour business.

One day in October, as Mulroney was settling into life at 24 Sussex, Verchere went to Toronto on business. This time the trip included a couple of client-related social events; one was a lunch, the other a party. To his surprise, he again bumped into the young woman he'd met at Winston's in May, Martha O'Brien. This time, at lunch, they had a chance to talk. "He was very charming," O'Brien remembered. "He turned it on like crazy. He was lovely, he was entertaining, he talked about food and I loved to talk about food. He was interesting."

When he saw her again at the party that evening he made a beeline for her, focused his full attention on her for twenty minutes, didn't talk to any other guests, then left quickly to get back to Montreal. O'Brien, a blonde in her late twenties, had never met anyone quite like him. Trying to pin down exactly what appealed to her, she shook her head with a rueful smile. "He was fun, that's what it was. I was interested in politics and he loved to talk about it. He was discreet but he was also extremely interested in what I had to say about politics. A lot of people like to talk but don't like to listen. When someone says, 'Well, what do you think?' and means it, that's very appealing." Here she was, half his age, left-wing if anything, much more interested in the arts than he was. He should have been anathema to her: an enthusiastic, outspoken Mulroney Tory, a middle-aged tax lawyer with all the prejudices of his age and position. Yet when he left the event so quickly, she was surprised to find herself disappointed. A couple of months later, she thought of him as she was doing her Christmas cards, and she sent one to him on a whim. "I remember asking myself, 'Why am I sending this man a Christmas card?'"

After the excitement of the election, Verchere turned his mind back to his dreams of an easier life. He tinkered some more with Manac's ownership structure. On December 10, 1984, he reorganized the share capital of the company once again. This time he created two new types of shares, common and preferred. He changed the 5,200 issued and outstanding Class A common shares he and Lynne owned (she had 4,000 while he had the 1,200 he'd bought with the $600,000 borrowed from the CIBC) to 5,200 issued and outstanding common shares. Then he exchanged Manac's 1,000 Class B common shares for 1,000 preferred shares. Two days later he took

$300,000 out of Manac — half the money he'd invested in the company — and used it to buy 300 shares of Niskair. In other words, he removed $300,000 from his wife's healthy company to invest in his own risky little charter airline business. The same day he instructed Manac to pay the Blue Trust a dividend of $48,000, the biggest dividend so far that Manac had paid to the trust. Up to now, the annual dividends paid into the Blue Trust had ranged from $16,500 to $22,000. The dividends had been intended to go towards David's and Michael's expenses, but Verchere gave no accounting of what he actually did with the money.

He wasn't through tweaking the Manac shares. Six days later he bought eighty-four of the common shares for $81,312; once again, he was looking for a research and development tax shelter. The company's earnings were climbing steeply, and the unaudited financial statements showed that in one year its assets had almost doubled to $978,387. Liabilities were down to $299,109; the working capital had ballooned from $48,013 the previous year to $679,278. Manac had term deposits of $562,000 and borrowing capacity of $685,206. Things had really started to cook in the two years since IBM licensed the Manac software, and the order book for 1985 already looking fat and promising. All those dinners at the Ritz with the IBM guys, all the seminars with law firms across the country, all Lynne's acumen and hard work had paid off. They were making serious money now, and Verchere increasingly turned his attention to a strategy for protecting, fostering, and controlling it.

TEN
A First-Class Affair

SOME PEOPLE CANNOT enjoy a great triumph or a spectacular win without feeling some nagging premonition of disaster. Do they really deserve their good fortune? Will it last? In some ways Bruce Verchere never had a better year than 1985, but he grew preoccupied about what might be lying in wait. In 1985 his friend and client Brian Mulroney was still getting a grip on his government, but already there were stories of sleaze in high places. Verchere's law firm, packed with powerful and wealthy clients, was doing better than ever, but a few messy lawsuits and ongoing threats from Revenue Canada were troubling. Manac was turning into a gold mine but Verchere was growing anxious about keeping its multiplying profits out of the hands of the taxman. And he would have liked more time for his hobbies and interests, but prosperity didn't mean less work; unfortunately, it meant more.

Nor did it mean that he and Lynne had more time for each other; on the contrary. Manac's extraordinary success had brought her numerous invitations to speak about her work, and by 1985 she was also doing occasional guest lectures at the Harvard Business School. Along with his busy law practice, Bruce was a director on several boards. Two were charitable boards which made him no money but were amusing and brought prestige. One was the Canadian Lyford Cay Charitable Association, set up to help the Lyford Cay Foundation educate Bahamian students. The foundation offered scholarships to eighty undergraduate students, twelve postgraduates, and thirty technical students; the Canadian group sponsored twelve undergraduates at Canadian universities. Proud of his membership in the Lyford Cay Club, Verchere was only too happy to help with this project. The second board was the Conseil du patronat du Québec, Quebec's largest employers' association. Not only was his position on this board a clear signal to the business community that he'd arrived, it was a well-stocked pond of premium clients.

Verchere's other board memberships were corporate and three of them were compatible, even complementary, to his work for the Swiss Bank Corporation. Aside from being a director of Manac, Camflo Mines, and Richards Melling (which, by now, had become a stinking albatross around his neck), he was also a director of two shipping companies, Cast North America, then Swiss-owned, and the Canadian subsidiary of Dutch-owned J. Lauritzen. Another Swiss-owned firm, Wild Leitz Canada, invited him to sit on its board. By the mid-1980s he was acting for more corporations than individuals; a number of these were international pharmaceutical companies.

Although there were lawyers around Montreal who were sceptical of Verchere's talents and a number who actively disliked and mistrusted him, the general view was that he was smart, successful, hard-working, and delightful. He never bragged openly about his work for Mulroney but was enormously proud of it and did not mind if the right people were aware of the connection. While the public didn't know him from Adam, the power brokers in Ottawa, Toronto, and Montreal certainly did.

In the federal tax department, Verchere had both detractors and supporters. One of the latter was Bob Beith, a director general at Revenue Canada. Beith, who had known Verchere for twenty years, considered Verchere one of Canada's top tax lawyers and liked him personally. As so many others did, Beith called him "charming." Their paths often crossed professionally; they would meet to discuss a Verchere client's file, whether to go over an appeal or to discuss what the audit branch called advanced rulings. "If lawyers can get favourable or 'advanced' rulings ahead of time," Beith explained, "they know they can carry out the transaction with certainty for the tax results." When Beith met with Verchere, it was often to discuss these tricky rulings. "In many instances you are into grey areas," Beith said. "They would not come for advanced rulings unless it was already grey." Verchere was always well prepared and Beith enjoyed the debate with him.

Like most tax lawyers, Verchere aggressively pursued tax-avoidance plans for his clients. By the mid-1980s, officials at Revenue Canada and the Finance Department were looking for ways to close loopholes on what they politely call "tax planning." They tried different strategies with varying success until they finally came up with a general rule that, said Beith, was pretty effective in slowing down tax avoidance. "Bruce was a respected professional, and one of the measures we would look at was someone's candour. I always found him candid. A good adversary."

The only file that Beith remembered leading to hard feelings between Verchere and government lawyers was the Special Risks Holdings case. For the most part, senior tax people in the government remembered with nostalgia

Verchere's hospitality, especially during the Canadian Tax Foundation's annual conference. The Toronto-based foundation, made up of tax lawyers and tax accountants, is a research organization that studies tax policy. Along with an annual three-day meeting for about 2,000 professionals, it runs regional conferences and puts out the *Canadian Tax Journal* every two months. Each year, when the foundation met at the Harbour Castle Hotel in Toronto or the Queen Elizabeth Hotel in Montreal, there would be a banquet on the second night; afterwards Verchere would invite at least 500 people back for liqueurs in the Verchere, Noël & Eddy hospitality suite.

Verchere moved smoothly through the crowd, spending a few minutes here and there talking to old comrades and colleagues. He had no trouble getting anyone's ear. It had got around that this was the prime minister's lawyer, and people hung on his every word.

MAYBE IT WAS a classic mid-life crisis, maybe something more complex, but all of Verchere's professional success, all of his board work and status and Tory connections did not give him happiness or peace of mind.

What was wrong? Few men had wives more attractive and successful than his, or finer sons, and few reached the professional heights he had, but he often felt friendless and lonely. He loved the Griffith Island Club; he'd take the boys there — sometimes individually, so that he'd have time alone with each of them — and they'd hike or fish. He taught them to shoot. But it was hard to find the time, and he was often preoccupied. He also enjoyed spending time in British Columbia but couldn't make it back more than a few times a year to see his father and to put in some flying time at Juan Air in Sidney. Usually he went by himself, and after his father's death in 1989 these trips tailed off to no more than once a year or so.

Part of the reason he spent so little time in B.C., Royal Smith felt, was that Lynne didn't feel comfortable with Verchere's friends, including himself and Pat Dohm. "She had no contact with us," Smith explained. "It seemed that Pat Dohm and I were a part of Bruce's life that was over — that, maybe, she didn't quite approve of any of us. We got the feeling she thought we were a little vulgar for them."

Linda and Royal Smith didn't know that their friend's marriage was eroding, evolving more and more into the "business arrangement" Peter Tolnai had observed. It wasn't anyone's fault exactly; two busy people, each travelling a great deal, each determined to achieve great wealth, simply didn't have much time to look after each other. Both felt isolated. For Lynne it was especially difficult; her natural shyness and reserve kept her from reaching out to others. She was comfortable talking to Sheila and Arthur Hailey, but even with them her pride did not allow her to speak openly.

There was one close friend from whom she hid little. Ann Bodnarchuk was one of the few people who actually understood exactly what Lynne did for a living; she'd joined Air Canada in 1970 as director of computer systems and become the airline's first female vice-president in 1979. She pioneered the development of computer reservations systems among airlines; it was her work, to a large extent, that led to Air Canada's Gemini reservations system. In 1984, as part of its celebration of 100 years of granting degrees to women, Queen's University included Bodnarchuk among six outstanding Canadian women given honorary degrees that year (the others were Sandy Johnstone, principal of the University of Toronto's Victoria College; Dr. Marguerite Hill, physician-in-chief of Women's College Hospital, Toronto; Kathleen Shannon, an executive producer at the National Film Board in Montreal; Ursula Franklin, professor of metallurgy at the University of Toronto; and Christine Rice of Perth, Ontario, a retired bacteriologist).

Bodnarchuk was a kindred spirit to Lynne, someone who understood the same arcane language of science and technology, an entrepreneur, a pioneer in her own field. A single woman, she was treasured by a wide circle of close friends for her compassion, good humour, and wisdom. She liked Lynne immediately — they came to know each other through their common interest in computers — and the two women saw each other often, sometimes with a group of other women who also worked with computers and turned up at the same technical conferences at Concordia. They enjoyed the same books, shared the same intellectual interests, played tennis together, and often went out to dinner. Over the years Lynne began confiding in her, and Bodnarchuk came to know about Bruce's casual infidelities and the pain they caused Lynne.

Another friend who gradually came to understand Lynne was Liliane Stewart, one of the most generous patrons of the arts in Montreal. Her husband, David Macdonald Stewart, was an heir to the Macdonald Stewart tobacco fortune and a passionate history buff who, with his wife, founded the Macdonald Stewart

Foundation to assist charitable causes. In 1979, they turned over the Château Dufresne, a large sixty-five-year-old house built in the Beaux Arts style that they'd bought six years earlier and refurbished, to the city of Montreal as a new museum of the decorative arts, displaying an international collection of furniture, glass, textiles, ceramics, and metalware. An honorary colonel of the Queen's York Rangers and president of the Macdonald Stewart Foundation, Liliane Stewart was a powerhouse and admired Lynne for her achievements.

With Bodnarchuk and Stewart, and with one or two others, Lynne could share her secrets; to the rest of the world she presented a dignified and graceful front. She seemed to have it all, and she played the role well. Their home was everything a Westmount house should be. Their sons were bright and good-looking; everyone remarked on their maturity and polite manners. Bruce was dazzled by her intelligence, her drive, her business sense. But did he love her? Did he even like her? She believed that he did, though the evidence of his affection, unfortunately, was in short supply.

By now, Verchere was fifty and by all the measures with which the world judges men, he had done well indeed. His role model had always been Heward Stikeman, and he'd made himself into something of a clone, outwardly at least — he flew his own plane, belonged to the Lyford Cay Club and the Anglican Church, ran his own firm, served as intimate counsel to a prime minister, lived in Westmount grandeur. He was one of those powerful, prosperous men who enter middle age repeating the mantra of their worldly success and wondering why they're so restless and discontented.

In the spring of 1985, he picked up the phone and called Martha O'Brien in Toronto. "It's Bruce Verchere," he said. A man less sure of himself might have said, "I don't know if you'll remember me," but Verchere was sure she would remember him and he was right. "I'm going to be in Toronto," he said. "Would you like to have dinner?" She was taken aback; she'd sent the Christmas card to his firm's Toronto office and this was her first inkling that he didn't live in Toronto. "I said yes to dinner because I thought of him as a business obligation." They'd met through shared business interests and she didn't want to offend him; the fact that she liked him was a bonus. They agreed to meet at Truffles, the expensive restaurant in the Four Seasons Hotel in Yorkville. When she arrived, Verchere ordered a $300 bottle of claret and went through the menu enthusiastically, although he ended up ordering a steak. And he was wonderful company. His conversation was far-ranging, but he particularly enjoyed talking about politics, which she found irresistible given his friend Brian's extraordinary victory a few months earlier. "He was a Conservative," she said, "but he wasn't right-wing."

As they sat talking, enjoying the wine, O'Brien was again flattered by his interest in her opinions, in what she thought of politicians and writers and other people in public life. It suddenly hit her that this was no business dinner. He was interested in her. She realized just as quickly that she was equally attracted to him, even though she knew he was married. "He wasn't handsome, but he had an enormous amount of self-confidence. That was appealing." He was in his element. He wouldn't let the waiter pour the wine. He was unconcerned that the meal cost hundreds of dollars. He tipped well. Intoxicating,

O'Brien remembered, for a twenty-eight-year-old, even one who was used to television's fast lane.

A week later they had dinner again and this time he didn't waste time. "I'd like to go away with you," he said. She started to say, "Don't be silly." After all, that's what most women would say to a married man almost twice their age whom they barely knew; that's what she knew she should say. But something stopped her. "I thought, 'Why not?'"

To his credit, Verchere didn't try to sell her on an exotic vacation. Once she had agreed, he said matter-of-factly that he'd make the plans. Except for his suggestion that they go to London, she knew little more until she met him at the Toronto airport. That's when he told her he'd booked them on the Concorde out of New York. They'd fly to New York, stay overnight, and go on to London the following day.

The trip was a revelation to O'Brien: first-class all the way. In New York, they stayed at the Carlyle, on the Upper East Side, one of the city's best hotels; in London, they stayed at Claridge's, one of the most expensive hotels in Europe. While they were there they went to the theatre — night after night. Verchere loved going to plays, especially in London, and crammed in as many as they could manage. When they returned to Canada, they continued to see each other almost every week, often for the whole weekend. It was simple for him to manage it; his biggest client by now was the Swiss Bank Corporation, based, as his family and partners in Montreal knew, in Toronto.

For the next two years, whatever spare time he had, he spent with her. Everything they did, they did first-class. He paid for everything — meals, hotels, wine, tickets, travel. "In retrospect," admitted O'Brien, "it was a kind of keeping. He thought he could maintain control as long as he paid. He wasn't interested in an equal relationship." Even if he'd allowed her to pay her share, of course, there was no way she could have done so. "He had extremely expensive tastes," she said. "He loved being a rich man. Except he wasn't rich. He was married to a rich woman."

Bruce made no secret of Lynne's success, nor did he pretend he could manage without her money. He had a plan, he told O'Brien, that he and Lynne would sell Manac as soon as they could realize a good price for it. Once that happened, he'd tell Lynne he was leaving her; he'd then have enough money to marry O'Brien and live well. In the meantime, they had their time together each week and that would have to do. And they had to be very cautious. Only one or two of her friends knew about the relationship; none of his did. He made sure that they never visited his old haunts or went near his own house in Montreal.

One day he told her he'd indulged in an extravagance he'd always longed for: a luxurious new $750,000 twin-engine prop-jet Cessna Conquest, a real jump up from his first tiny Cessna. Because this one could seat eight people and had an impressive interior, he justified it by arguing that it could be used for a profitable small charter business; all he needed to do was figure out a way to pay for it so that he could write off its costs. On November 3, 1985, he fiddled around with the shares of Niskair to make this work. First he issued Niskair shares he stated were worth $500,000 (U.S.). He didn't have the money to pay for the shares, so he borrowed it from the

CIBC and then used the cash — $685,000 Canadian — to help pay for the plane. He confided in O'Brien that his powerful Ottawa connections had helped him obtain a charter licence for the new Cessna; it meant he could rent the plane out and begin to recoup his costs.

What his clients didn't know was that Verchere frequently scheduled himself as the pilot. High-level diplomats, government bureaucrats, politicians, wealthy businessmen would come on board and he'd be waiting for them, wearing a dapper new uniform. As they left, they'd thank him for the flight. "Good flying, Bruce," they'd say, and he'd grin and nod. "He loved to do all that bowing and scraping, pretending to be a service person," O'Brien said. "And he'd laugh at them all afterwards."

Verchere's mentioning that his political clout in Ottawa had helped him with the charter licence was a rare indiscretion; even with O'Brien he was careful not to talk about the specific work he did for the prime minister or the personal and political secrets they might share. Not that the relationship with Mulroney was a secret; on December 9, 1985, for example, Lynne and Bruce were among a small group of insiders invited to the Mulroneys' private Christmas party at 24 Sussex Drive. But by his very nature Verchere was a tight-lipped man with few intimates; O'Brien often asked about his friends and he always evaded the question.

"I don't have close friends."

"You must have some friends," she'd insist. "Who do you relax with? Who do you call when you want to go out and have some fun?"

"I have no friends," he'd say. "I only have business acquaintances."

Pressed, he said, "Well, I suppose I'd call Frank Moores. Frank's fun."

Sometimes he and Moores would go fishing together.

"Or maybe I'd call Fred Doucet."

Perhaps Mulroney's most trusted advisor, Doucet now worked for the prime minister in his Ottawa office, handling the Mulroneys' money and personal issues.

Verchere was not the only one who enjoyed hanging out with Moores, who was revelling in his new life as Ottawa's most feared and influential lobbyist. As one of Mulroney's inner circle and a fundraiser, he was on the board of Air Canada, to which he'd been appointed on March 13, 1985. Later that year, however, when it became known that he was lobbying for two other airlines, Wardair and Nordair, there was a public scandal over his conflict of interest in representing two private airlines while serving on the board of a government-owned carrier. On September 6, 1985, he was forced to resign from Air Canada's board.

During this period, Moores was also working closely with the German-Canadian businessman Karlheinz Schreiber on a number of lucrative deals involving the Canadian government. Both men were working for two German companies, Messerschmitt-Bolkow-Blohm (MBB) and Thyssen AG. On March 18, 1995, MBB signed a sales agreement with Schreiber for helping to sell thirteen helicopters to the Canadian Coast Guard, a contract which eventually resulted in $1,241,475.52 in commissions for him. Thyssen paid Schreiber nearly $4 million after he landed an agreement with the Mulroney government for a military vehicle plant in Port Hawkesbury, Nova Scotia. (The plant and the anticipated hundreds of millions in military contracts never materialized.) Moores's lobbying firm, too, was handsomely paid for its work on the projects; in July 1987, for instance, MBB paid the firm over $350,000. But Moores and Schreiber had another much bigger deal on their minds: selling Airbus Industrie's aircraft to Air Canada. Schreiber was working actively to pitch the new Airbus passenger plan to the Crown corporation, and by the summer of 1985 Moores was attending meetings in Ottawa and Montreal to discuss the deal.

When Moores wanted to open two bank accounts in Zurich to handle money he was making on his European-based projects, in March 1986, he and Schreiber visited the Zurich headquarters of the Swiss Bank Corporation, where Schreiber had an account already. They were accompanied by Schreiber's business partner, Giorgio Pelossi, an accountant, who later said the new accounts were opened to handle the commissions from the German companies. Pelossi also said Schreiber told him that some of the money was intended for Mulroney. No one has been able to prove that Mulroney received any of this money or knew about these accounts. (Pelossi's statement, in 1995, sparked a formal investigation by the RCMP, one that was still ongoing as of August 1998. However, the Mounties and the federal government apologized to Mulroney in 1996 after he sued them for libel for allegations they had made in a letter to the Swiss government seeking information about his role in the affair. They also paid more than $2 million for Mulroney's legal and public relations expenses. Although such RCMP letters to Swiss authorities alleging wrongdoing and asking for assistance are commonplace, this was the first time one had ever been leaked to the media.)

Verchere, of course, did legal work for the Swiss Bank Corporation and sat on its board. He was probably the only man in Canada who knew exactly what kind of money Mulroney had, although Fred Doucet (who was soon to leave the Prime Minister's Office to work with Moores as a lobbyist for MBB, Thyssen, and other companies) was the person in the PMO who actually handled Mulroney's money there. One example was the monthly payment to Mulroney made by the Progressive Conservative Party's fundraising wing, the PC Canada Fund, run by David Angus (coincidentally, another Air Canada board member). These payments were made to Doucet in trust; Doucet cashed the cheques and turned the money over to the Mulroneys to help them pay their expenses. As Mulroney's financial trustee, Verchere would likely have dealt with Doucet over these payments. He would also have been in close touch with Bernard Roy, Mulroney's principal secretary, who was Verchere's main contact in Mulroney's office. "He was always talking about Bernard Roy," O'Brien confirmed.

Whether Verchere worked with Moores or advised him on the Swiss Bank Corporation accounts is not known. A Supreme Court of Canada decision in May 1998 allowed the Mounties to trace Schreiber's accounts in the same bank branch; someday that information may be made public. In 1997, German police issued an arrest warrant for Schreiber in connection with financial transactions involving Thyssen and other companies, and Swiss authorities have also agreed to let the Germans see Schreiber's bank accounts.

How much Verchere knew of all this is a question Lynne could probably answer. Martha O'Brien, for her part, knew little about her lover's business secrets. Only once did he let her in on something, and then only in a limited way. Except for paying all her travel costs and meals — things that could be claimed as business entertainment expenses — Verchere was unable to give her money or expensive gifts. There would have been awkward questions in the accounting office; it might have got back to Lynne. But he wanted to do something for her, and one day an opportunity arose.

Verchere told her to buy shares in Horsham, a company owned by Toronto entrepreneur Peter Munk. Verchere had met Munk a year or two earlier when Munk started to make a takeover play for Camflo, Bob Fasken's gold mining company, which had been sinking fast under a $100-million debt load. Verchere was on the Camflo board that backed Fasken's refusal to accept Munk's offer. In 1986, when Camflo's bankers finally pulled the plug, Fasken was forced to turn the company over to Munk. It was about this time that Verchere and O'Brien ran into Munk at Brownes Bistro in Toronto.

Soon after this encounter, Verchere turned up at O'Brien's home in Toronto and thrust a pile of gold coins at her. "Listen here, have these," he urged. "I've had them lying around for a while and I want you to sell them." He instructed her where to sell them, where to get the best rate. "Then buy shares in Horsham. I'll tell you when to sell them." She did as she was told. She sold the coins for between $4,000 and $5,000 and bought Horsham shares with the money; later, when Verchere told her to dump them, she did — and earned a handsome profit of

$14,000. It was his tidy way of giving her money without Lynne finding out.

As the months of their affair stretched into years, O'Brien grew disturbed by the complexities of Verchere's personality. He had only one real prejudice, she said: his intense dislike of aboriginal people. "He had no time for them. He totally misread the swell of interest in that issue and he was just waiting for them to die in the cities of alcoholism. He said if you come from B.C., you hate Indians because they're on the streets everywhere." It took Verchere a long time to reveal his prejudice to her; he sensed it would shock her, and it did.

Once, when he was late meeting her, he explained that he'd been with former U.S. general Alexander Haig, who was speaking at a high-technology conference in Toronto where Manac's software was showcased. "Oh," O'Brien mocked. "I'm-in-charge Haig." She was referring to the time when Haig, then Ronald Reagan's national security advisor, reacted too quickly after the president was shot, telling people not to panic; with the president out of commission, he said, he was in charge. Verchere was only mildly amused at her irreverence. She got the feeling he was disappointed that she had failed to be impressed. On such occasions the difference in their ages showed clearly, and it made him cranky. Most of the time, though, they understood each other well, and what she increasingly understood was how deeply troubled he was about his life. "It wasn't much of a marriage. I don't think he liked his wife," O'Brien said bluntly. "Bruce was enormously proud of her and he admired her, but I don't think he liked her much."

Still, when Lynne had serious medical problems with her eyes and went to Boston for treatment, Bruce went with her.

During the long days of waiting while she recovered in hospital, he looked for an interesting way to pass the time. It occurred to him, as he was staying at the Ritz-Carlton Hotel and enjoying the first-class meals there, that he might be able to arrange cooking lessons from the hotel's chef. The chef was happy to oblige and they arranged for regular two-hour lessons; the next time Verchere was in Toronto, he arrived at O'Brien's funky house in the Beaches area and took over her woefully inadequate kitchen. He was eager to show her the proper way to roast a bird. "You chop all these vegetables," he said, "then you put the bird on top." In spite of all his fancy training, though, and his eagerness to display his gastronomic knowledge, his tastes remained simple: good wine and good red meat, served with Keene's hot English mustard.

As time went on, O'Brien began to understand what so many women do when they have affairs with married men. He told her that his relationship with his wife was businesslike; living with her in the house on Montrose, he said, was like living in a hotel. "I think he was jealous that she was making more money than he was," O'Brien said. "He told me that he was making about $500,000 a year, but that's not the same thing as building up a company. She had fifty employees by then; he only had about thirty."

By the end of 1985, it was clear that Lynne's upward financial trajectory was no fluke. Audited financial statements showed that Manac enjoyed assets of $1,658,736, liabilities of $433,510, working capital of $609,658, term deposits of $922,220, and borrowing capability of $1,387,091. And earnings were skyrocketing. The statements put the company's income from systems licensing and networks at $3,157,296 and from systems technical support contracts at $1,296,041, for total revenues of $4,453,337 and after-tax profits of $1,005,001.

On January 20, 1986, Manac paid $96,800 in dividends to the Blue Trust, a huge jump from the dividends paid a few years earlier. And by June of that year, Verchere was so confident about Manac's profits that he arranged for Manac to give $1,590,000 in term deposits to Niskair — in effect, to give Niskair an interest-free loan of nearly $1.6 million. A few days later, on June 23, Verchere quietly took $500,000 of that money out of Niskair for his own use. Lynne didn't know what he was doing; all the transactions he explained away as "estate planning."

In the meantime, O'Brien was growing frantic. She loved him and had always believed they would marry. Soon, he promised, soon. They had to wait for Manac to become profitable enough that it could be sold for a fortune. The figure he had in mind, he told her, was about $12 million. He would get half the money — which he said he was entitled to — and then be free to retire from law and marry her. He talked quite openly about the money. "He had this romantic view that we were going to have this wonderful life together," she said. "He would quit work. He didn't like working."

Still, he fretted. Would half the proceeds be enough? Half would be only $6 million. "To him, that was a real worry," O'Brien said. "I used to say, 'Well, what would we need?' And he'd say, 'You can't live the kind of life you'd want to live on $6 million.'"

Which sounded ridiculous to her until she discovered exactly what his dream of retirement was. It included a waterfront summer home in Maine. A new sailboat, from the upper-crust Hinckley boat works near Bar Harbor in

Maine. A ski cabin in Colorado. Holidays at the Lyford Cay Club. Maybe a place in Switzerland. He was right; $6 million would not be nearly enough to generate the kind of return he'd require to keep him in such style.

Despite his repeated promises to leave his wife and marry O'Brien, despite the fact that he spent all his spare time with her, he did not seem able to screw up the courage to ask Lynne for a divorce. In the meantime, he took credit for asking Mulroney to give her a fine patronage appointment at Christmas 1986, even though she was well qualified for the job. It was a two-year stint on the board of the Export Development Corporation, a government organization with great prestige. The announcement, in the December 18 edition of the *Globe and Mail*, was brief.

> Mr. V. Edward Daughney, Chairman of the Board of Directors of the Export Development Corporation (EDC), is pleased to announce the appointment of Ms. Lynne Verchere to the EDC Board. Ms. Verchere, of Montreal, is the founder, President and Chief Executive Officer of Manac Systems International Ltd., the largest supplier of law firm computer software in North America. EDC is a Canadian Crown corporation that provides a wide range of insurance and bank guarantee services to Canadian exporters and arranges credit for foreign buyers in order to facilitate and develop export trade.

Although the corporation was not well known outside Ottawa, it was a powerful organization, and EDC appointments were one of Mulroney's favourite ways to reward friends. Established in 1944, the EDC helped Canadian exporters compete internationally by offering them help with insurance and financing. The insurance was especially important; it allowed Canadian exporters to send their goods to foreign countries almost risk-free; it meant, for example, that goods entering a country in a volatile political situation are indemnified. The biggest advantage of the EDC was its ability to negotiate secret, very political deals under cabinet order to suit the government of the day through a special part of the EDC, Section 31. No bureaucrat could get in the way of a Section 31 deal. Once the cabinet decided to support a company looking for financial help on a foreign contract, it was a done deal. Many viewed Section 31 as nothing more than a slush fund for projects dear to politicians' hearts; that was why government liked to have its friends on the board.

Lynne's appointment was not the first time Mulroney had personally arranged for the appointment of a friend to the EDC board or even to EDC contracts. In 1985 a scandal had erupted when his close crony Toronto lawyer Sam Wakim was given the lucrative legal work for the EDC and used it as a dowry to find himself a good job in one of Toronto's leading law firms. Then, when other fundraisers were going on the Air Canada board, Mulroney put another good friend, Jonathan Deitcher, on the EDC board. (Mulroney later larded in another old pal on the EDC board, Montreal publisher Brian Gallery. The president of a federal Tory fundraising organization, the 500 Club, Gallery had had to resign in disgrace when he was the acting chairman of Canadian National

Railways and was found to have threatened CN executives with the loss of major new transport contracts if they dropped advertising from his little shipping magazine.)

It was in this 1986 Christmas season, during Lynne's euphoria about the board appointment, that Verchere told her about the affair. It was a painful scene, one the children soon found out about. Terribly upset, especially because it was Christmas, their son David, who was only seventeen, begged his parents to see a marriage counsellor. Partly to calm him, they agreed and visited their Anglican priest, who arranged regular counselling sessions. These were futile. Verchere didn't want to be there — the last thing he knew how to do was confide in his parish priest — and didn't want to save his marriage. An uneasy status quo developed, Lynne telling her closest friends that Bruce would come to his senses and that, in the meantime, she had her company to look after. "I don't think Lynne knew what Bruce's plans were," O'Brien said. "I think she thought it was still a happy marriage — it's just that her husband was fooling around."

It was a dreadful, awkward time for all concerned. Verchere, in particular, grew deeply depressed. He began drinking more heavily than usual and became remote and uncommunicative. He was not a man who could open up to anyone about his feelings — not his wife, not his priest, not even his lover. It took her three years to see what was happening. "He'd talk about politics and about books because they were impersonal," she said. "But he couldn't talk about feelings."

During this difficult period, Verchere and O'Brien went on holiday to a remote island. One day, she remembered, he sat down to read a biography of Winston

Churchill and didn't move for eight hours, didn't say a word, just sat there staring at his book. O'Brien wasn't sure that he even turned the pages. That night he drank more wine than usual, growing garrulous and drunk, rejoicing over the year-end results from Manac. Manac, he kept telling her, was the key to their freedom.

Manac's balance sheet at the end of 1986 suggested that the dream wasn't far from reality. Sales added up to $3,469,635 while revenues from the technical support contracts came in at $1,354,470. Total revenues were $4,824,105 and after-tax profits $1,036,373. Verchere began to wonder if it wasn't time to sell. Maybe, he thought, $6 million would be enough after all. In all his plotting and manoeuvring and fantasizing, there seems to have been one simple question he never stopped to ask himself: Why was he entitled to any of the Manac money?

ELEVEN
Cashing Out

MARTHA O'BRIEN had made the same sad calculation that so many women make in a long affair with a married man. When the time is right, they tell themselves, he'll leave his wife; the deception, the sneaking around, won't last forever. From Verchere she heard the predictable clichés: When Lynne's feeling better. When I can afford to leave. When the kids are older . . . "It was," O'Brien said ruefully, "a dumb position to get myself into."

Early in 1987, Verchere told her that they were looking for a buyer for Manac. She didn't know whether to welcome or to dread the prospect. Would Bruce decide that half Lynne's money was enough and leave her? Or would he decide he couldn't afford to go, forcing O'Brien to carry on in the netherworld of the affair? Would Bruce follow his heart, or would the luxuries that Lynne's money could buy ease his pain at giving up his mistress? These calculations were drumming in Verchere's brain and O'Brien understood it, all of it.

In self-defence, she started to pull back, to think about life without him. This kind of relationship, she grimly concluded, was impossible to sustain. Verchere himself was so preoccupied that he gradually let her drift away. Their calls slowed to once every week, twice a month. They saw each other every few weeks, instead of every weekend; then every month or two. She got the impression that he was too busy even to notice.

What he was busy with — besides his work for Swiss Bank, Arthur Hailey, Mulroney, and his remaining clients — was the prize he and Lynne had dreamed of all their lives: wealth. In anticipation of selling Manac, Verchere restructured the Blue Trust once again. Lynne paid little attention. Manac was making enough money that she was able to indulge her fantasy of renovating the big house on Montrose, a project that soon consumed her. She could afford to do more than just renovate; she could turn it into a showplace. The work, which cost close to $800,000, included a new outdoor eating area and patio on the east side of the house. Her curriculum vitae proudly laid it out, noting that in 1987 she supervised the "restoration, reconstruction and decoration of a 20-room traditional vintage 1920 home in Westmount along with several other private residences." The project was so big, Verchere told a friend, that the family moved into the Ritz-Carlton for a year while the contractors were doing the work.

Verchere had his own corporate renovations to attend to. Back in 1985, he had registered a new numbered shell company, 147626 Canada Inc., which remained inactive for the next couple of years. But on January 27, 1987, it awoke with a bang when Verchere used it to begin engineering a complicated set of transactions for the family assets. Again he explained the manoeuvring to Lynne as routine estate planning. As of January 1987, their real property consisted of the house on Montrose, the furniture and paintings in the house, and their cars. They also had the following companies:

- The Blue Trust, set up to minimize the family's income taxes. Although Arthur Hailey was the settlor for the trust, he had played no role in it since it was founded. Verchere was the trustee and controlled it. The Blue Trust owned 1,200 preferred shares of Manac.
- Manac Systems International Ltd., Lynne's software company. She owned 4,000 common shares; the 1,200 preferred shares, as noted, were owned by the Blue Trust.
- Mancor, Lynne's management company, which ran Verchere's law firm and owned the couple's collection of paintings.
- 147626 Canada Inc., a federal shell company, inactive until now.
- Niskair, set up as a private air charter service, which owned the float plane and the Cessna Conquest and was owned by Verchere.
- Verchere, Noël & Eddy, the law firm he had founded in 1976, in which he was one of several partners.

On January 27 Verchere took three major steps. First, he sold 1,000 of the Blue Trust's preferred shares of Manac to 147626 Canada Inc. for $968,000. The numbered company paid for the shares by creating and issuing 968 preferred shares of itself. It was a share-for-share exchange. Second, Lynne transferred 405 common shares of Manac to 147626 Canada Inc. in exchange for 169,173 common shares of the capital stock of Manac. Finally, Lynne transferred her 100 shares of Mancor to 147626 Canada Inc. Again the numbered company paid for the shares by creating and issuing 73,240 common shares of itself, the final share exchange of the day. A blizzard of paper was generated by all this shuffling; Bruce spun dozens of pages of legal text for each transaction, all of them duly signed and dated by himself and Lynne. The upshot of all this shuffling was to make the previously inert 147626 Canada Inc. a major shareholder in Manac and the full owner of Mancor.

The next stage began on February 9, 1987. The difference this time was that real cash was involved. It came from the only company that actually had some to spare. Manac bought back its 1,000 preferred shares from 147626 for $968,000, the amount Verchere had decided they were worth. Then Manac bought back the 405 common shares from 147626 for $845,565.

The numbered company was now in possession of $1,813,565 it hadn't held two weeks earlier; Manac was that much poorer. It didn't matter, perhaps, in the sense that the assets all belonged to one family. But Lynne wasn't paying attention to what her husband was doing, accepting his vague explanations and assuming he was using his tax-planning expertise with the family's best interests at heart.

Now that 147626 was cash-rich, Verchere directed it to lend him some money interest-free. Over the next few months, he signed promissory notes to 147626 three times. The first loan was for $350,000, the second for $75,000, and the third for $60,000. These loans added up to $485,000; to obtain them, he needed Lynne's signature. For two of the loans, he got it. In the case of the $75,000 loan, he simply signed her name to the loan documents and obtained the funds at the CIBC's main branch on Dorchester Boulevard, where they kept most of the family accounts. Why bother her with it? He was in charge of all their tax and estate planning, after all, and the loan was merely a part of that. Besides, he needed some cash, and given the tempestuous scene a few weeks earlier when he'd told her about Martha O'Brien . . . well, doing it himself was simpler and less aggravating.

Forging her name was small beer compared with what he did with the money he had steered into 147626 from Manac. On February 9 Verchere also directed 147626 to put $1.2 million interest-free into Niskair, his own company. He had thus arranged for the previously dormant 147626 — which he alone controlled — after cash infusions from Lynne's company, to move $1,685,000 in interest-free loans into Niskair, which he alone controlled. It was all breathtakingly simple. As the person solely responsible for all the tax, legal, and corporate work for Manac, Mancor, 147626, Niskair, and the Blue Trust, he could move the money around at will. No need to tell Lynne what he was doing, or that his law firm charged these companies stiff fees for the legal work. After all, even that made a kind of sense: his legal fees were a business writeoff for the companies.

Verchere was employing the sophisticated money-shuffling techniques that often catch the attention of tax authorities and the police. Former law partners had left his firm because they didn't like the ethics of what he was doing; Arthur Campeau spoke for many of them when he said, without hesitation, that Verchere was a man capable of laundering money.

"Laundering is a crime," said Campeau, "but there's a very fine line that tax lawyers walk. At a certain point you cross the line and it's fraud. I mean the fraudulent concealment and non-disclosure of money that you have earned, and its removal from Canada, and hiding it abroad in countries that have laws that prohibit banks from disclosing the nature of their transactions with their clients. In Canada, this would be considered fraud. Was Bruce capable of providing that kind to advice of clients? Yes, I think so. The chameleon that I knew, yes. The many facets of Bruce . . . the deceit that characterized him. That's the way I characterized his relationship with me, and it's certainly the word used by others in the profession who had had a similar experience working with him."

Verchere's motivation for the shuffle in early 1987 was simple: he desperately needed money. Although he and Lynne had agreed they'd live on his income while hers went to investments, the brutal truth was that, even though his remuneration was handsome, he couldn't manage from day to day without her money. Moving paper around to cash in on Manac's profits, he knew that Lynne had a hot company on her hands, one that was getting more valuable by the day. Most law firms were computerized; at the very least their billing departments were on computers. Manac was still under licence to IBM, which put it in an enviable position, but now that new companies were starting to offer legal software packages, Verchere believed that Lynne couldn't take her strong lead for granted any longer and that it was the ideal time to sell.

Lynne agreed. Sure, Manac would continue to grow, but Lynne was also beginning to think there were other things she wanted to do with her life. She and Bruce had paid a heavy personal price in pursuing their careers;

maybe it was time to cool down, spend more time together, travel, and enjoy life. She too had plenty of other interests. She loved fixing up the house; maybe she could do more of that kind of thing. Music was another interest she could perhaps develop. One thing she knew for sure was that she didn't want outside investors in Manac. It was her baby. Either she would own it and run it, or she'd sell it and do something else. Consulting and teaching were tempting alternatives; she was already doing a fair bit of both, and such work could also keep her involved in the business and academic worlds.

By the summer of 1987 they had a serious suitor, the publishing company Prentice-Hall Canada Inc., which was owned by the giant American conglomerate Gulf + Western. On December 8, 1987, they finally closed the deal. Prentice-Hall and its sister corporation, a Delaware-based company called PHPS Acquisition Corporation, agreed to buy Manac Systems for $13 million (U.S.). According to the complex sale documents, they calculated the U.S. dollar at $1.30 Canadian, which resulted in a sale price of $16,900,000 Canadian. Once the deal closed, Prentice-Hall would own Manac's business, its unfilled orders, inventories, accounts receivable, equipment, machinery, book plates, office supplies, fixtures and furnishings, vehicles, computer chips, data bases, trade secrets, know-how. Everything. Even Manac's logo: an owl with the Latin motto "Tempus Pecunia Est" (Time Is Money). Verchere, Noël & Eddy didn't do badly on the deal either; the firm charged Lynne more than $300,000 in legal fees for tax and legal advice.

As soon as the deal was struck, Verchere resigned as a trustee of Manac. This, he explained to Lynne, was the beginning of his strategy to do for themselves what Arthur and Sheila Hailey had done nearly twenty years earlier — move to a tax haven. If they didn't, he warned Lynne, half the money would disappear in taxes. What they had to do, and quickly, was cut their ties to their Canadian companies and relocate offshore.

Verchere was again doing what he loved best, spinning bundles of paper into an impenetrable web. The whole exercise was intended to mask the truth, but here are the essentials of what happened. On December 10, when the asset sale was complete, Verchere placed the proceeds in a company called 159409 Canada Inc., which he and Lynne continued to refer to as Manac. Ten days after that, on December 20, Verchere arranged for Manac to start paying out the Prentice-Hall money in fat little parcels, each earmarked for a different purpose. Lynne received the first payment, a cheque from Manac for $3,500,000, as "consulting fees" for her role in negotiating the deal. That same day she received a second cheque, this one for $3,750,000, as an eligible capital amount. This money, $7,250,000 in all, was a splendid Christmas present; what made it even better was that Lynne by this time was fairly secure in her belief that Bruce was no longer seeing his mistress. The affair was over. What a different Christmas this would be from the tense, sad holiday the family had endured the year before.

Verchere wasted no time in sentimental celebration. He had to hurry, feeling the breath of the taxman hot on his neck. A day or two after Manac paid the cash to Lynne, Bruce changed Manac's share capital again. This time the common shares became convertible to any other class of shares at the option of the holder. He created a new class of shares consisting of an unlimited number of Class A shares to which several generous rights were attached: the right to vote, the right to non-cumulative discretionary dividends, and the right to receive the rest of the corporation on the winding-up or dissolution of the company. Legal gobbledygook; in plain English, what Verchere managed to do with this step was allow himself the privilege of converting the shares in the capital stock of Manac, shares he controlled through the Blue Trust, into a class of shares different from Lynne's.

On December 22, he changed the Manac shares he controlled into the new Class A shares he'd just created. The next day he arranged for Manac to pay dividends of $1,128.82 (U.S.) a share on both the Class A and the common shares of the company for a total payment of $5,507,500 (U.S.). Once the amounts were translated into Canadian dollars, Lynne received another $4,057,925 as a capital dividend and another $2,600,000 as an ordinary taxable dividend. Verchere himself received $1,449,575 as a capital dividend.

Somewhere along the way, everyone seemed to have forgotten that this instrument was originally set up as a trust for Michael and David. Add it all up, and Lynne had been paid $13,907,925 Canadian for her share of Manac. Her husband's portion added up to $1,449,575. The total amount he arranged to pay out to Lynne or to himself from the Manac sale came to $15,357,500; another $1,542,500 was left in their bank account.

Just before Christmas, while Bruce was pushing through the chunks of Manac money, he told Lynne it was time for her and the boys to move to a tax haven. As soon as he could organize his own business affairs, he promised, he'd join them and they'd start their prosperous new life beyond the reach of the taxman. But to turn Lynne into a non-resident, there were steps they had to take immediately. Aside from resigning from clubs and boards (including the EDC board) to help prove she was no longer a resident of Canada, she had to take certain financial steps.

First, he said, she'd have to transfer ownership of the house on Montrose Avenue to the Blue Trust. The trust would pay Lynne $940,000 for the house. It seemed straightforward to her, although she was unaware that the deed stated clearly that the transfer was made to Bruce Verchere personally, not to the Blue Trust. When he finally did move the ownership of the house to the Blue Trust a few days later, it really made no difference; as the sole trustee of the Blue Trust, he controlled all its assets in any case.

The next step was taken on December 23, when Verchere directed that $5 million (U.S.) of Lynne's money be wired to a joint account he'd opened at Pictet & Cie, a prominent private bank in Geneva where James Crot, a close friend and frequent business colleague, was a senior official. Then he wired another $5.4 million (U.S.) of Lynne's money to a joint account he'd opened at Darier Hentsch & Cie, another large private Swiss bank. The $10,400,000 (U.S.) meant that Verchere had sent about $13,520,000 of Lynne's money to Switzerland, about $400,000 shy of what she'd been paid. The idea behind moving the money to Switzerland was that Lynne would now be able to support their sons with money from the Swiss accounts. Verchere would set up more bank accounts in New York, he told her, to serve as conduits for the money. And, he added, he would act as the manager of her assets.

A few weeks later Verchere wrote a letter to the Pictet Bank in Geneva stating that his wife was entitled to all the interest in their joint account, acknowledging that the money was hers. He told her he would write a similar letter to Darier Hentsch.

On Christmas Eve, Lynne resigned as a director of 159409, of 147626, of Niskair, and of Mancor. Two days after Christmas, she left Montreal with the boys to establish their non-residency status outside the country. She and Bruce were extremely secretive about where she was planning to settle; most people thought she'd moved to Switzerland. A few others believed she'd gone to Boston. (Some thought she'd simply stayed quietly in Montreal, keeping a low profile. "You didn't see me," she cautioned a friend she ran into on the street. "I'm not here.")

From that moment on, it was Lynne's money that paid all their expenses — hers, the boys', and his. Bruce used all of his share of the Manac money, as Lynne told Arthur Hailey, "to pay his debts for the way we were living." The biggest of these was the $1.2 million he had borrowed from Manac on February 9 and put into Niskair, the little company he was using like a private bank account. "This left Bruce with no personal capital," Hailey noted in his diary and, "according to Lynne, he still has none. However, she says, their joint concept at the time of the Manac sale was that Bruce's legal work would pay for their regular living and she was supplying the capital which would make it possible for them to invest and live comfortably on the proceeds from that investment."

Bruce told Lynne he repaid the Niskair loan in December 1987. She later discovered he had used money from the Manac sale to do this, not money he'd earned from the law firm. Maybe it didn't really matter, she told herself. After all, wasn't it all the same pool, more or less? Weren't they in this together? What was important now was to put their worries behind them. They'd achieved the goal for which they'd worked so hard, cashing out of Manac and protecting the proceeds thanks to Bruce's ingenuity. They were wealthy now, set for life, and it was time to enjoy the fruits of their labours.

TWELVE
The Shell Game

BRUCE VERCHERE'S law partners don't remember him actually leaving his practice; they just remember that as time went by, he was around the office less and less. He seemed to have just drifted away. The truth was that Verchere didn't leave Verchere, Noël & Eddy, nor did he stop practising law, nor did he leave Montreal. But from late 1987 on, from the time the Manac sale was wound up, he started maintaining a very low profile, trying to keep up the fiction that he and his family were resident offshore.

In fact, he still had clients, the important ones — the Swiss Bank Corporation, Arthur Hailey, Brian Mulroney — as well as the file that wouldn't go away, Fred Melling's. Although Melling went back to Revenue Canada to ask for relief, the department would not give up its demand for $1.2 million in taxes. The urban legends were growing around Special Risks. The tax world is small, and just as gossipy as any other legal specialty. A tax lawyer who appeared to be having a spectacular failure as a result of being too clever by half was the subject of gleeful chat by everyone in his field. Criminal lawyers, arbitrators, judges — all love to dish the dirt about each other. Verchere knew people were talking about the case, though the sting was soothed somewhat by the Manac windfall; it gave him some distance. Besides, he had more important fish to fry. Mulroney, for example, was facing an election in 1988 and Verchere expected their relationship to continue.

Still, politics and law came second to Verchere's main preoccupation in 1988: protecting the new family wealth from capital gains taxes and squirrelling it away. Once again, he found Niskair the perfect corporate vehicle. It was convenient and it was his; Lynne wasn't even a director any longer so she didn't have to sign anything.

Lynne, meanwhile, set herself up as a software consultant, and it wasn't long before she had three clients. Not surprisingly, Gulf + Western, the parent of Prentice-Hall, was one; it wanted her nearby for advice while the new owners took over her company. The second was the Anglican Church of Canada (presumably she gave them advice free); the third was the Conrad Foundation, a small private charity. She also kept busy with the continuing renovation project on the house.

Verchere created more companies, more shells, more paper; and he did it further and further afield. Layers of foggy obfuscation clouded plain words; thick seals and ornate stock certificates dressed it all up.

First he needed two new corporations to own his dream vacation property, a waterfront retreat in Maine, and his much longed-for Hinckley sailboat. While he and Lynne looked for the property and while he thumbed through specs of different yachts, he talked to Horacio Alfaro and Rodrigo Moreno, lawyers in Panama City, about setting up the two shell companies. Their firm, Alfaro Ferrer, Ramirez & Aleman, was one of the biggest in the country. (In the 1970s it represented John C. Doyle, the Newfoundland financier who fled to Panama after the collapse of his scandal-plagued company, Canadian Javelin Ltd.)

Panama was a good choice for the kind of secrecy he wanted. One of the most notorious tax havens in the world — or, more politely, what McGill crime expert Tom Naylor, in the 1994 edition of his book *Hot Money*, called a "peekaboo financial center" — it is a country where few questions are asked and the world's tightest secrecy laws apply. Everyone understands the game. Not only do depositors not have to give their names or addresses to Panamanian banks, but, as Naylor explained, "one of the principal occupations of Panama City's several thousand lawyers is to create and subsequently to administer shell companies on behalf of offshore clients who designate 'nominee' directors." These lawyers were stamping out shells a hundred at a time in the 1980s, so many that they turned them over to brokers for resale. With no owner of record, Verchere's shell companies could deposit money in bank accounts protected by Panama's infamous secrecy laws. On March 7, 1988, Verchere arranged for Alfaro and Moreno to incorporate a new Panamanian company for him called Shore Operations S.A. Alfaro became the president of Shore; Moreno became the treasurer. The deed, number 3442, was duly witnessed and registered.

Now that he had a corporate vehicle in place, Verchere went shopping. For years he had wanted to own a boat made by the famous Hinckley Company in Maine's Southwest Harbor on Mount Desert Island; in fact, a few years earlier, he'd even given one of his girlfriends a Hinckley boating cap when they took sailing lessons together. If you were going to buy a luxury yacht,

Hinckley's was the place; the company had been in business since 1928 and its boats were prized around the world. The one he ordered was a 42-foot Sou'wester, "perfect for weekend races to extended cruises," as the brochure says, to be custom built to his specifications. Verchere had a choice of cherry, mahogany, or ash for the cabin's luxurious interior. The price for a 42-foot boat? Only $600,000 U.S. It cost extra to equip it with sails and other necessities; fully loaded, the price was closer to $700,000 U.S. Verchere told the men at the boat works in Southwest Harbor that he'd wanted this boat for a long time, but Hinckleys are custom-fitted and they told him it wouldn't be ready until the end of the summer.

Verchere had brought his son David with him to Southwest Harbor. Though it was still winter, and though they had arrived in a pelting snowstorm, they liked the area. Verchere couldn't resist having Gary Fountain, a local real estate agent, show them around. This was not the time of year to go house-hunting in Maine, but it wasn't long before he decided Mount Desert was where he'd like to buy a weekend retreat. Reached by a causeway from the mainland, it's a mountainous island — at 1,532 feet, Cadillac Mountain is the highest point on the Atlantic coast of the U.S. — and so beautiful that it attracts millions of tourists each year; three million visit Acadian National Park. Others come to hike through the island's trails, kayak in the coves, or join whale-watching trips. Then there are the bird watchers; Mount Desert is famous for its puffins and eagles. The permanent residents of Mount Desert, which was discovered by Samuel de Champlain in 1604 and originally named Isle de Monts Deserts, make their living on tourism, lobster fishing, blueberries, and boat building. Bar Harbor is the largest town on the island; the picturesque villages in the area include Southwest Harbor, Northeast Harbor, and Pretty Marsh.

For generations, wealthy Americans have come here for the summers; in 1997 the whole island was buzzing over the purchase of the old Edsel Ford estate in Seal Harbor by lifestyle guru Martha Stewart, who was rumoured to have paid at least $4 million for the twelve-bedroom, three-storey granite house. And, sniffed the natives, notwithstanding all the Rockefellers who had lived nearby, it wasn't even in the best part of the island. Bar Harbor has attracted Mellons, Pulitzers, and Morgans, but the "best" part of Mount Desert is generally conceded to be Northeast Harbor, where you'll find Fords and former U.S. secretary of state Caspar Weinberger. This is where the billionaires live, explained one real estate agent.

This particular patch was too expensive for the newly rich Vercheres, so Gary Fountain drove them a bit further afield to the west side of the island, where the properties were slightly cheaper and you had to be only a millionaire. "It's much more beautiful than Northeast Harbor," Fountain said later, "and there's much more old Philadelphia money, larger tracts of land, and no cocktail circuit."

Here, in Southwest Harbor near the village of Pretty Marsh, the Vercheres found a 17-acre shorefront camp with three cabins high on a rocky bluff, overlooking the ocean. "To this day it's one of the favourite places I have sold up and down the Maine coast," Fountain said. "It has these little Hansel-and-Gretel cottages, it was tucked in the woods, and it was very unassuming." The middle cabin housed the kitchen, living room, dining room, and bathroom, while the other two contained bedrooms. Along with the highly prized waterfront, which ran 700 feet, the view, with its western sunsets, made the property spectacular. And the place came with some local lore attached; this was the camp once owned by one of the state's best-known ornithologists, a man called James Bond. Working in one of the cabins on the property, he'd written a number of bird books which had found readers around the world; one of them was the British author Ian Fleming, who was staying in Jamaica while he planned a novel about a British spy. Fleming needed a name for his hero. On the coffee table in his living room, he noticed a bird book by a man called James Bond. Bond — James Bond, Fleming thought. That's what I'll call him.

But it had been many years since the real James Bond had worked here in Pretty Marsh writing about his beloved birds, and the rundown old cabins needed a lot of work. The price? About $685,000 U.S., or $900,000 Canadian. It might have been less fashionable than Northeast Harbor, but the deep-water docks were ideal for his new sailboat, and the float — a floating platform, used as a landing and attached to the wharf — had water and electricity. The airport was only ten miles away. Verchere figured it was a bargain.

A few weeks later Verchere phoned Nathaniel Fenton, a lawyer in Bar Harbor, to handle the purchase of the camp. Lynne later mentioned that her husband was a lawyer, Fenton remembered, and that he worked for the prime minister. "I never met Mr. Verchere," he said. "I only talked to him over the telephone. He was extremely personable — he had a wonderful voice, a very melodious voice, very soft-spoken. And he was very kind." He was also a good client who made sure that Fenton understood what he had to do. Verchere's complex scheme was launched at 10 a.m. on April 26, 1988, in Panama City, when Alfaro and Moreno held the first shareholders' meeting of Shore Operations S.A. to take over power of attorney from Bruce and Lynne Verchere. Thirteen motions and thirty minutes later they adjourned. The same day, under Verchere's direction, Fenton set up a Maine holding company called Blue Wave Inc. to become the titular owner of the new camp. Although Fenton also became Blue Wave's president and director, he said all he really ever did was complete the real estate transactions and do the title search.

It was a heady time for Verchere. He'd found his camp, he'd picked out his sailboat, and on April 27, the day after Fenton set up the company in Maine, he and Lynne accompanied their friends the prime minister of Canada and his wife to a dinner at the White House. It was Brian Mulroney's fourth visit to Washington and the last during Ronald Reagan's presidency; because the two leaders, always celebrating their Irishness, had become such pals, it became a sentimental farewell, launched with a nineteen-gun salute on the lawns of the White House. Ostensibly, Mulroney went to Washington to lobby President Reagan and the Congress for tougher controls on acid rain, an issue that had often strained relations between the two countries. This visit seemed as futile as all the others; for years, Canadian diplomats had worked unsuccessfully to get the Americans to cut smokestack emissions of the sulphur and nitrogen oxides that cause acid rain. Although the few members of

Bruce Verchere (left) graduated from the UBC Law School in 1962, but he always enjoyed partying more than studying. Warren Mitchell (centre) and Bill Britton were Verchere's classmates at UBC Law School, graduating the same year. Mitchell worked with Verchere as a government tax lawyer in Ottawa; Britton would eventually head the firm of Bennett Jones Verchere.

Royal Smith and Bruce Verchere, fraternity brothers and lifelong friends, as young men at UBC. Smith went on to become a wealthy Vancouver businessman. *(Courtesy Royal Smith)*

Lynne Walters, Lady Stick and president of WAKONDA, graduated from the University of Manitoba with a commerce degree in 1961. *(Courtesy University of Manitoba)*

Heward Stikeman, Verchere's role model and former boss at Stikeman Elliott, at the controls of his Cessna in 1985. *(Copyright Len Sidaway,* The Gazette*)*

Arthur and Sheila Hailey in the living room of their dream home in Lyford Cay, the Bahamas tax haven that became their residence in 1970, soon after Arthur became a client of Bruce Verchere.
(Michael Arnaud for Town & Country*)*

puter counsel for lawyers

e office system

On their own

A 1979 *Financial Post* profile of Lynne Verchere admiringly described the potential of her software company, Manac Systems International, and the "steel will and razor-edge mind" of its president. *(Courtesy* Financial Post*)*

4481 Montrose Avenue, the twenty-room house the Vercheres bought in Westmount in 1975 for $150,000 and spent hundreds of thousands of dollars renovating.

Bruce Verchere shows off his new twin-engine Cessna Conquest, a lavishly appointed jet-prop aircraft, in 1986.

In 1988, Verchere acquired a luxurious 42-foot sailboat from the Hinckley Company of Maine at a cost of more than $700,000.
(Courtesy Hinckley Company)

When Fred Melling, the Vercheres' neighbour on Montrose Avenue, hired Verchere for tax advice, he had no idea his case would become a seventeen-year nightmare.

Arthur Campeau brought the controversial "God's Banker" file with him when he joined Verchere's law firm. Here he is seen with Brian Mulroney, who later appointed him Canada's ambassador for the environment. *(Courtesy Arthur Campeau)*

Relaxed and seemingly carefree in this photograph taken by Diane Hailey, Verchere strolls along a beach during a holiday in 1993.

Royal Smith and Verchere, reunited in May 1993: "Bruce was the happiest I'd seen him in twenty-five years." *(Courtesy Royal Smith)*

Arthur Hailey in his book-lined study in 1996, the year he was finishing work on *Detective*, a novel that began as a distraction from the turmoil of his family's problems. *(Michel Arnaud for* Town & Country*)*

Arthur, Sheila, and Diane Hailey pose proudly with four-month-old twins Paul (left) and Emma at Lyford Cay for the Haileys' 1994 New Year's card. *(Courtesy Arthur and Sheila Hailey)*

Diane with two-year-old Emma (left) and Paul on the golf links at the Lyford Cay Club in 1996. *(Michel Arnaud for* Town & Country*)*

Congress who bothered to show up listened to Mulroney's acid rain speech with sour indifference, they did perk up when it came to the second item on his agenda, the virtues of a new free trade deal between Canada and the United States.

"The dispute over acid rain," the *Toronto Star* reported, "didn't deter Reagan from offering a sumptuous feast for Mulroney and friends at the White House last night. Nor did it restrain Mulroney, in his toast, from heaping praise on the 77-year-old president who retires in January." The report went on to note exactly who these Mulroney friends were, and the list was a little odd. It didn't include senior cabinet colleagues from Ottawa like Finance Minister Michael Wilson or External Affairs Minister Joe Clark, nor even Mulroney's closest political cronies like Frank Moores and Fred Doucet. The small group at the White House was made up of his closest personal financial advisors. David Angus, there with his friend and fellow lawyer Louise Pelly, was now chairman of the PC Canada Fund and ensured that the Mulroneys received monthly expense cheques. Jonathan Deitcher, who brought his wife, Dianne, was the Montreal broker who had handled Mulroney's personal investments. Montreal businessman Paul Desmarais, the chairman of Power Corporation, one of Canada's wealthiest men and a long-time financial mentor to Mulroney, was there with his wife, Jacqueline. And, of course, Bruce and Lynne Verchere. It was quite an evening for the kid from Kamloops, one of those moments by which he charted the course of his life.

Back on Mount Desert to inspect his new property, he told people there about his visit to Washington. "He talked about the feeling he had walking into the White House," remembered one businessman. "The architecture and sheer size of the building struck him, fully revealing the wealth and power of the world's most powerful nation." A few days later Nat Fenton closed the sale of the camp at Pretty Marsh, and on June 1 the Vercheres took possession. In mid-June Verchere arranged for Blue Wave's control to go to Shore Operations in Panama by issuing one common share of its capital stock — or 100 percent of the company — to Shore. Before long, Verchere had approved plans to put in a new septic system and redecorate the cottages; Lynne's cabin was to be done in a light, feminine style with lace frills; the cabin Bruce shared with his sons was more rugged and included home gym equipment.

No matter how enchanting this phase of Verchere's life, however, reality had a way of rearing its ugly little head. That spring, Melling's legal team was back in court yet again. In April 1988 Guy Du Pont, one of the tax litigators at Verchere, Noël & Eddy, had written to Monique Giroux, an administrator at the Federal Tax Court in Ottawa, to plead with her on behalf of Melling. The case had been dragging on for almost ten years, he pointed out, and despite all Melling's legal appeals, he'd been told to pay up $1.2 million or else. Repeatedly raising Melling's "precarious financial situation," Du Pont begged, unsuccessfully, for swift action in settling the case.

And over the summer there was unpleasantness on Montrose over the ongoing renovations. The Vercheres had ordered $87,204.91 worth of new windows from a company called Meubles de Québec. The windows were supposed to be installed by September. The Vercheres had the old windows removed, but the delivery was late and as winter approached they had to put them back.

The new windows didn't arrive until early in 1989. Verchere refused to pay more than $75,634; the company sued him for the balance of $11,570. Small change, but a nuisance they could have done without, and for a perfectionist like Lynne it was maddening.

While the renovations were going on and the Hinckley was being fitted up, Verchere found himself short of cash. On August 19, 1988, he helped himself to another interest-free loan from 147626, this time for $180,000. The next day, August 20, he added to his kitty by having 147626 declare a dividend of $31,254 on the outstanding preferred shares registered in the name of the Blue Trust. Three weeks later, he went back to the well again. This time, on September 13, he directed Manac to lend him $1,534,000, effective the next day, saying he needed the money to repay loans he and Lynne had taken out to do the renovations on Montrose. (They'd borrowed the money from the CIBC to do the work.) In less than a month he'd borrowed $1,745,254 from family companies.

During this period Mulroney was re-elected to his second majority government. Once again, Verchere was his financial trustee. Though delighted by his friend's victory, Verchere was slightly detached at the same time, preoccupied with getting all his own ducks in a row. On September 23, he arranged for Nat Fenton to set up another company with a registered office in Bar Harbor to own his new sailboat, called *Niska*. In December he turned again to his agreeable Panamanian friends for help. Moreno and Alfaro set up a shell called Thunder Investments Inc., which would control Niska Inc.

Verchere wasn't through with his financial manipulation of the camp and the yacht. He needed another layer of insulation, and in early December he moved control of both Shore Operations and Thunder Investments to Darier Hentsch & Cie, one of the private banks he used in Geneva. This made Darier Hentsch — where a year earlier he'd deposited $5.4 million from the Manac sale — the controlling trustee for the camp and the yacht. This is how the ownership structure looked:

Darier Hentsch & Cie (Geneva)	Darier Hentsch & Cie (Geneva)
|	|
Thunder Investments Inc. (Panama)	Shore Operations S.A. (Panama)
|	|
Niska Inc. (Bar Harbor)	Blue Wave Inc. (Bar Harbor)
|	|
42-foot sailboat	17-acre oceanfront camp in Maine

To shift control of Shore Operations and Thunder Investments to Darier Hentsch, Verchere ordered the two companies' share capital transferred to the bank. The bank was instructed to hold it in trust for Bruce and Lynne Verchere. Lynne actually had no control over Shore or Thunder, but Verchere assured her she could have access to them at any time. Even more reassuring was that he gave her power of attorney, which he told her would give her access to all their Swiss accounts. He did not tell her she had no access to half the money from the Manac sale, which he'd deposited into an account he alone controlled. Nor did he tell her that he alone controlled Blue Wave and Niska and could, at his sole discretion, direct Blue Wave and Niska to dispose, transfer, pledge, or otherwise deal with the ownership of their assets.

It was great to have a terrific new place in Maine and a sailboat that was the envy of all their friends, but one question remained. How were they going to pay for them? Isn't that why Verchere had taken the interest-free loans from the family's numbered company and from Manac, and why he took the dividend from the Blue Trust? Apparently not. At the end of December, Verchere directed his bankers at Pictet & Cie to transfer enough money to pay for the camp and the boat. Pictet wired $1,650,000 (U.S.) to cover the costs. It had been a cheerful Christmas in the Verchere household, and no wonder. Verchere had just arranged for a total of $3,395,254 to come his way; it costs millions, after all, to live like millionaires.

Looking back on 1988, Verchere reflected that it had been a very good year. The election had won Mulroney a second term; working as his trustee was challenging and rewarding. His directorship on the Swiss Bank Corporation board had brought him great prestige. Michael was at one of the best coeducational private schools in the States, Deerfield Academy in western Massachusetts, while David was enjoying life at McGill in Montreal. His financial worries were over; he and Lynne were set for life. What he'd like to do now was retire. He'd hang on to his best clients, sure, but he didn't want to work hard any more. He'd paid his dues.

There was only one problem, and it seemed insoluble. He was not in love with his wife but was irrevocably tied to her. He admired her, of course, was happy to be seen with her, but he was not happy to be spending his life with her. Lynne knew it, had put up with his philandering for years. But their relationship became more strained than ever, and the friends they'd made together also began to take notice. One Geneva-based banking friend remembered that he and his wife had become fond of the Vercheres over the years and saw them whenever they visited Montreal. They also saw them often in Switzerland, where the Vercheres regularly went to ski. But sometimes, the banker said, they acted oddly. On one occasion, the banker discovered that he and his wife would be at the same Zermatt hotel at the same time as the Vercheres. "We arrived before they did," he said, "and I ordered some flowers sent to their room. Then I didn't hear from them at all. We sort of bumped into them in the corridors once or twice but we didn't see them for supper or anything." Baffled by their coolness, the banker finally stopped Lynne in the halls to ask her if she'd received the flowers. "Oh, yes," she said flatly. "That was it," said the banker.

Three months later, the banker and his wife were in Montreal; this time Lynne and Bruce took them to one of the finest restaurants in the city, ordered the best Champagne, and charmed them with their attentive conversation. "It was as if the thing in Switzerland never happened," said the banker, who found himself wondering whether the Vercheres' marriage was as secure as he'd thought, and whether, beneath the charm, his friend was not, in fact, a deeply unhappy man.

THIRTEEN
Visible Means

By 1989, THE FACT that Verchere had almost withdrawn from his law practice had become an uncomfortable issue for his partners at Verchere, Noël & Eddy, both in Montreal and in Toronto. Because he was so secretive, no one knew the financial details, but they all understood that Lynne had made a killing on Manac and that the Vercheres were preoccupied with building a new life outside Montreal. Lynne had started doing some guest teaching at the business school at Stanford University in California; added to her occasional lectures in Harvard's MBA program, these kept her busy and involved. She had to be careful to restrict her activities within Canada to maintain her non-resident status.

Except for his directorships on corporate boards, Bruce had no comparable opportunities, no cultural or academic gigs with business-school prestige, and the last thing that interested him was any kind of philanthropic do-gooding. Whatever looked nice in the social pages, whatever burnished his image, fine; beyond that he was indifferent. His arrogance, which was usually overlaid with charm, started to surface, infuriating some of his board colleagues. Even on the Swiss Bank Corporation board, he made enemies. "Bruce was very cold and nasty and tough," said a former associate there. "He wasn't popular. He could be very mischievous, and he was always trying to make trouble for people."

He also made mistakes dealing with his partners in Montreal. What he did all day was a mystery to them; they had no idea he was spending much of his time power-shopping and then shuffling money around to pay for — and hide — his purchases. Between 1989 and 1991 he spent as much time as he could at the camp in Maine and as little as possible in Montreal. Not that he was trying to pretend that he was a non-resident for tax reasons; clearly, he was still a partner at Verchere, Noël & Eddy, and still Mulroney's trustee. That, if nothing else, ensured his status as a resident. Rather, he seemed preoccupied with other interests: people would hear of him visiting Michael at school in Deerfield, or getting his plane serviced at the Cessna repair centre in Binghamton, New York, or living for long periods at the Ritz-Carlton in Boston, where he got physiotherapy for a shoulder he'd injured in a ski accident in Switzerland.

When he was at the office, it was often as a commuter. He would get up in the morning at seven o'clock in Southwest Harbor, drive to the nearby airport where he kept his plane, clear customs at Bangor, Maine, and fly up to Montreal. He could be in his office by ten and back in Pretty Marsh by six. In Maine he liked to sink into a chair in the main cabin and read one of the new novels he was always bringing back. He'd listen to opera and classical music; over the years he collected thousands of albums. In particular he indulged a passion for the operas of Wagner. If he had several hours, he'd take out the boat for a day sail. More and more, Maine was where he wanted to be.

People in the area grew fond of him. "I loved the man," said Gary Fountain emotionally. Fountain remembered calling him once to say he and his wife were going to Montreal for a weekend of shopping; could Bruce recommend a hotel? You'll stay at the Ritz, Bruce said. When the Fountains arrived, the manager, Fern Roberge, greeted them personally and treated them, said Fountain, "like visiting diplomats." There were hockey tickets waiting in the penthouse suite that Bruce had reserved for them, tickets at centre ice for a game in which Wayne Gretzky was playing. "Any friend of Bruce's is a friend of mine," Roberge told Fountain. And when they checked out, Fountain discovered that his bill came to less than he would have paid at a Holiday Inn.

Verchere's partners, meanwhile, became crankier with his absences, especially given what was going on around them. Canadian law firms, large and small, were in a massive state of flux, propelled by the free trade agreement with the United States and by the forces of globalization. Mega-firms were gobbling up small and medium-sized firms south of the border, and the same was happening in Canada. Among the high-profile small firms with anywhere from eight to eighty lawyers, only the ones specializing in criminal defence were safe; none of the corporate boys wanted them on board. It was always handy to know a good criminal lawyer or two, but you didn't want them down the hall. Killers and serial rapists leafing through the Financial Post and sipping coffee from the firm's old Worcester in the waiting room didn't add to the sort of atmosphere Bay Street lawyers hoped to create in their downtown lairs.

What you did want in mergers were blue-chip firms with lucrative tax practices, or patent and trademark experts, or a growing list of clients in intellectual property, entertainment law (a movie star in the waiting room was something else entirely), or — best of all — mergers and acquisitions. "Economies of scale" was the phrase always used to explain why Canadian firms were conjoining so lustfully in 1989. "Full-service law firms" was another expression of the day. Senior management committees were convinced that their much-merged clients wanted everything done in-house, from a takeover bid to the pre-nup with the CEO's new trophy wife.

McCarthy Tétreault, the result of a merger in the late 1980s between Clarkson Tétreault of Montreal and McCarthy & McCarthy of Toronto, had 450 lawyers; Fasken Martineau Walker had 480. In 1989 Osler, Hoskin & Harcourt of Toronto formed an international partnership with Montreal's Ogilvy Renault; not long afterwards, they were joined by Ladner Downs of Vancouver to form the international partnership of Osler Renault Ladner with offices in London, Paris, Hong Kong, and New York. Fasken & Calvin in Toronto joined with Campbell Godfrey & Lewtas to create Fasken Campbell Godfrey, while three slightly smaller firms decided to join forces: Byers Casgrain of Montreal and Ottawa merged with Bull Housser & Tupper of Vancouver and McMillan Binch of Toronto to form McMillan Bull Casgrain, with a total of 280 lawyers. Blake, Cassels & Graydon in Toronto merged with Calgary's Duncan Collins. And these are only a few examples. In the late 1980s law firms were so frightened about being left on the shelf that the long legal courtships of yesteryear were replaced by whirlwind engagements.

With the new mega-firms sagging under the weight of 200 to 500 partners and associates, overheads were astronomical and frazzled young associates were expected to bill between 2,000 and 2,500 hours a year. Big-city lawyers, overwhelmed by the greed-is-good philosophy of the day, started thinking there was something wrong if they weren't pulling in $350,000 or $400,000 a year. Why should the partners at Verchere, Noël & Eddy be any different? They chafed as they watched their rainmaker become more and more detached, and unavailable. He guarded his Mulroney files ferociously and didn't want anyone near his Swiss Bank Corporation work, but Ross Eddy became the custodian of the Calvi file and another partner in the Toronto office, Janice McCart, often dealt with the Haileys when their day-to-day business needed attention. That was fine with Arthur Hailey; as far as he was concerned, McCart was competent and well informed.

Simply put, Verchere had lost interest. He knew it, Hailey knew it, Verchere's partners knew it. When the partners started to talk, very delicately, about hopping on the merger bandwagon, he didn't object. Maybe he'd make some money, sell his stake in the firm and stash that away, too. "There was just so much merger and acquisition work going on out there [in the late 1980s], and we, as exclusively a tax firm, weren't part of it," one partner, Bernie Morris, told the Toronto journalist Jack Batten, who wrote a history of the firm in 1997. "We could get into it by growing from within, but that would be the slow way to expand. We could buy new people, but that would be expensive. Which left merger."

It didn't take the partners long to figure out who they should be romancing. Calgary's Bennett Jones, which began as Bennett, Hannah and Sanford in 1922, was a desirable target and a more than nodding corporate acquaintance. The firm's roots went back to 1897, when R.B. Bennett, an ambitious young Tory lawyer from Chatham, New Brunswick, moved to Calgary to join forces with James Lougheed, a wealthy Calgary lawyer who needed someone to run his practice while he spent several months each year as a new Tory senator in Ottawa. Long before he moved to Alberta, though, Bennett had been a close friend and legal advisor to another New Brunswicker, Jennie Eddy, the widow of E.B. Eddy, who had founded a huge company in Ottawa based on pulp, paper, and logs. Eddy matches became the company's best-known product, but the newsprint, toothpicks, sawmills, and real estate kept the money rolling in. Eventually Jennie Eddy left R.B. Bennett a substantial share of her fortune. Like Lougheed, Bennett began to take an active interest in federal politics. Lougheed, Bennett & Company imploded in 1922 in what they still call "the Great Schism," after scandals and quarrels divided the partnership, but Bennett built a new Calgary firm he called Bennett, Hannah & Sanford. Within a few years he was deeply involved in federal politics as leader of the Conservative Party, and he won the 1930 federal election, becoming prime minister of Canada, a position he kept until 1935. Bennett retired in relief to a country estate in England.

In 1939, the firm, then called Bennett, Hannah, Nolan, Chambers & Might, brought in twenty-one-year-old Maclean E. Jones as a new articling student. One of the small trials he endured early on was a brief encounter with Bennett, who had dropped in unexpectedly. Bennett's message to Jones was that he shouldn't get too big for his britches; he might be only twenty-one and the youngest person in the firm, but he should remember that William Pitt the Younger had been called to the English bar when he was only eighteen. The exchange was memorable, wrote Batten, because their situation was unique: "R.B. Bennett was the father of the firm and Maclean E. Jones was the father of the modern firm."

Over the next thirty years the firm grew and prospered, bringing in many young lawyers who later went on to high honours; one was Jack Major, who became a justice of the Supreme Court in Ottawa. Another catch was former Alberta premier Peter Lougheed, who turned down offers from six other law firms after leaving politics in 1985; it was his grandfather, James Lougheed, who had brought in R.B. Bennett in 1897. Although he wasn't famous, Mac Jones had become the dean of oil and gas lawyers in Alberta and the guiding hand of the firm, which was known, by the late 1970s, as Jones Black.

A less well-known partner, but someone who was extremely capable, was Bill Britton, the UBC Law School classmate of Bruce Verchere who had joined the firm in 1962. Britton and Verchere had remained in touch over the years and Britton was also friendly with Ross Eddy, who had excellent connections in western Canada. Before setting up Verchere, Noël & Eddy with Verchere in 1976, Eddy had spent several years as a young lawyer in Calgary working for Shell; he knew everyone there who mattered.

Lynne also had strong ties to the Calgary law firm. In the late 1970s Jones Black had decided it needed to modernize its accounting and administrative systems, so with high hopes and a great deal of inconvenience it brought in computers to do the job. After two years of frustration and glitches, Jones Black gave up and returned to old-fashioned typewriters and adding machines; still, it clung to the hope that someone out there would save it. That person turned out to be Lynne. Brought in by a computer expert in the early 1980s, and welcomed by Bill Britton, who knew her, Lynne sold the partners on Manac Systems. Jones Black became the tenth firm to buy the package from her company. It worked brilliantly, and as far as the Calgary lawyers were concerned, Bruce Verchere's wife was golden.

With bloodlines like these, with old friendships and excellent business relationships, with political loyalties that stretched back nearly 100 years, the union between the Calgary and Montreal firms seemed ordained. Bennett Jones, as it was now called, had expanded into Edmonton and was hungry to cash in on the new business Toronto could offer. Ross Eddy spearheaded the merger talks from the Montreal office and the deal was signed in November 1989. The new firm would be called Bennett Jones Verchere. "The merger brings together the energy, finance and trade strength of Bennett Jones with the taxation expertise of Verchere Noel & Eddy," the *Globe and Mail* noted sonorously. "Bennett Jones has been involved in finance, energy and resource matters for many years, and its international trade group is headed by Peter Lougheed, former premier of Alberta."

That was the public face of the merger. It was not the story Lynne gave Arthur Hailey when they talked on the phone. Bruce simply didn't want to have to work so hard, she explained. "He doesn't like law any more. He doesn't want to have to work at it."

Perhaps it was the continuing nightmare of the Special Risks Holdings case that had soured him on practising law. The bloody file just wouldn't go away. Tenacious tax prosecutors hung on like grim death, and Fred Melling was beside himself. Remorselessly, like the terrible lawsuit in Dickens's *Bleak House*, it ground on and on, greedily chewing its way through billable hours. It certainly didn't make Verchere happy, whatever his earlier billing practices, to see his client racking up legal bills caused by his own reckless tax strategies. He wanted the case over as much as Melling did; the nasty odour of the thing wafted gently through the legal offices up and down McGill College Street; Verchere could almost hear the snickering. He might have been relieved to have his firm merged with Bill Britton's, but instead of being soothed by moving into the big time, the deal left him with a bitter taste. He wanted the world to think — and he encouraged people to believe — that he'd made some real money on the merger. To his immense chagrin, however, he did not. Not one cent. This was a blow; he had never allowed himself to think his shares in Verchere, Noël & Eddy would ever compare to Lynne's coup, but he expected to get something. It just didn't work out that way.

A piece of information that did not appear in the *Globe*'s respectful story was that not everyone at Verchere, Noël & Eddy was happy to join a big western firm. Guy Du Pont, who had been with Verchere since 1980 and a partner since 1984, was one of those who disliked the merger. "Bruce," he said, "was an excellent person when it came to marketing. He had a great deal of talent in marketing his product and he brought in a lot of good clients, a lot of big clients." And at first, he conceded, the idea of the merger was okay with him. "We were following, or leading, the big national movement. After all, there is a lot of business shaking in Toronto, then as now." But Verchere didn't want to live in Toronto himself and opted instead for flying back and forth in the Cessna. Du Pont often went, too, but tried to avoid flying with Verchere: "I prefer big planes. I am uneasy in the little ones."

Maybe it was the flying, maybe it was the fact that orders seemed to emanate from Toronto, maybe it was Verchere's indifference, but the steam went out of the Montreal office. Miserable, Du Pont decided to leave the firm. Four other lawyers marched out after him. If some of the partners in Montreal weren't thrilled with the merger, the sentiments were reciprocated in Toronto and Calgary. As a tax practice, the firm was doing well, but the big corporate, commercial, and securities business they all expected to flow in the door didn't materialize. The reason, Bill Britton told Jack Batten, was that they didn't understand the marketplace. They hadn't seen that if they had no partners involved in the corporate-commercial or securities world in Toronto, they couldn't bring in the work.

It took years before Britton was able to turn the situation around; to his disappointment, Verchere did nothing to help. Mentally, emotionally, he was out of there. As the months went on, he appeared in the office less and less frequently, four or five days a month. "He did his work on the phone from wherever he happened to be,"

Lynne confided to Arthur Hailey. Verchere's standard of living was rising, but he'd dropped most of his clients. His earnings from his law practice were only about $100,000 a year, but he needed much more than that. His biggest self-indulgence, his passion, was the Cessna, which cost $150,000 annually just to maintain. Verchere wasn't concerned; as things had been structured, he was able to access the money from the Manac sale without Lynne suspecting a thing.

FOURTEEN
With Love and Gratitude

IT WAS A LOVELY summer evening in Montreal, the time of year when Montrose Avenue was at its prettiest; the thick old maples shaded the street, softening the hauteur of the great houses arrayed side by side in grand dignity. Each lawn, each privet hedge, each perennial bed was neat and healthy, trimmed to a fare-thee-well by armies of professional gardeners.

At the end of the block, where his house was a neighbourhood showpiece, Bruce Verchere could hardly contain himself. He seethed. He didn't ask much, he told himself, he certainly didn't make demands on his neighbours. But the least he had the right to expect was peace and quiet when he went out on his new patio in the evenings to sip a glass of wine. Why buy in Westmount, where real estate prices are ridiculous, why spend hundreds of thousands on renovations and furniture, when you can't enjoy your surroundings? He was furious.

The object of his wrath was Michel Kaine, his next-door neighbour at 4477 Montrose, who'd had the temerity to install a new air-conditioning unit and a heat pump. Kaine, a thirty-five-year-old engineer who had recently married Paul Desmarais's daughter Sophie, hadn't skimped; he paid $750,000 for the house in 1989, invested $150,000 on renovations, and poured another $20,000 into the air-conditioning. The new unit was the best that money could buy. Installed on his western wall, behind some large, leafy bushes, it hummed and throbbed all day and night and it drove Bruce Verchere nuts.

One approach to the problem would have been to knock on Kaine's door, perhaps with a bottle of good wine in hand, and ask for a chat. If you were naturally surly, or if you had a history of bad relations with your neighbour, you might instead write a stiff letter complaining about the noise. Not Verchere. He went nuclear. He complained to Kaine's real estate agent, he harassed officials at Westmount City Hall, and he launched a lawsuit, demanding that the court grant him an injunction to stop the Kaines from using the system. "The defendant," huffed his statement of claim, "has installed a heating and air-conditioning system with an outdoor unit which is adjacent to the plaintiff's property and emits a great deal of noise pollution, thereby preventing plaintiff having peaceable enjoyment of his property." Verchere described the beautiful new eating area, patio, and garden they'd installed in 1988 and claimed that the "intermittent noise and vibrations" from the Kaines' system were intolerable. He and his wife, he pointed out, didn't have air-conditioning in their own lovely house; in summer they simply kept the windows open.

The noise was so bad, Verchere declared, that he'd listed his house for sale (for $4.5 million). That didn't stop him from getting his architect, Paul Bender, to write Kaine a letter threatening to build a high fence between their properties "that would have the effect of seriously blocking direct sun and natural light from the west windows and garden of your property." Kaine had covered the unit with sheet metal but that didn't lessen the noise, the suit stated; it made it worse. "The noise and the vibration levels are so high that if they are not terminated right away the plaintiff and his family will suffer damages related to their health and well-being."

Kaine fought back vigorously, and the two neighbours brewed up a tempest in a teapot. Each side hired noise experts who determined that the noise was about the same as an electric kettle at three feet and considerably less than a bath being drawn at the same distance. In an examination for discovery Kaine explained that Westmount bylaws forced him to put the unit where it was. But what really irked him was that Verchere had never even bothered to talk to him about it. "He never tried to contact me, to notify me." And his lawyer's response in the statement of defence was equally sharp. "Mr. Verchere never came to meet with the defendant to inform him of his grievances. To the contrary, he hounded Kaine for reasons that Kaine cannot understand, by multiplying his complaints to the city of Westmount, by going to court despite Kaine's good faith." Kaine's lawyer, Jocelyn Poirier (of, ironically, Stikeman Elliott), also forced Verchere to admit he had never met, spoken to, or telephoned her client.

Despite the efforts of the lawyers to bring the silliness to an amicable conclusion, Verchere angrily pursued his neighbour into Quebec Superior Court, where he finally met his match: the even angrier Justice Gérald Ryan. As cantankerous, impatient, and unpretentious as his more famous brother, former Quebec Liberal leader Claude Ryan, Justice Ryan could hardly believe it. People all over Montreal, he snapped, put up with the hum and whir of air-conditioners, "even in apartment buildings where the requirements of good neighbourliness are less exacting than in the present case." Verchere couldn't prove any physical or psychological harm had come to him or his family, nor could he prove his claim that his property had lost value. He hadn't even had a dinner party or reception on the patio to demonstrate the noise nuisance, and no one in the family seemed to have trouble sleeping. Try living next to a discotheque or a factory, like many Montrealers, suggested Justice Ryan, and see what real noise is like. Scolding Verchere for his ham-fisted method of dealing with a normal neighbourly issue, the judge impatiently dismissed the case and, rubbing salt in the wounds, ordered Verchere to pay the costs. Verchere tried to appeal but gave up when his request to bring new evidence before the Court of Appeal was refused.

To Martha O'Brien, Verchere's behaviour in this wretched mess was entirely predictable. Although they were only occasionally in touch, and she was now seriously involved with someone else, she remained fond of her former lover. "Going to the neighbours and saying, 'Let's talk about your heat pump,' would be impossible for him," she said ruefully. "He wouldn't be able to do it. Because he had no idea how to have a give-and-take conversation. He knew how to give orders and how to control stuff, but he didn't know how to have a conversation." He wouldn't have known, with Kaine, how to control the discussion or what might happen, and wouldn't take that chance. "He couldn't have an open-ended conversation," she said. Almost as an afterthought, she added quietly, "It's difficult to have a relationship if you don't have that."

As O'Brien understood, the ridiculous lawsuit with Michel Kaine was not about noise, it was about control. Verchere did not like to be crossed or challenged and, at home at least, he had his way on all the important issues — finances, for instance. Whatever he decided was fine with Lynne; she signed one document after another without inquiring too closely. Verchere spent the summer of 1990 moving more of her money under his control through a series of moves that would baffle anyone but the shrewdest corporate or tax lawyer. His manoeuvres that year were reminiscent of the tax strategies he designed for Fred Melling's company.

On July 20 he directed Manac to reduce the stated capital of Lynne's common shares by $175,079 and move that money to increase the capital of Manac's Class A shares. By now, Manac's shares had been split so that Verchere controlled the Class A's and Lynne owned the common shares.

In August he persuaded Lynne to transfer 242,343 shares of their numbered company, 147626, shares worth $250,000, to the Blue Trust in exchange for $1. Then, on August 9, he directed Lynne to ask their bankers at the CIBC to transfer $1,023,236 (U.S.) to the Blue Trust.

The day after that, Verchere directed Manac to reduce the stated capital of its Class A shares by $340,656 and pay the money to him. He also arranged for Manac to pay dividends to both Lynne and himself. He received $217,499 on his outstanding Class A shares while Lynne received $608,863 as an ordinary taxable dividend, subject to Canadian withholding tax. His dividend was not subject to tax. Lynne had no idea her husband was manipulating the shares to put them under his control, no idea he'd arranged matters so that his dividends were tax-free while hers were not, and no idea of the consequences of signing the endless pieces of paper.

Despite the fact that Lynne owned 74 percent of Manac's shares, Verchere received $558,155 — almost as much money as she did — and his was tax-free. And that money was on top of the $1,449,575 he'd already received as a capital dividend, and on top of the interest-free loans he'd arranged for himself.

At this point Verchere repaid the money he'd borrowed from Manac. He didn't use any of the money he'd just moved out of Manac; instead, he helped himself to money from Lynne's account at Darier Hentsch & Cie in Geneva. On August 31 he directed Manac to issue a statement saying he'd paid back all his loans from the company and granting him full and final discharge in consideration of such payment.

His tinkering hadn't ended. On September 6, he returned to manipulating the share capital of 147626. He changed the numbered company's 968 preferred shares registered in the Blue Trust into one single issued and outstanding common share. Then he changed the 242,353 common shares registered in the name of the Blue Trust to 999 common shares. The stated capital of the preferred shares was reduced to zero; the stated capital of the 1,000 new common shares was fixed at $1 each, a total of $1,000. And he did this without repayment of the capital in the company to its shareholder — Lynne.

This kind of paper shuffling was what he loved best. Move it, hide it, obfuscate, confuse, control. At the end of the day, only one person understood what had gone on and only one person controlled the money. If Lynne asked for an explanation of what she was signing, he soothed her, as usual, with comforting bromides about estate planning and tax shelters. She may have been a software genius, but she had lost interest in business, and though she knew he was unfaithful to her, she trusted him with their wealth. After all, they'd designed the Blue Trust together to ensure their security and that of the boys. She knew that his moves were intended to place all their assets under the control of the Blue Trust; what she didn't understand was that she had lost any control over those assets. Verchere controlled the Blue Trust and so controlled all the money.

If Lynne harboured the slightest suspicion in the back of her mind, it vanished on October 19, the day she came home from a visit to her doctor with some bad news. She was shaken and frightened. Tests had shown that she had a congenital heart condition; it was serious and she would need major open-heart surgery. When Bruce had been involved with O'Brien, and Lynne had spent weeks in Boston having medical treatment for her eye problems, he'd been wonderful. This time, the news was much worse, and he was even more solicitous and helpful. Once again they decided that Boston offered the best surgeons and the best hospitals, so she made plans to go there after Christmas. In the meantime, the wait was long and anxious.

Verchere wanted to do something to cheer her up. He'd always wanted his own ski condo, the kind many of his old law school buddies now had at Whistler, near Vancouver, or the kind his Montreal colleagues kept around Mont Tremblant or Saint-Sauveur in the Laurentians. But he wanted to go one better. He thought about Switzerland, then someone told him about

Telluride, the spectacular Rocky Mountain ski resort in southwest Colorado. A seven-hour drive from Denver, Telluride enjoys "the greatest concentration of 14,000-foot peaks in the United States," according to boosterish local tourist literature. It would be a great Christmas present for Lynne and the boys; after all, they loved to ski. On December 12, 1990, Verchere arranged for 147626 to spend $550,000 (U.S.), or $715,000, on a large luxury condominium at 134 Lost Creek Lane in Telluride. Their new three-bedroom, three-bathroom retreat, Unit H in the Telemark Condominiums, was among the most desirable in Telluride Mountain Village. With a spectacular view of the mountains — the private deck overlooked the Misty Maiden ski slope and Competition Hill — it boasted its own hot tub, wood-burning fireplace (condos in the $300,000 range had only gas fireplaces), cable television with HBO, maid service, and underground parking. It was, as they say, "steps away" from all the ski lifts, shops, and restaurants.

Even in the slow season Telluride has become a popular resort; thanks to its cultural activities there's no off season any more. It has a renowned film festival, museums, and art galleries as well as dance and theatre companies. It began as a little gold and silver mining town back in the 1870s and one of its charms is its Victorian street scenes, the old houses and picturesque storefronts clustered in the Telluride Historic District. Telluride had something for everyone in the Verchere family. It was sophisticated enough for Bruce, cultural enough for Lynne, and challenging enough for David and Michael.

Once again, Bruce did not let the kick of owning a wonderful condo deter him from the routine of hiding the ownership from Lynne. On February 1, 1991, he set up a company called Ride Investors Inc. with one million shares, with his son David as president. Verchere directed 147626 to pay Ride Investors $563.88 (U.S.) per share and issued 1,000 shares for a total of $563,880 (U.S.), thus covering the cost of the condo. Then, on February 19, he hired a Telluride businessman, David Hoffman, to incorporate Ride in Colorado. The deal closed on March 28. When the dust settled, the Blue Trust controlled 147626, which in turn controlled Ride, which in turn owned the condo.

Before the deal closed, Lynne had been admitted to hospital in Boston for heart surgery. The operation was successful, but her recovery slow; it took her six months to recuperate and it wasn't until summer that she started to feel well again. Let's go to Maine, Verchere urged, where you can get some rest. It seemed like a wonderful idea to a woman who had had little time in her career for a long vacation, even an enforced one. She agreed to go with him to the coast. Shortly before they left, they ran into the Haileys at the Lyford Cay Club and discovered that they'd all be on Mount Desert at the same time. Friends of the Haileys had offered them the use of their summer home. How delightful, they all exclaimed. We'll see lots of each other, get caught up.

Verchere arranged to pick the Haileys up in Boston when they arrived and fly them over in the Cessna; as soon as Hailey, who had not lost his love of airplanes, sat beside Verchere in the cockpit, he noticed how richly furnished the plane was and how sophisticated the navigational equipment. His lawyer hadn't spared any expense. He was also, as Hailey recalled later, "a damn good pilot."

In Maine that summer, another sort of reunion took place. One of the Haileys who turned up was Diane, who had worked for Verchere and Lynne as a nanny back in 1975. Now, sixteen years later, she was thirty-three, tall, slim, and gorgeous, with blue eyes and thick, streaky blonde hair highlighted by the sun. Like her sister and her brother, Diane had done well. None of Arthur and Sheila Hailey's kids expected to be looked after by their parents. They'd all been given good educations, then expected to support themselves. Each time one of the kids needed money for a business investment or a house or some project dear to their heart, their parents weighed the decision carefully, sometimes declining. The kids had to make it on their own.

Jane, the oldest of Arthur and Sheila's three, was now a pediatrician in Vancouver with a thriving practice. She was married, though she and her husband, Robert, had no children. Steven and his wife, Susan, lived in Menlo Park, California, where he worked in the computer business. Diane, still single, worked as director of creative affairs at Universal Television in Universal City, California. She was responsible for evaluating screenplays coming in from recognized screenwriters for possible development as movies and television series. While she was there Universal was producing *Northern Exposure* and *Murder, She Wrote*. Diane would usually work with writers; when the script needed a fix, as most did, she'd hire a script doctor who would rework it until it was usable. Like her father, she had a strong story sense and an eye for the movie that words on the page could become. It was the sort of job young people entering the movie business would kill for.

It was always pleasant for the two families to get together; it was especially satisfying for Verchere to be able to show off his wonderful new property and sleek new sailboat to the Haileys. They, gracious and loving, generously rejoiced in the Vercheres' good fortune. When Arthur and Sheila were alone together at night, though, a time when he always jotted down the day's events in his diary and talked things over with her, they wondered if everything was all right with their old friends.

They could tell there was a real strain between Bruce and Lynne. Maybe, they thought, it was her heart operation; she was still very tired. But they couldn't help notice that Lynne's bedroom was in one cabin while Bruce and the boys stayed in another. To put it bluntly, it looked as if Lynne was deliberately living apart from her husband. None of our business, they decided, though they couldn't help worrying a bit. Lynne had so few friends in whom to confide. The Haileys sensed her reserved isolation and her sadness but were reluctant to intrude. In any case, it was a pleasure to sail and swim and read, and to watch Diane enjoy herself with the boys. Verchere was also in good form, seeming to have renewed vitality around the young people.

Aside from the suspected marital problems, the Haileys were astounded at the way the Vercheres had been spending money. They knew pretty well what the Manac sale had brought in, knew it was less than the capital they themselves used to live far less ostentatiously. The plane, the sailboat, Mount Desert, Telluride, Westmount, the fine wines and lavish entertaining and trips to Switzerland — there was simply no way they could live like that indefinitely on just $13 million U.S.

Doing so would eat up their capital, and fast. The Haileys assumed that Verchere must have made a fortune on the merger of the law firms.

As the summer moved on, Verchere took time off from his holiday to tie up a number of loose ends with all the family companies. On July 8 he bought 634,217 common shares of Niskair at $1 a share. Where the money came from to do this began to worry Lynne; he told her it came from his own funds, and with that she had to be content. In fact, it seems to have come from Lynne's Swiss accounts. That same day, as part of his "estate planning" for the family, he arranged to transfer ownership of the Cessna Conquest from Niskair to himself, though the money he'd used to pay for it originally had come from Lynne's company. By the end of September a financial report for Niskair showed the plane had just been valued at $1,029,655. At the same time, Verchere set up a leasing plan so that any tax benefits he could wring out of Niskair would go to him. Again, the bottom line was that Lynne had paid for the plane but Verchere was getting all the benefits, including the tax credits.

HAILEY WAS ONE client Verchere never overcharged. He liked and respected the writer; he was grateful for the introductions around Lyford Cay — few club memberships could have been more valuable to an international tax lawyer working for the Swiss Bank Corporation. Most of all, though, Verchere envied the older man. Like Heward Stikeman, Hailey was living the kind of life Verchere wanted for himself, and up to now he had always worked hard to ensure Hailey's continued approval.

One day in Lyford Cay he met with the Haileys, who wanted to change their wills. As they worked out the Haileys' legacies, Verchere suggested that they might consider leaving something to their lawyer. Hailey was taken off guard.

"I'll think about it," he replied, his brain all the while calculating the fees Verchere had been paid over the years, and the fees he had worked out for himself to act as the executor of their wills.

"It's customary, you know," Verchere pressed.

"I'll think about it," repeated Hailey, who later asked old friends about such a practice and was told it was not customary at all. Until that moment, Verchere had always been able to cloak his greed behind a thick veil of charm and bonhomie. Perhaps his new wealth made him less cautious and more audacious. In any case, the Haileys decided not to leave him anything. The more Hailey had turned it over in his mind the more it bothered him, especially when he remembered the time he'd agreed to be the settlor for the Blue Trust. On that occasion Hailey had paid $1,000 of his own money to set up the trust — a small amount, but it was an irritant that Verchere had never paid him back. It still annoyed him to think about it, and now the suggestion of a bequest was over the top.

It wasn't long before Verchere was tapping the Manac well once again through Niskair, which allowed him to wash money in and out at will. Every time he ran short of ready cash, Niskair was there to provide it. As the trustee of Niskair, Verchere simply wrote a promissory note to himself and removed cash from the company. When the company ran short, he'd top it up with money from

Manac. On October 31, 1991, for example, he needed walking-around money and removed another $28,000 from Niskair. As always, the loan was interest-free.

At the end of October Verchere went to Switzerland and had a talk with his pals at Darier Hentsch and at Pictet Bank, where he and Lynne had their joint accounts. (Lynne later told Hailey about Jim Crot, Bruce's close friend at Pictet. According to Hailey's notes, she described the two as "cronies who work closely and do things for each other.") He and his wife were following separate investment strategies, Verchere explained, and so needed to separate the joint accounts. Back home, when he casually explained this to Lynne, she raised no objections and signed the necessary documents; it was only an administrative issue, he explained, and didn't really change anything. She would still have access to the accounts being opened under Bruce's name because, after all, it was her money and she hadn't turned it over to him for his own use. His new account at Darier Hentsch was designated J.F.K.33.260.

As December grew closer, Lynne started to plan for a ski holiday after Christmas with the boys in Telluride. Because of her slow recovery from heart surgery, the family hadn't used the place much. She looked forward to spending a week with David and Michael in this magical setting. They settled on late February. Bruce wouldn't have time to join them, he said, but he was delighted she was getting away with the boys.

Verchere's own mood was much improved. His despised neighbour, Kaine, had decided to sell his house. He took a beating on the sale; it went for $735,000. Given that he'd paid $745,000, mortgaged it for

$1,046,000, and spent $170,000 on renovations and the infamous air-conditioning, it had not been a good investment. But Kaine was as happy to leave Montrose Avenue as Verchere was to see him go.

Verchere's good mood did not last long. In early December, Fred Melling's tax case, *Special Risks Holdings, Inc. v. The Queen*, was heard in Ottawa before Justice Francis Muldoon of the Federal Court of Canada. Melling, bitter about the pounding he'd taken over the years, had decided to fight back without Verchere; he'd pulled the file from Bennett Jones Verchere and turned it over to Dick Pound at Stikeman's, an embarrassing move for Verchere.

Pound did his best, but Justice Muldoon ruled that Melling had to pay up the $1.2 million (plus interest) that Revenue Canada had deemed he owed for Hogg Robinson's $3-million investment in his company, and the court threw in costs as part of the judgment. "This is a complicated tax case which should never have had to be litigated," wrote Muldoon in his decision. "It has, however, been much litigated." Thanks to his tax advisors, Melling had entered into a series of what Muldoon described as "frightfully complex" transactions, and while it was accepted in law that taxpayers are allowed to arrange their affairs so as to reduce, lawfully, their tax burden, what had happened here, he said, was ridiculous.

Muldoon disliked the two-step 50-50 ownership deal that Verchere had set up when Hogg Robinson first poured the $3 million into Richards Melling — which had been transformed, a few days later, into a 51-49 percent ownership in favour of Melling. The word Muldoon used to describe this manoeuvre was a "ruse."

The deal, he concluded, "was a contrivance at best, and a deliberate sham at worst, being a ploy to pretend that control was lost without possibility of retrieval, except by Hogg's act of grace." Melling, added Muldoon contemptuously, "is hoist on his own petard." Muldoon hadn't finished with the miserable carcass of Melling's pride. Taxpayers were not expected always to be right in figuring out their taxes, but they were required, the judge scolded, "not to be duplicitous, or deceitful, or knowingly to evade the duty to make a reasonable attempt to meet the standard of correctly determining the tax [to be] paid. The taxpayer fell woefully short of that statutory standard."

As if having Justice Muldoon's scornful ruling on the record for all the world to see wasn't enough, Verchere had the added humiliation of a few words from Pound in court, a statement deliberately made to become part of court record. Pound, after all, was determined that no lawyer searching legal precedents ever consider this mess of a case as a Stikeman Elliott failure. He wanted everyone to understand clearly who was to blame. "As Your Lordship will get into the evidence," he stated, "you'll see the relevance of this particular admission, but the agreement between counsel [the lawyers acting for Melling and for Revenue Canada] is that Bruce Verchere and the Verchere firm are recognized as tax specialists in income tax matters, for purposes of this litigation. Counsel agree it will not be necessary, therefore, to introduce evidence to the effect that Verchere and the Verchere firm are known to be specialists in the field." Pound was telling the court, in no uncertain terms, that his former partner was to blame for Melling's $1.2-million mess. Though

Verchere didn't want to practise law, he certainly didn't want anything to stand in his way if he felt like returning full-time, or needed to. Muldoon's decision was going to make it difficult to regain his lustre among the top Canadian tax lawyers. If Verchere was unhappy about the way this long case ended, Fred Melling took it even harder. Melling had hero-worshipped Verchere. They'd been close, lived near one another on Montrose, seen each other socially.

Melling regretted having mixed business with pleasure, and although he felt Revenue Canada had dealt with him unfairly, and was angrier with the taxmen than with Verchere, it was obvious the whole subject remained terribly painful. He lost a huge tax judgment and paid hundreds of thousands in legal fees, all because his lawyer was too cute. He asked Pound to appeal Justice Muldoon's decision and the case staggered on, waiting for an appeal court date, for another two years.

The Vercheres, meanwhile, spent a quiet Christmas in 1991, and two days later they celebrated their twenty-eighth wedding anniversary. They'd come a long way together over nearly three decades, the kid from Kamloops and the lovely, shy girl who'd turned herself into a computer expert long before most people ever imagined the impact such machines would have. Verchere could not let the occasion pass unremarked. He picked up a Christmas card, crossed out the stale "Seasons Greetings" message with his pen, and wrote, "For dear Lynne, 27.12.63 — 27.12.91. With love & gratitude from Bruce."

FIFTEEN

A Woman Scorned

JANUARY AND FEBRUARY in Montreal are never easy. Once the pleasures of Christmas are over, there is only the long, grim slog ahead of icy streets, deep slushy snowbanks, and fierce winds whistling between the city's downtown office towers. Anyone with the time and the money tries to get down to Florida or the Caribbean for a few weeks, to sit in the sun and bake the chill out of their bones. Hardier souls head for the Laurentian ski resorts or drive south to Vermont's ski areas around Stowe.

Few Montrealers, even those nestling in splendid Westmount houses, could boast a ski property in Telluride, and Lynne, David, and Michael looked forward to their week's holiday in the new condo. Verchere told them he couldn't manage it but would fly them all down. Though disappointing to Lynne, it was nothing new; the whole marriage had been a history of the couple spending holidays apart.

Just before Lynne and the boys went off, Bruce asked her to transfer $170,000 (U.S.) to him from her Swiss Bank Corporation account in New York. He needed the money, he told her, for the boys' expenses. It seemed a large amount for expenses, but he must have had his reasons. In fact, Verchere didn't use more than $20,000 of the money to cover costs for his sons; the rest he kept for himself. His personal extravagances had escalated; for example, he built up a wine collection eventually worth nearly $500,000. He had no money to pay his bills unless he took it from Lynne's accounts.

On February 21 he flew his family to Telluride for their holiday and then returned to Montreal. A week later, on February 28, Lynne and the boys returned home.

When they got back to the house, it seemed oddly dark and quiet. Nobody was home. "Bruce?" Lynne called. "Bruce?" She went into their bedroom.

"Bruce?" No sign of him. Slowly, dread mounting, she began to see that something was wrong. For years, she realized, she'd almost expected something like this, but even so it was a dreadful shock. His clothes weren't there. Frantic, she rushed into his study. Here, too, many articles had disappeared, personal items from his desk. His bathroom was beside the study — she saw that all his things were missing, not just the shaving kit and toothbrush but everything. He was gone. He'd left her.

Any woman who has gone through it knows exactly what it feels like. For anyone as private and reserved as Lynne Verchere, the embarrassment of having to tell people, of having to explain the "separation" to family and friends, was mortifying. Even informing casual business acquaintances was a trial, especially after so much effort, for so many years, had gone into maintaining the fiction of a happy marriage. Bruce's leaving was a failure for a woman who knew little of failure. It shattered the picture of the couple who had everything. One could ask how great a loss it was for a woman whose husband had been having affairs for years — except that Lynne loved him, and much preferred life with Bruce, even on his terms, to life without him. She wasn't sure who the other woman was; she only knew there had to be one.

For two or three days Lynne was in shock. "I'm devastated, just devastated," she told close friends. "So are the boys." It didn't take long, however, before her formidable brain clicked into gear; along with grief, rage had started to boil up, and fear. She thought about friends whose husbands had walked out and taken up with other women. Change the locks on the house, clean out the bank accounts before he does, get a killer lawyer: that was the mantra of the wronged wives.

Thinking about her money, Lynne became even more distressed. She realized how little attention she'd paid to it; thought of all the times Bruce had slid papers under her nose for her to sign, papers she often didn't understand because of their complexity. Estate planning for the Blue Trust. For the good of the boys.

She felt a complete fool. She, of all people, should have known better. She with her MBA and a business success story that had become a case study at Harvard Business School; she with her obsessive, nitpicking passion for detail; she hadn't even had the wit to keep an eye on her own money. Of course, there was a good chance Bruce hadn't done anything untoward — surely he wouldn't be that reckless. But he'd already been reckless with some investments, and it was her money they'd been spending to support their lavish lifestyle, and her rage and panic grew until she was on the verge of hysteria. A few days after Bruce left, she asked David to pack himself a suitcase.

"I was so mad that I got on an airplane for Switzerland," she later confided to Arthur Hailey, "and went to our bank account there and transferred everything I could get my hands on into an account in my name only, so that now Bruce cannot touch it. When he found out about it he was furious."

Her satisfaction in stripping out that account evaporated with another shock. When she and David arrived at Darier Hentsch in Geneva, she found that Bruce had split their old joint account and opened a new account for himself, blandly forging her signature on one of the bank's application forms. She had no access to the bearer bonds they owned jointly. Only he could get at them. In disbelief, she demanded to talk to senior management at the bank. Look, she insisted, this signature, supposedly mine, is a forgery.

"They clammed up and would not discuss it," she told Hailey in despair. Hailey knew from his own experience of Swiss banks that clamming up was precisely what the officials would do when caught in a corner. From their point of view, it made perfect sense to behave this way; if Lynne were to sue the bank for negligence, the less said the better. The last thing the bank wanted was to be held responsible.

At Pictet the story wasn't much different. She discovered with shock and dismay that Bruce had moved half the Pictet account — $1,641,295 (U.S.) — into a new account for himself; the rest stayed in the old joint account. And all this after he'd been paid his share of the Manac money. Whatever remained in the Pictet Bank actually belonged to Lynne, even when the accounts were joint. Wildly, she remembered him telling her she'd have access to all the accounts in Switzerland, but when she tried to use the new ones he'd set up at Pictet, the response was the same as she'd received at Darier Hentsch: "Sorry, Madame."

Except for the one account she'd been able to strip out, Bruce had blocked the Swiss accounts. He was the only one able to withdraw money from them. Lynne realized she had no knowledge of all the accounts he had opened in Switzerland; in fact, she had no clue what accounts he might have opened in other countries. Where were they? How much was in them? She knew there were several accounts at the CIBC in Montreal, as well as a safety deposit box; she knew there were more accounts in Maine, and more in Geneva, and some in New York. Maybe Panama? Were there others? Again and again she chastised herself. She had trusted Bruce. Why wouldn't she have trusted him? They were married, for God's sake, had been a wonderful team, transforming themselves from aspiring professionals into wealthy, accomplished members of the elite.

She'd wake each morning in Switzerland, her mind in overdrive, with the sick realization that it wasn't a bad dream. Bruce wasn't there any more. Neither, she feared, was her money. When she and David got back to Montreal and told Michael what they'd found, they all struggled to come to grips with the real possibility that Bruce was going through the fortune they'd made from Manac. This was not only the fortune meant to generate the income on which they'd live, it was also the patrimony the parents had worked so hard to build for their sons.

She needed a lawyer. She also needed a smart accountant with a nose for fraud, someone on her side, someone far from the clubby lawyers' world that might feel protective towards her husband. The man she found was Jacques Grandmont, a senior audit partner at Raymond Chabot Martin Paré, a well-known accounting firm in

Montreal. Grandmont, who lived in Repentigny, east of Montreal on the north shore of the St. Lawrence, was given the job of tracing all the money she and Bruce had earned from the Manac sale and figuring out what assets her husband had parked in all the different companies he'd set up over the years. She paid no attention to Bruce's earnings as a lawyer or his partnership shares in Bennett Jones Verchere; she knew that his own assets were negligible.

She focused instead on the money she'd earned and the things they'd bought with it. What, legally, did they own as a couple? Who controlled those assets? The house? The paintings? The Cessna? Maine? Telluride? *Niska*? Those debentures in the Griffith Island Club — whose money had paid for them? How much money had Bruce actually spent over the years? How much was left? Would she ever get it back?

═

ALTHOUGH VERCHERE had planned his getaway for some weeks, he'd only had the one week at home alone, while the others were in Telluride, to cover his tracks. His strategic disadvantage was the singular situation of having had a wife for a business manager. Lynne, the gifted businesswoman, the computer whiz, the woman scorned, was not going to take this lying down. She assembled an army to help. While Grandmont began going through documentation and working out flow charts, she retained lawyers at Langlois Robert in Montreal to take charge of the battle. The firm's best-known partner was Michel Robert, a former national president of the Liberal Party of Canada, a savvy and tenacious litigator; so was his partner, another

Liberal, Raynold Langlois, who took on Lynne's file. Once Langlois saw the way the Blue Trust had been set up, under the laws of Prince Edward Island, they brought in James Macnutt, a prominent lawyer from Charlottetown, to act for her there.

A partner at Macnutt and Dumont, another active Liberal, and a volunteer in many of P.E.I.'s charitable and cultural activities, Macnutt was a credible choice — he too was an experienced litigator, especially in the often dicey area of wills, trusts, and real estate. Still, few files he'd seen were as dicey as this one. He settled in to study how P.E.I. law applied to Lynne's situation. If Verchere needed any more signals to show how serious his wife was, the choice of prominent Liberals for her army should have alarmed him more than it did.

Lynne, meanwhile, added up all the promissory notes her husband had casually signed and tucked away. In doing so, she began to see the size of her problem:

- $1,590,334.65 signed on June 11, 1986
- $209,665.35 signed on June 20, 1986
- $445,200 signed on December 15, 1987
- $306,212.26 signed on December 23, 1987
- $40,000 signed on January 3, 1987
- $300,000 signed on January 7, 1988
- $28,000 signed on October 31, 1991

These loans were all interest-free; if Verchere paid them back, he always used money from the Manac sale to do so. But there was more. As Grandmont put the picture together for her and as she made her own calculations, she concluded that on separate occasions from 1988 to

1992 her husband had squandered — "illegally," as she said to close friends — the sums of $363,898, $244,528, $219,684, $230,368, and $264,993, largely for his own benefit. Lynne didn't tell her friends how he had spent these amounts. She may not have known. Wine, music, travel, clothes — the lavishness was endless. Not only did he have a Jaguar convertible, he'd bought three Range Rovers, one of them for the camp in Maine.

Even as Lynne worked her way through the figures, Bruce, with breathtaking insouciance, continued to pull money out of the Blue Trust. On March 19, 1992, for example, he directed the trust to issue another promissory note to pay him personally $1,454,399.

Beside herself over the way he'd spent her money and managed their accounts, she was even more hurt about the spineless way he had walked out. Two or three close friends kept her informed about what he was doing. She heard he was living in a modest flat in downtown Montreal; "a dump," as she described it to friends. He was involved with someone, she knew, but wasn't sure who. His colleagues at Bennett Jones Verchere had closed ranks against her, she felt; in particular she thought Bill Britton, the firm's managing partner in Calgary, was protective of his old college chum. Her only comfort came from women like Ann Bodnarchuk and Liliane Stewart.

By May she knew she had to confront her husband. She couldn't stand it any longer; she had to know. Just what was he doing? What were his plans? Finally, after her repeated entreaties, he agreed to meet and to tell her everything. When she also demanded a full accounting of their money, he began, reluctantly and slowly, to give her some information.

If she thought her life couldn't hold more cruel surprises, she was wrong. When she asked why he'd walked out, Bruce told her he had fallen in love with Dianc Hailey. She barely registered the words as he told her bluntly he wanted to marry Diane. When he said that the affair had started in October, after the summer reunion in Maine, she realized that his unfaithfulness — this round of it — had begun while she was still recovering from open-heart surgery.

Calmly, her husband laid it all out. When the Haileys were in Maine for their summer holidays, he'd got to know Diane for the first time since she'd worked for them sixteen years before. During that week in Pretty Marsh he'd been drawn to her, amusing her, charming her, winning her friendship. Not long after she returned to Los Angeles, he was on the phone to say he was coming out on business; any chance she'd be free for dinner? Lynne found herself almost unable to comprehend her husband's story. As if stealing her money wasn't enough, how could he have betrayed her again, so callously, so brutally? Seducing a woman twenty years his junior, the daughter of one of his oldest and most cherished clients, who was also one of Lynne's best friends?

To Diane Hailey, Bruce Verchere had seemed at first like a nice older man, a friend of her father and mother, Lynne Verchere's rather brisk and businesslike husband. When he phoned her in Los Angeles, he seemed to be taking an avuncular interest in her career; maybe he was even a little starstruck. Showing visitors around Los Angeles and taking them to the stars' favourite restaurants was nothing new for Diane, and she was happy to make time for Verchere.

Once they had talked for a while, she understood that he was powerfully attracted to her. He was white-haired and looked every one of his fifty-five years; she was twenty-two years younger, exceptionally lovely, and could have had her pick of attractive men. But when Verchere turned on the charm, he was irresistible, witty and attentive, fascinating and well-informed. On the delicate subject of his marriage, he was forthright. He told Diane he hadn't been in love with his wife for a long time. In fact, he said, he'd been on the verge of leaving her once before and had stayed only because of their closely entwined business interests. Intrigued and sympathetic, Diane knew at once she would see him again. "He seemed very strong and dependable," she says. "He was very open. But he was also a lot of fun. He loved to cross-country ski, he liked running, he liked sports. He was very physical." So was she.

All her life she had been a good athlete who kept slim and fit with swimming, sailing, and tennis. A man who enjoyed sports as much as she did was very appealing. As for the difference in their ages, she had always preferred older men; falling in love with Verchere was as natural as love could be. And it wasn't long after that first dinner, just a few weeks, that she realized that was exactly what had happened. As she got to know him more fully, his quirks seemed all the more endearing. She smiled to think of how he enjoyed getting all dressed up to go out for dinner. She loved his passion for good food. She cherished the fact that he also liked solitude and reading and quiet. The same qualities that Martha O'Brien had loved, she loved too; it could not have been lost on Verchere that Martha and Diane were, by now, almost exactly the same age.

For Verchere, Diane was everything he had ever wanted, all the different elements in one package. He always admired brains in a woman, and, like Lynne, she was smart and successful. He admired women who were optimistic and cheerful and warm; Diane was all these things. He could never have loved a woman who wasn't beautiful and chic, someone who made other men's heads turn enviously; Diane had that quality, too. Soon after their affair had started, Verchere knew this was the woman he wanted to spend the rest of his life with. The other women he'd had merely reinforced his conviction. He'd felt something similar for O'Brien, but had messed it up; this time, he promised himself, he'd get it right.

In November Verchere had told Lynne he was going away on a secret mission for Brian Mulroney; he'd be gone a few days. Instead, he flew his Cessna to Los Angeles to spend the time with Diane, staying with her in her Brentwood apartment. As he had almost given up his law practice, no one really noticed that he was gone. He'd spent the Christmas holidays with his family, and had ferried them down to Colorado, but all the time he'd been desperate to get back to Diane and sorting through a profound dilemma. Did he have the courage to end his marriage? He adored his sons; were they old enough to understand? Could they cope? He'd been at the brink of this decision once before, with Martha, but hadn't had the guts. Did he now? Slowly his determination grew. This time, he reasoned, there was one important difference; this time he could afford to go. Ever since Lynne had sold Manac, he had worked diligently at safeguarding the money. The Blue Trust now controlled all the other shell companies, all the bank accounts, all the property, even the art on the walls of their house.

And he controlled the Blue Trust.

It was time. This was what he'd wanted for years and nothing need stop him. Diane was the woman he'd been waiting for all his life. Her parents, unlike O'Brien's, were wealthy, and she had money of her own. Thinking back to his conversation with Arthur Hailey, when he had asked to be remembered in the Haileys' wills, gave him pause. He knew his old client well, knew Hailey was uncompromising about many things. But he also loved Diane, and even if Arthur was not going to like this he'd eventually come around, if only for her sake.

However he rationalized the situation, Verchere couldn't find an easy way of telling the Haileys. Finally, on May 19, when Hailey called to talk about some paperwork, Verchere drew a deep breath and broke the news: he and Lynne had separated, he said, and he and Diane were "seeing each other seriously."

Arthur Hailey was at that stage of life when little comes as a surprise or a shock, but this news set him back on his heels. When he and Sheila sat down in their glass-walled porch in Lyford Cay that afternoon to have their usual cup of tea, he told her what Verchere had said. Immediately, Sheila called Diane. The relationship was as big a surprise to them as it had been to Lynne, and they needed time to think it over.

As always, Sheila, whose common sense and good humour had kept the family on an even keel for decades, took the events in stride. For her, it seemed almost inevitable that Diane would fall in love with someone like Bruce; most of her adult life she had chosen men who were much older than herself. As a mother, Sheila wanted her daughter to have the kind of strong and loving husband she had in Arthur; age mattered less to her than character and personality. If they were well suited, she felt, the age difference wasn't such a big deal. And Diane was certainly old enough to know her own mind.

SIXTEEN
A Fine Mess

ARTHUR HAILEY was a familiar sight in the early mornings in Lyford Cay as he walked briskly along the quiet boulevards lined with palm trees, past the thick stucco walls protecting the deep lawns and pink and grey villas of the super-rich. Slim and wiry, dressed in crisply ironed tan shorts, T-shirt, and thick-soled jogging shoes, he stopped for no one, only lifting his hand briefly to friends who might be pulling out of their driveways to catch a plane to the mainland, drive to their offices downtown, or play a little golf or tennis before it got too hot. A few cars would pass him, bringing management staff, chefs, maids, and gardeners to work from their homes in Nassau's suburbs.

Hailey's power walk lasted forty minutes; it took him into the private yacht harbour and down the pier to a sandy beach at the end, where he wheeled around and started pounding back. While he walked, he took quick note of who had come in overnight. Ted Rogers's yacht, the *Loretta Anne*, might be tied up, or the one that belonged to the family of his late neighbour Stavros Niarchos, the Greek shipping billionaire who died in 1996. And all the time he was pounding along the pavement, he was thinking. Usually he thought about what he was going to write that day. This morning, however, he was thinking about Bruce Verchere.

Only once in a long while do most of us catch a glimpse of an earthly paradise. For Arthur and Sheila Hailey it was an almost permanent condition. Here, in the most exclusive corner of the 700 or so diminutive islands that make up the Bahamas, they had lived in a gorgeous little Eden year-round since 1969. Guiding a visitor around in his car at 20 miles an hour, Hailey would point out its people, its palaces, and its privileges with all the boosterism of the newest, proudest homeowner. Clearly, even after thirty years here, he had never taken it for granted.

It was an extraordinary community. There was something of the small town about it, with old-fashioned values and virtues, neighbourly friendliness. It was a place where people knew each other and worried about each other and spent pleasant evenings in one another's homes. At the same time, it was one of the most sophisticated communities in the world; just when you thought you could typecast the members of the Lyford Cay Club as WASP, you discovered the place was integrated and members could be white, black, Jewish, Arab, you name it. The pale pink Colonial clubhouse, fronted with graceful pillars and surrounded by golf greens and tennis courts, would have more Toyotas and Volkswagens parked in front than Rolls-Royces or Porsches.

Taylor himself had provided the money to build a small hospital in the community; he donated more to build a school. Both are open to Bahamians who live outside the area, and both have helped to influence this wealthy citizenry to think beyond their own privileged estates. Even though Taylor himself kept a mistress close by — Lady Annie Orr-Lewis, a talented interior decorator, who worked on many of the houses in Lyford Cay — there was a sense of decorum about the place. One of the least pretentious houses was a long low bungalow belonging to the actor Sean Connery and his wife, Micheline, great favourites in the community. One of the largest was a work in progress for the Canadian fashion magnate Peter Nygaard, who put together a personal theme park on two hectares with a 35-foot pyramid and an 80-foot artificial mountain, overrun by peacocks, in which nestled sixteen guest cabanas. Somewhere in the middle of all this was the Georgian-style house (now demolished) which once belonged to Edward Plunket Taylor, known around here as Eddie but to most Canadians as E.P., who built the house for his wife, Winifred. It all felt a little . . . Canadian. Not flashy (except for Nygaard), not vaunting, but a place so cheerfully self-confident, so beautiful, and so underplayed it would steal your heart. Many of the houses were the same gentle pink of the clubhouse, and they were low and not so big that they'd frighten you. If the houses weren't pink, they were white or pale grey. And yet each of the 352 properties in this part of New Providence Island was different from its neighbours, so if there was any uniformity among them it was in the explosion of ruby and carmine and rose in the wild tumble of bougainvillea, poinsettia, hibiscus, frangipani, and oleander that twisted around gates and fell over fences and perfumed the soft, warm air.

═══

WALKING ALONG purposefully, Hailey reflected on the fact that he wouldn't be here, wouldn't be enjoying such a splendid life, were it not for the prudent counsel of Bruce Verchere. If Verchere hadn't advised him in 1969 to move to a tax haven so that he wouldn't be paying most of his book royalties to governments, and hadn't shown him exactly how to do it, where would Hailey be? He certainly wouldn't have had the same level of wealth, the same wonderfully pleasurable existence. He and Sheila wouldn't have become close to Bruce and Lynne, an enduring friendship the Haileys treasured. Hailey felt enormously indebted to his tax lawyer.

He also felt enormously troubled. As a father he would have done anything for his children. He had always treated each of them with scrupulous fairness. But Diane was his youngest, the one who had prompted the conversation about taxes and leaving the Napa Valley so many years before. He couldn't forget the image of her as a little girl. Now that she was a grown woman, he rejoiced in her success, her beauty, and in the deep love she felt for him and for Sheila. No daughter was closer or more adored. All he wanted was her happiness and, like Sheila, he had long wanted her to find a husband who'd love her and help her bring up a family of her own.

What he couldn't wrap his mind around was the idea that Verchere should be the one. Hailey himself had been no saint, he'd be the first to admit; he'd had affairs. But his own lawyer, a close confidant of long standing, a man so much older, in such a muddle back in Montreal? Was this not a man with more baggage than any young woman needed?

Something else stuck in Hailey's craw. He couldn't put out of his mind Verchere's suggestion that he and Sheila remember him in their wills. Was it merely a tactless aberration, the sort of thoughtless, foot-in-mouth blunder we all make from time to time? Or had his true colours finally shone through? Verchere was well aware of Diane's status in the Haileys' wills, of course, and Arthur couldn't help wondering if Verchere would have found his daughter quite as compelling if she did not stand to come into a small fortune of her own one day.

If Verchere had thought through his affair with Diane as carefully as he ought to have, he might have seen that Arthur Hailey would become a redoubtable opponent. Instead, Verchere's calculations were self-centred and shortsighted. He reasoned that Arthur and Sheila were, after all, part of the international jet set. They were sophisticated and worldly and famous. When they stayed in the Fairmont Hotel in San Francisco or ate Bahamian specialties at Compass Point near their home or attended an event in London or New York, these small events in their lives often found their way into the newspapers. Raffles Hotel in Singapore, a place beloved of famous writers — Somerset Maugham, Joseph Conrad, Rudyard Kipling, and Noël Coward were just a few — named one of its suites after Hailey. The Haileys lived in one of the world's most exclusive communities, where few eyebrows went up when older men acquired beautiful younger wives.

Verchere imagined that Arthur, as a man of the world, would accept his affair with Diane. And if there was a little strain — well, surely his client's gratitude would help to smooth the way; after all, Verchere was well aware that Hailey had often told people how much he owed his lawyer. And because Sheila was so quick to accept her daughter's happiness, Verchere assumed Arthur would join her. What he utterly failed to understand was his client's character. Arthur Hailey, a man who did not believe in God and had no place in his life for organized religion, was an extraordinarily moral person. Old-fashioned, courteous, hospitable, diplomatic. A man who wore his heart on his sleeve — especially when it came to family — and remained intensely loyal to old friends. He was like a character out of an old *Boy's Own* magazine, someone who valued steadfastness and honesty and fairness. In his world at Lyford Cay, there were many other people who shared those values.

Arthur Hailey turned out to be not quite as sophisticated as Verchere had counted on. Verchere had also seriously failed to calculate the depth of his client's love for Diane. Hailey wanted only the best for his child, not a scheming older man who'd just flattened a perfectly good wife and two nice boys in Westmount and who may have had one eye on the Haileys' net worth. Arthur brooded about what had happened; Sheila, meanwhile, gamely decided to accept it. Her attitude was simple: "Let's make the best of it," she urged. "No," he responded gloomily. "I can't."

Not surprisingly, the tension between them grew, adding to his grief; never was any man more happily married, and he despaired as Sheila took the side of Diane and Bruce. The cosy morning breakfasts when they planned their days, the afternoon tea time when they talked things over and discussed their evening plans became times of silence and sadness. When Diane spent the U.S. Memorial Day holiday in May at Lyford Cay instead of with her lover, as she'd hoped, it was a miserable time for all of them. Arthur hadn't been able to give her his blessing, and Sheila was heartsick about this rift in the family.

Hailey's sympathy for Lynne Verchere, like his suspicion of Bruce, was considerable. Thus, when Diane returned to California after the brief holiday, nothing had been resolved.

═══

On June 11, 1992, Hailey called Lynne Verchere, and when she learned that he was not taking Bruce's side, she responded warmly. Hailey listened with compassion and for the next little while they talked frequently. As he continued to learn how appallingly Lynne had been treated by Bruce, the angrier he became, the anger extending to his own daughter. Sheila wasn't there to pitch in with her own steadfast counsel; she had gone to London for ten days because her eldest sister was seriously ill.

Sheila had hoped this meant she'd be able to get a break from the misery and move into the Beaufort in Knightsbridge, her favourite hotel when she was in London on her own. She might never have left the Caribbean; everyone knew her phone number and the calls from her agitated husband and children followed her.

On his own, Hailey continued to grieve over the double betrayal of his daughter and his lawyer. Soon he was back on the phone to Lynne, who poured out her heart to him about many things — the state of her marriage to Bruce, the money they'd made from the sale of Manac, how Bruce was squandering their capital, even the tax and legal problems they were facing. The more Hailey heard, the more upset he got. Each day Hailey plodded through his daily work schedule before taking another call from Lynne with her litany of woe. One day he called his daughter Jane in Vancouver to talk about what was happening in the family, then called Lynne, giving her advice. On June 13, after a chat with his son

Mark, Hailey spoke with Lynne again, continuing their earlier discussion, before having another talk with Jane. All in all, a fine mess.

When Jane phoned again, on June 16, she was acting as a go-between for Diane and Sheila. His objections, Jane told her father, were threatening the relationship between Diane and Bruce. Not true, Arthur replied. If they are indeed breaking up, I'm being blamed for problems entirely of Bruce's making. He faxed a note to Sheila at the Beaufort to tell her his side of the story, and they agreed to let things cool down until she got home.

Then it was time to talk to Jane again. "Jane understanding," he recorded in his daybook, then phoned Lynne again. Lynne assured him she hadn't talked to Bruce about their long conversations. "Therefore Bruce has lied," he jotted. "Detailed notes explain."

Hailey's conversations with Lynne had depressed him. As he thought over what she'd told him, he decided to go over the notes he'd made as they talked — he made notes every time he spoke on the phone — and put everything into some kind of order. Maybe then he'd understand what was happening, make some sense of it all.

> The notes which follow are an attempt to put into perspective and sequence a series of events which are connected and which, in their later stages, have caused great unhappiness to several people. Most of that unhappiness persists and some effects will remain for a long time. Also, there have been misunderstandings, accusations and confusion. Not all of these have been resolved.

Comment by A.H.: Most of what is set down here is the result of several long phone conversations between A.H. and Lynne Verchere. Until nearly the end of these conversations Lynne was unaware that detailed notes were being taken and it is possible that if she had known of this, she would not have spoken as freely or revealed as much as she did. However, there is nothing wrong with having taken notes. At no time, in advance or during the conversations, were promises about confidentiality asked or made; therefore no promises have been broken. If a recorder had been used on the phone line (one was available) that would have been something else. But it was not.

Near the end of the conversations, when A.H. revealed existence of these notes and ran over them with Lynne with the objective of correcting any errors, she seemed totally taken aback by how much ground and detail had been covered. But soon after, she agreed to help with corrections (there were very few) and asked specifically for the deletion of two items (paragraphs) which contained what seemed to Lynne especially sensitive material. A.H. agreed to this and the deletions have been made. He also promised not to reveal to anyone else what they were.

Something else: At several points A.H. tried to "catch out" Lynne concerning things she had told him during earlier conversations, using a method he had developed for book research. But as it proved, there was nothing to "catch out."

> Lynne was consistent and convincing in all that she said and where, in these notes, her words are in quotes, they are exactly as she said them.

Lynne began by telling Hailey about the sale of Manac Systems, which she described as her own creation. With Bruce's legal help, she said, they'd sold the company to Gulf + Western for about $17 million in Canadian dollars and divided the proceeds so that one-quarter went to Bruce and the rest to her. She talked about Bruce's debts and how he'd used his share of the Manac money to pay them off, leaving him without any capital of his own. The last thing she expected was that he'd then try to take half of the remaining capital to go off and live with another woman.

Neither Lynne nor Hailey knew that taking half of Lynne's capital to go off and live with another woman had been Verchere's plan for years. It was his plan in 1985 when he was promising Martha O'Brien he'd leave his wife as soon as they'd sold Manac. Even without this knowledge, Hailey knew in his bones that Lynne was right when she summed her husband up with one astute remark: "Bruce is obsessed about money, but no longer wants to work for it."

She took Hailey through all the financial stepping-stones of the past years, including the merger between Verchere, Noël & Eddy and Bennett Jones, explaining that the merger hadn't brought her husband any money at all, despite his attempts to give the impression he'd done well by it. She explained that he had only three or four clients left, drifted into his office only three or four days a month, and kept his practice alive on the phone;

that he was earning not more than $100,000 a year, she said, a trifling sum given his lifestyle. "Lynne says Bruce needs access to the capital they once intended to share, and without that access (which Lynne has largely blocked) he does not have enough money to keep their airplane and boat." As Lynne outlined what they owned, and what her husband had paid for the properties and the boat, Hailey's suspicions that his daughter had stepped into a snake pit were confirmed.

Verchere controlled all Lynne's money, Hailey soberly concluded, but wouldn't share financial information with his wife. "When she inquires, he replies, 'Why do you need to see those?'" Hailey noted. "Or on another occasion, 'It's weird that you want to see them.' (A.H. Note: This is especially convincing because 'weird' is a favorite word of Bruce's.)" The Vercheres' marriage had been so different from his own that Hailey felt uneasy. He and Sheila were a team. She would sit at her computer in her office updating financial charts while he went to the library in the Lyford Cay Club to check the *Wall Street Journal* for the latest currency rates. He and Sheila discussed every investment together. Every financial step he took, she took with him. What was Diane getting herself into with a man like Verchere?

Lynne continued her confidences, holding back nothing. Because of her husband's financial misdeeds, she said, she'd retained her own lawyer; she also needed a lawyer because of Bruce's relationship with Diane. Not that she expected it would last long, she added; his affairs never did. Indeed, they agreed, this one may have ended already.

For Lynne it was very convenient having her rival's father as a confidant; it gave her a way of delivering messages she had no intention of sending directly. Through Hailey, she could state her position on ending the marriage. It was a non-starter, she made clear; she had no plans to give up Bruce and if he wanted a divorce — well, her lawyer had told her there were ways to delay a divorce for years, maybe even forever. Lynne also let Hailey know that she had several confidential sources who kept her well informed about what her husband was up to, at all times.

Lynne knew, for example, about her husband's trip to Los Angeles to see Diane when he'd told her he was on a secret mission for Mulroney. She also knew that her husband had planned to spend the Memorial Day weekend the previous year with Diane in Los Angeles. When she found out about it, she said, she blew her top and demanded that he stay home. "If you go," she stormed, "you are telling me that our marriage is over." Verchere caved in to his wife's ultimatum and cancelled. Even though Verchere clearly wanted the marriage to be over, her warning had set him back on his heels; when it ended, he wanted to be the one in control, the one calling the shots.

Hailey, hearing all this from Lynne, wondered whether Bruce could afford to leave. He felt desperately sorry for Lynne, angry with Diane, and isolated from his wife, who had been his closest companion for so many years. The more he talked to Lynne, the worse it got — she completely undermined any faith he might have had in Verchere's integrity. "Nowadays Bruce lies to everybody," Lynne told him. "He lies to me. He lies to the boys. He probably lies to Diane."

Lynne pointed out that Bruce had lied when he had told Hailey a few weeks earlier, on May 19, that he and

Lynne had separated and that he and Diane were seeing each other seriously. The part about Diane was true; the part about the separation was not. Although he had walked out on her in February and had rented an apartment for himself, he had returned home for a few days. The very day he gave Hailey the news, said Lynne, they were still sleeping in the same bed in the Montrose Avenue house. We weren't separated, Lynne insisted; Bruce was living only part-time in "a crummy walk-up" in Outremont.

When Verchere was home, of course, it didn't mean he and his wife got along. One morning Verchere went out early to jog, leaving his wallet and his appointment book lying on his dressing table. Lynne went through them. What she found couldn't have been more hurtful. Not only was there a record of all Verchere's meetings with Diane, but her husband's wallet, she told Hailey, was "bulging with condoms. Of course, Bruce would never want to get Diane pregnant," she added. "The fact is, he can't stand babies and small children, even having them near him. When David and Michael were small he wanted no part of them, almost ignored them. I did everything. Only when they were big enough to throw a ball did he want anything to do with the boys. But if he had children now, by the time they could throw a ball he would be too old to catch it."

Other people are adamant that Verchere adored his sons and always tried to be part of their upbringing. In fact, that same summer Bruce took his sons and some of their friends to New York in the Cessna for a holiday, and everyone had a wonderful time. Bruce was particularly close to David, who not only resembled him but was as charming and charismatic as his father. When David told his parents he was gay, both were understanding even though it was difficult for them. Bruce even attended a Gay Pride march with him to show his solidarity.

Lynne may have suspected that a young woman like Diane would want children, even if she was taking precautions for the time being. The very idea of her husband starting another family, this time with Diane, was clearly more than Lynne could endure. After finding the condoms she confronted him again. She was ashamed, she confessed tearfully, that she'd snooped through his personal things — but it was his own fault. "This is what you've reduced me to!" she wailed.

It was a terrible situation for Lynne. Their friends in Montreal knew the marriage was in trouble, and news of his liaison with Diane was seeping out. Lynne told close friends that they discussed the possibility of a reconciliation. "In unguarded moments he admits he's feeling old," she told Hailey. "Diane makes him feel young. He is going through a mid-life crisis and cannot come to terms with growing older. But it won't work. He would never be able to keep up with Diane."

And, Hailey noted, "Lynne believes her own heart surgery contributed to Bruce's awareness of growing old and his reacting to that feeling, though she adds, 'He was absolutely wonderful to me, and caring, while my heart surgery was happening.'"

According to Lynne, Verchere sought to reassure his wife that his affair with Diane wasn't serious. "It's insignificant, just a fling," he'd say. "It's not important. I've never been serious about Diane. She knows what she's getting into." How Lynne could take him back after his long history of philandering was another question; she excused her weakness by saying that she'd been married to Bruce for twenty-eight years, she loved him, and she wanted him back. Period. Meanwhile, David and Michael, who by this time were almost as upset as their parents, begged them to stay together. "From all of this," Hailey wrote briskly, "it is clear that throughout Bruce's affair with Diane he has kept his options open. Equally clearly he has not wished to draw a hard line between himself and Lynne and — since the two go together — Lynne's money."

SEVENTEEN
The End of the Affair

WITHOUT HIS WIFE'S optimism and sunny cheerfulness to hang on to, Arthur Hailey's mood worsened. Waiting for her to return from England, he grew more and more depressed about the mess Diane was getting herself into. Diane, not surprisingly, didn't think it was a mess. She was very much in love with Bruce, and while the inconveniences of an angry rival and a protective father made her unhappy, they were not reason enough to give him up. She wanted to marry him and have his children.

On June 17, however, it looked as if the decision had been taken out of her hands. Early that morning Lynne phoned Hailey in triumph. "Bruce and I had dinner together last night," she told him joyfully, "and we've decided to work on a reconciliation." Hailey noted dispassionately in his daybook, "BV's affair with Diane is over." Then, knowing he could count on his older daughter to be level-headed and comforting, he called Jane in Vancouver to talk it over. She knew that Verchere was blaming her father for everything, saying it was Arthur's fault that he and Diane had ended their affair. Hailey couldn't contain himself: "BV is a cowardly, hypocritical bastard!" he stormed in his diary. "He told Lynne many times the affair was not serious."

He waited until the next day, when his temper had cooled down and he'd thought things through, to talk again to Lynne. This time she gave him some of the details. Her husband and Diane had intended to have "one more holiday" together — she thought they meant to go to Harbour Island in the Bahamas — but they'd cancelled it for several reasons. First of all, Michael and David had pleaded with their father to "come to his senses and come home," she said — just as they had six years earlier when he'd planned to leave Lynne for Martha O'Brien. Once again, Lynne had brought in an Anglican priest they were close to to talk to her husband, and this time Bruce had listened to him carefully. Some of his relatives from Vancouver had also called him, said Lynne, begging him to return home and give up his mistress. What might have been the final push, though, came from a comment Lynne made to her husband: "Some of your friends are laughing at you." As those who knew Verchere could have predicted, the idea of being an object of ridicule was insupportable.

Hailey found Lynne's explanation of her husband's remorseful about-face vague, confusing, and unconvincing. Heartsick himself, though also relieved, Hailey didn't press for more details. But he wanted to set the record straight: he told her bluntly that he knew Bruce was blaming him for the breakup. This was not only untrue, he told Lynne, but it was causing, as he described it, "severe strains and accusations within the Hailey family." Lynne didn't allow herself to be drawn into the Haileys' problem; instead she simply agreed that her husband was only behaving true to form. "Bruce is very clever at that sort of thing," she said. "He needs someone to blame — anybody but himself. You happen to be convenient."

Hailey was tired of being the conduit for information from Lynne. He asked her if she'd be willing to talk to Sheila when Sheila got home from England. Sheila wasn't trying to be fair about the situation; this was her cherished youngest child who was under attack and her own loyalties were plain. But Lynne didn't seem to mind. "I would love to talk to Sheila," she replied calmly.

During these harrowing weeks that were taking such a toll on both families, another problem had come up for Bruce and Lynne. Perhaps because they were both so preoccupied with their personal unhappiness, they hadn't been paying attention to business as carefully as they should have. Suddenly they found Revenue Canada on their doorstep, asking unpleasant questions about tricky issues such as the Manac sale and their residency. The questions ballooned into a nightmare when the Revenue Department took Lynne to court, claiming she owed the government $7 million: $5 million in back taxes, the other $2 million in accumulated interest.

Although it was her name in the court record, Bruce was jointly responsible, she told Hailey, and had even signed a document accepting this. The Vercheres confided in the few people who knew about their problem that they weren't too worried; they thought they could win because a similar case was before the Supreme Court in Ottawa and it looked as if Revenue Canada would lose. If so, Bruce assured Lynne, it would create a precedent that would favour them in their case. Lynne, for good reason, wasn't so confident; privately she worried about their plight. One thing she had decided, however, was that she was not going back to life as a tax fugitive, hiding out in Switzerland or the Bahamas, so that she could hang on to her cash. Even if it meant risking the money in the tax case, she was going to live in her beautiful house on Montrose Avenue. "I've had enough!" she told Hailey. "I'm a Canadian and I'm going to stay here. When all this began, Bruce promised me he'd give up his memberships and connections in Montreal — as I had to — and would come with me. He didn't. Now I'm staying too. I want my own life with some continuity."

Hailey asked her if making that point was worth the possibility of losing $7 million. "Especially since," he added, "from what you tell me, Bruce would not be able to pay his share." Lynne didn't hesitate. "I don't care about the money. I don't need a lot of money to live on. I can live a lot more cheaply than Bruce, and will if I have to."

They both knew that Bruce could not imagine a life without money; such a life was simply not part of his plan. Besides, he was certain that they'd win their tax case. Only at the end of one conversation with Hailey did Lynne allow doubt to creep in. "I don't think Bruce is paying attention to it," she admitted. "Sometimes it seems he's in a dream world."

Hailey found it difficult to believe that it hadn't been so long ago, less than a year, that they'd all been together in Maine, enjoying a family holiday and a reunion of old friends. That summer, Lynne told him, had been among the happiest she and Bruce had ever spent. "Really?" he asked. "It looked to us as if you and Bruce were actually living apart there; you even seemed to have separate quarters."

"Absolutely not!" she retorted. "We were living together and had never been closer." The only reason she kept her clothes in the second cottage, she said, was that the main cottage was crowded. They had an extra building — why not use it?

The fact that Hailey was talking regularly to Lynne at this time was awkward and painful for his family. For Diane, heartbroken about Bruce's decision to end their affair, it was intolerable. She had always been close to her dad and they loved each other so much. How could he be so rational and even-handed at a time like this? How could he take Lynne's side? Wasn't he her father? Where were his loyalties? Furthermore, she was nearly thirty-four, independent, with a good career. On June 20, when father and daughter finally talked to each other openly about how they felt, it just got worse; Hailey told her everything he'd discovered about Verchere, and everything he suspected. Diane was deeply hurt and immediately defensive. Later that day she faxed her father a note.

> Dear Dad,
> Our conversation this afternoon was awful for both of us. And I feel if we don't try desperately hard, every conversation will wind up a hurtful, damaging, shouting match. I don't want that.
>
> I think the best course of action is to put this all behind us and move forward. Please do not tell me what you have found out about Bruce: true or not, it is too painful to hear.
>
> We may never resolve this and it is not my goal to do so. My goal is to keep my family whole. I will, however, ask you one favor. Please, in the future, allow me to make my own

mistakes. I know you love me and mean well, but I must know that I control my own life.

I want to always be able to wish you a Happy Father's Day. I do love you and care about you. Please let this go.

Love, Diane

(Just so you know, I'm also faxing a copy of this to Mom.)

The next few days were terrible. Sheila came home, but that almost made it worse; she and Diane were united, making Arthur feel like the outsider, resented and disliked. A few days later, tired and worried, Hailey had to drag himself to Houston, Texas, for a three-day trip to the famous Texas Heart Institute where he'd had his quadruple bypass in 1980. The visit had been scheduled long before; Hailey wasn't the kind of man to cancel an obligation, and he'd become a supporter of the institute and its doctors. Even meeting Linus Pauling, the famous California scientist, and Everett Koop, the U.S. surgeon general, at the institute couldn't take his mind off the troubles at home. Sheila was with him, but her company didn't help. On July 1, he made a brief note in his daybook: "Began dinner but abandoned it. Depressed by criticisms and argument. Didn't sleep much." The next day he was back home in Lyford Cay but nothing was better: "Dinner at home w/S.," he wrote; "v/tired; still depressed." When Diane called from Hawaii, where she was taking a brief vacation, all he could manage in his diary was a scribble to say she'd phoned.

By July 4, Hailey's sadness had almost undone him. Alienated from the people he loved more than his life, disillusioned by the betrayal of one of his most trusted friends, he went for long walks around his beloved Lyford Cay, trying to think of what to do. Here he was, at seventy-two, living in paradise with a woman he adored, with six successful children who loved him dearly, with more money than he could ever spend, with good health and good friends, and yet he'd rarely felt so blue. All the optimism and courage that had kept him driving ahead had drained away. As he walked up and down the fragrant boulevards and inspected the incoming yachts in the harbour, he decided he'd better get a grip on himself. He needed something to take his mind off his problems, he decided, something therapeutic.

It's not as if he wasn't busy. Although he considered himself retired, he was actively involved with the Lyford Cay Property Owners' Association and the Lyford Cay Club's activities, still wrote the Cay's quarterly newsletter, and had just started to research the area's history, all pastimes that gave him pleasure. He was always in demand for speeches; in early June, for example, he'd been asked to speak to an audience arranged by the publishers of Reader's Digest Condensed Books. He and Sheila also enjoyed an active social life, though they didn't feel much like seeing people just now. Maybe, he thought, I should do another book. Another novel.

In the spring of 1990, when he was seventy, he'd published *The Evening News*, a thriller about how a major U.S. television network dealt with the crisis when Peruvian terrorists, members of the Shining Path, kidnapped members of the family of a famous U.S. television anchorman. Like all his other books, it had been an international hit. And, as with all his other books, the research, which began in 1986, six years after the quadruple bypass, had been exhaustive. To understand how security forces deal with terrorists, Hailey had taken a five-day anti-terrorist course in England that trained him in unarmed combat and pushed him through a gruelling military obstacle course. He learned how to handle rifles, submachine guns, and handguns. They'd even taught him what to do when taken hostage. After the British training course, he'd gone to Ayacucho in Peru to climb a mountain in Shining Path territory; as he told the Toronto writer June Callwood, an old friend, who was interviewing him for the *Globe and Mail*, "I'm going to be writing about terrorist activities. To do that I need to see and taste and smell the environment in which terrorists live."

He had intended that book to be his last; *The Evening News* had been particularly strenuous, and he and Sheila thought it was time to enjoy retirement while they were still healthy. They never imagined this kind of personal crisis, however, and the only way Hailey could think of coping with his distress was to immerse himself in another novel.

In his daybook, he began to make notes about what it would be. Something about police work, he thought. He spoke to an old friend and former reporter in Miami, Connie Crowther, about some ideas. The one they liked best was a book about the Miami Police homicide department. Now, in the early 1990s, readers everywhere were gobbling up crime fiction; they couldn't get enough of it. And one of the most popular forms was the police procedural, tales of the day-to-day work of cops as they tracked down "perps." Police procedurals were certainly not new; among the earliest examples were those of Arthur Conan

Doyle, whose hero, Sherlock Holmes, worked as a private detective with police forces to find his villains. During the 1950s, another British author, John Creasey, wrote dozens of "PPs," as they were called, about his two most popular square-jawed heroes, Gideon of the Yard and Roger West. By the 1970s and '80s, such books had become so popular with the reading public that many former police officers had given up law enforcement for mass-market fiction, and in the 1990s specialty genres had mutated out of the simple tale of how a cop solved a crime. Patricia Cornwell, for example, churned out one bestseller after another about Kay Scarpetta, a medical examiner who worked with the FBI's Behavioral Science Unit, books which taught eager readers everything they wanted to know about profiling serial killers.

By the time Hailey was thinking of a police procedural, the plots had become far more complex, the murders more gruesome, the issues more sophisticated, the science more precise. Hailey would have to learn about computers and DNA and forensic accounting. And he'd need to find a locale that would work for him. The most convenient, because it was just half an hour away by plane, would be Florida — somewhere with a high crime rate and a large police force, the kind of place that would yield the best research. That meant Miami; he knew the city well and it was just the right size.

It started to feel like fun again. Bustling around, Hailey ordered new computer upgrades and a new office chair from Miami. He arranged for new carpeting in his study and was irritated when the workers arrived without the underpad it needed — because it meant he couldn't get going on his work yet. When he talked to Anne

McCormick, an editor at Knopf in New York, she told him that Michael Crichton's latest book, *Rising Sun*, another crime thriller, was selling very well. All of this made him feel he was back in the thick of things again.

The new book would be about a homicide detective who was trying to solve a series of brutal murders in Miami. The first thing he needed to do was get to know some policemen. Connie Crowther knew a retired homicide detective in Miami, a man named Steve Vinson, who would be willing to help. Hailey arranged to go to Miami for meetings. This was the start of a big Hailey book — getting acquainted with experts in the field who could teach him everything he needed to know about their work. Once the research was under way and he was beginning to do interviews and make notes, Hailey finally started to cheer up. The problems with the Vercheres had not gone away; in fact, they seemed to be getting worse. But, fully engaged with the new project, he now had a way to keep some mental distance from the turmoil.

EIGHTEEN
New Life

By MIDSUMMER, as Hailey went about researching his new novel, the Vercheres' efforts to mend their marriage had collapsed. Bruce, preoccupied with money, arranged for staff from Walter Klinkhoff's gallery to appraise all their paintings. The number that came back was only about $79,000 for the whole collection. Klinkhoff sent the bill for the evaluation to Verchere through Mancor's corporate shell; it was Mancor that actually owned the art.

Verchere had begun adding up their assets to see how they could be divided. He knew his marriage was finally, irretrievably over. It wasn't even the deteriorating relationship with Lynne that made him want to end it for good; they'd fashioned a marriage of convenience for so many years that he could probably have carried on indefinitely. What he could no longer abide was a life without Diane. "I've met the love of my life," he told Royal and Linda Smith during a trip back to Vancouver. "I'm going to marry her."

Early in September, Verchere left the house on Montrose again. He wasn't going back to the "crummy walk-up" Lynne had mentioned to friends. He'd looked in Outremont, the exclusive residential area favoured by the city's French-speaking elites, central but far enough away from Westmount that he wouldn't be running into his neighbours, not to mention his wife. Here he found a

1,500-square-foot condo, Suite 604, in the Tournesol, a modern, seventeen-storey building with sixty-three apartments at 205 Chemin Côte Sainte-Catherine. The owners tended to be professionals: doctors, lawyers, and professors, for the most part. The apartments cost $160,000 and up; Verchere was able to find one worth about $325,000 to rent. Once he'd sorted out finances with Lynne, he and Diane planned to start over again in Vancouver. The flat on Côte Sainte-Catherine was a place to camp until he could leave the city. In the meantime, he planned to visit Diane as often as possible in Los Angeles.

During these months of despair and worry, Verchere felt guilty about Arthur Hailey. He knew his client was furious, his trust shaken; Lynne had not spared him any details about Hailey's reaction and Verchere wanted to see if he could repair the friendship. On September 29, 1992, Verchere sat down at his desk at Bennett Jones Verchere and wrote Hailey a short letter, by hand, on the firm's letterhead.

> Dear Arthur,
>
> You & I have not spoken since May and I am concerned that our lack of communication may have led to misunderstandings. After twenty years, I'd like to try and retain our friendship.
>
> Lynne & I are in the process of separating our lives and divorcing. This is inevitably painful and the support you have shown Lynne has been kind. But regrettably, some doubts about me have been raised in your mind. And while I don't intend to defend myself against allegations I don't understand, I would suggest to you that

there are usually two sides to every story. In retrospect, one could always have done better and been wiser but if I had it to do over again, I'm not sure I would have acted much different.

As you know, Diane and I are once again seeing each other from time to time. Believe me, Arthur, I would have preferred to come to her without any strings but life and timing are rarely that cooperative. Still, you should know that I wouldn't do anything to create unhappiness for Diane.

Yours sincerely,

Bruce

SUDDENLY IT WAS AUTUMN. Mulroney's second government was now four years old and the prime minister would be required to go to the public within the next year. Everyone wanted to know whether he'd lead the unpopular Tories, stained by eight years of scandal and controversy, into a third federal election, or whether he'd retire to go into business and take advantage of all the international offers and powerful contacts he'd made in office. Most well-informed Conservative Party insiders were betting on his leaving, and some discreet jockeying was going on behind the scenes for his job. Aides and cronies who had been close to him were now searching for safe berths in law firms, consulting companies, or corporations; some, just to be on the safe side, were lobbying assiduously for Senate seats.

The Vercheres, who were normally political junkies, paid less attention than usual to politics that fall. Lynne was playing tennis with Ann Bodnarchuk as often as they could manage; Bodnarchuk was recovering from intensive treatment for breast cancer and had joined the Hillcrest Tennis Club, where Lynne was a member. With this dear friend, Lynne felt no need to keep up the pretence of a happy marriage; she talked freely to Bodnarchuk of her husband's infidelities. The women also went out to dinner often, sometimes joining other close women friends. "Although she was very protective of her good name," said one of them, "she turned 180 degrees when she discovered what Bruce had been up to. She wanted a divorce. She said, 'He wants me to be the mistress of the house while he carries on with another woman.'"

Prudently, Bodnarchuk urged Lynne to check on all the property she and Bruce owned. Lynne wrote to a property manager at Telluride to make sure she understood what the condominium was worth. By this time, she was almost beyond grief; she was waiting for Jacques Grandmont's report on how her husband had dissipated and hidden her money — and what she had to do to get it back. She was steeling herself to act aggressively if she needed to.

Verchere himself was made nervous by Grandmont's sleuthing, but in the case of Lynne's money, he rationalized, it was no more than he had deserved for his work in making Manac profitable. He kept his fingers crossed that their own tax problems would be resolved in their favour. Special Risks was the monster crouching in the corner, waiting to pounce on him and ruin his reputation. It was still crawling through the courts.

Beleaguered as he was, he looked forward to joining Diane soon, this time for good. Until then, they made do with regular visits, fitted in around the board meetings he attended and his work for Mulroney and the Swiss

Bank Corporation. Money was becoming a problem, especially with Grandmont hounding him, and by mid-October he needed another transfusion. This time a promissory note allowing him to raid the Blue Trust was too risky. Instead, on October 19, he borrowed $350,000 from the CIBC for an "investment loan"; in return he gave the bank a lien on the Montrose Avenue house as collateral, along with a further lien on the Cessna. In a graceful letter making clear how much the CIBC valued his business, the bank also noted, with exquisite tact, that should he sell the Cessna, the money should be used to pay off his bank loan "permanently." It also noted that he would be required to sign a letter stating that if he and Lynne sold the Montrose Avenue house, that money too would be used to pay the loan.

Aware that he owned 87,939 shares of a company called Mission Resources Ltd., the bank also asked him to assign the shares "as evidence of good faith." His investment in Mission, a speculative Alberta company, had long been a sore point with Lynne; she viewed it as money down the drain. He'd bought 67,000 shares a few years earlier for $235,171 and the investment had upset her terribly. She blamed his friends on Mission's board — Fritz Baehre and Garth Rhodes, both Calgary businessmen, and Gregory Hiseler, a Toronto businessman — for talking him into putting so much money in the company.

During these weeks Lynne had been demanding a full accounting of all the money he'd spent and all the money he'd moved offshore; when he dodged her questions or refused to answer them directly, she became angry and impatient. Her particular obsession was the investment in Mission Resources. Verchere had originally told her he'd put only $205,000 into the company; when she found out he'd invested $1,138,368 in all, she couldn't believe it. She felt even $205,000 was far too much to put into such a speculative venture; when she discovered he'd lied to her about the amount, she was not only terrified they'd lose every cent but furious with his deceit.

Mission's board was tiny: Verchere, Baehre, Rhodes, and Hiseler were the only directors. Baehre sat on two other boards with Verchere, the Swiss Bank Corporation and a private company called Chartwest, where Ross Eddy was also a director. Despite the intimate setting in which the Mission directors made their decisions and despite their other board connections, Fritz Baehre said he barely knew Verchere. "I wouldn't give an opinion," Baehre stated icily, "about a person I really did not know well." Baehre said Mission, which was privately held, was still a going concern and that Verchere had not been a major player in it.

The extent of Verchere's investment in Mission Resources upset Lynne, but a more bitter blow came when she discovered what he'd done with their house. Lynne understood clearly that she now had no control over her own home; only he did, as trustee of the Blue Trust, which actually owned the house. Suddenly the place she'd renovated and furnished with such care and pride, her sanctuary from the humiliations of her private life, was burdened with debt. Not only did it have the CIBC's new lien on it for $350,000, it was already encumbered with the old lien from Revenue Quebec for about $92,277 plus interest, a total of about $200,000. Her home, her pride and joy, was weighed down with liens and debt totalling $550,000.

The time had come to stop rationalizing Bruce's behaviour. She had to make sure he didn't steal all her money and leave her ruined. She didn't know if they'd win their tax case, or what new liens he might be piling onto their properties. She had to fight back any way she could. The way she chose — working closely with the lawyers and the accountant who were making their way through the maze of transactions and companies Bruce had used to hide the money — was expensive and time-consuming, but it was the only way to stop him.

Down in Lyford Cay, Hailey continued work on his new book, making frequent visits to Miami to see Steve Vinson. This new project kept him going; with Sheila still very much on Diane's side and Arthur on Lynne's, family life continued to be tense. As fall turned to winter, the Christmas holidays, for both families, became a season just to get through.

By December the talk of the town in Montreal was the expected resignation of Mulroney; all the signals were there that he was going. Everyone in political circles, whether Tories or Grits, had watched with cynical amusement as Mulroney carefully fixed appointments for all his old friends and supporters, renewing well-paid jobs for years into the future, improving salaries for others, tucking some people into the Senate or into judgeships. During two weeks over the 1992–93 holiday season he rammed 178 appointments through the Privy Council Office, only a few of which went to regular civil service members. The vast majority were for friends. If this tsunami of patronage hadn't made it clear that he was leaving, the other big story around Montreal confirmed it: senior businessmen were quietly passing the hat to provide a retirement gift for him, widely believed to be about $4 million. According to people close to his family, Verchere was on board to advise on tax strategies. (Mulroney later denied receiving any such retirement purse.) The prime minister spent January in a rented villa in Palm Beach, consulting with his allies about many issues, including the best timing for his departure. The decision was that he'd resign as prime minister on June 25 after a leadership convention.

Both Vercheres were well enough plugged in to know all the inside stories and the details of Mulroney's plans. On February 24, when Conservative Party president Gerry St. Germain issued a press release announcing Mulroney's intention to step down, he was only telling the rest of the country stale news as far as Lynne was concerned.

The next day brought a story she hadn't heard, one that turned her world upside down and made her frantic with jealousy and humiliation. Diane, she heard from her confidential sources who were close to her husband, was moving to Montreal to live with Bruce in the apartment on Côte Sainte-Catherine. And that wasn't all; that day there was more bad news for Lynne. It was just as bad for Arthur Hailey.

Diane wrote her father to tell him everything.

> Dear Dad,
> Please forgive me for writing you with this news but after much consideration, I feel it's better than talking over the phone. I would give the world for you to greet this with joy — but I simply can't be sure. And a negative response would devastate me.

Yes, it's true. If all goes well, I will be having a baby in October.

Bruce and I told Mom when she was out visiting and though she was elated and anxious to share the news with you, I begged her to wait so that I could tell you myself when I felt that you would be happy. But I don't like asking either of you to keep anything from the other. I haven't told anyone else yet (my doctor says it's a good idea to wait, since the first three months are precarious, especially at 35.) Still, it was important to me to tell you and Mom first. Soon I will share the happy news with Jane and Susan and Steven.

The pregnancy is not unexpected, though I never imagined it would happen so fast. Because of my age, I knew the sooner I had children the better.

I know you haven't come to terms with this (and I accept your feelings because they're real and they're yours) but I know that my life is with Bruce. He is everything I have dreamed of and the man for whom I have waited so long. For us, the prospect of a family is a joyous revelation. I hope you, too, will be happy about it.

It saddens me that I feel anxious and afraid to tell you this. But then again, I never dreamed this phase of my life would pull us apart instead of bringing us closer.

I hope and pray that one day you will all share my happiness.

From your loving daughter, Diane

Later that same day, Arthur faxed Diane a response.

> My dearest Diane,
> Yes, you were right in thinking it was better to write the letter as you did, rather than talk over the phone. I could not have handled it.
>
> Quite frankly, I do not want to react at all. I simply cannot.
>
> Obviously, this is because of certain feelings which have not changed and will not. But there is no point repeating them here. I realize this will be hard for you, but there is no point in my lying, pretending or otherwise dissembling.
>
> My only wish — and this I truly mean — is that all goes well with you and that you have everything you want, both now and in the future. I believe it will be a while before we see each other again, and I think that any more communication would only make you unhappy, which I do not wish. So, as much as you can, put me out of your mind. You have your life to live, which is the more important. But I shall always love you.
>
> Dad

Both father and daughter, who adored each other, were bereft. Arthur's elegiac letter, final in tone, seemed to Diane a harsh response to her passionate plea for understanding. Though she continued to keep in touch with him, mostly through Sheila, her letter was her last attempt to reach out to her father for a long time. His response had wounded her deeply. "It was unimaginable," she said later. "Having grown up with a father who was so enlightened, I couldn't believe he would react this way." What upset her even more was that her dad had never replied to Verchere's note to him; instead, she said, during the height of the crisis "he was on the phone every day with Lynne, listening to her side."

By early March Diane and Bruce were planning their lives together. With two siblings and three half-brothers, she was comfortable with the idea of a large family and knew they'd have to hurry, given Bruce's age. To their delight and consternation, they soon discovered she was carrying twins, which would certainly speed up the process of creating a family. She would live in Montreal with him while he and Lynne sorted out their affairs and while Bruce saw the Special Risks Holdings case through to the bitter end. They expected the babies to be born there, but as soon as they could leave they would move to Vancouver to live near Jane and near Bruce's old friends and family. Diane had grown up in the American West and knew she'd be comfortable in British Columbia. Both of them wanted a new life, far from the politics, personal complications, and bad memories Montreal now held.

Diane faxed her parents a note on March 16 saying she'd be leaving Los Angeles for good on March 22. Her new address and phone number, she said, were "#604, 205 Chemin Cote Ste. Catherine, Outremont Quebec, H2V 2A9, 514-277-3049 (no fax yet)." At the bottom she added, "I hope the Caymans were fun and that you didn't get too battered by the storm. Much love, Diane XX."

Lynne, of course, was aware of each development from her own sources in Montreal and found it excruciating. Bruce was no longer even trying to conceal the affair; he and Diane had been travelling together, and Lynne heard accounts of friends running into the couple in shops, airports, restaurants. "I saw them together in an airport," said one of Lynne's closest friends, "and he introduced Diane to me as his fiancée. You could have knocked me down with a feather." Marc Noël saw them together in Birks in Montreal but decided not to intrude, nor to ask Verchere to introduce him. It didn't take long for the news to get around Westmount and the legal community. People were fascinated. Verchere was happy and proud, not in the least hesitant to show off his pregnant new girlfriend. "We didn't hide anything," said Diane.

It was more than Lynne could take. Hurt, furious, mortified, she thought the situation through carefully and then sat down to write her husband a letter he would never forget.

> 19 March, 1993
>
> Dear Bruce,
> After the twenty-eight years of our marriage and my fidelity, during which we loved and trusted each other, raised our sons, shared our lives and built our place in the world; it devastates me that you must end our life together in such a tawdry, arrogant and deceitful manner.
>
> In 1987, the profits and sale of Manac delivered us from a position of debt to a position of wealth. The enormous tax burden on the funds from Manac and on the income generated by these funds was assumed entirely by me under the premise that we would both stop working, become non-residents and that we would use

the funds to continue our lives together. Under your professional instructions my business and financial life in Canada was terminated. Unbeknownst to me your associations continued as did your Canadian residency.

In March 1992, a need for self-examination led to your unannounced departure from the family. Initially we tried to understand your decision to leave. After a four-month charade of attempted reconciliation, it became apparent that instead of self-evaluation the real reason for this departure was an on-going relationship with a thirty-three year old daughter of a client and family friend. This deception began the erosion of the trust which had previously existed between husband and wife and a father and his sons.

At this point regaining control of my assets, separating our lives and reestablishing my Canadian residency became my priorities. Since 1987 you were entrusted with the management and control of my and our family's assets and financial information. The limited financial information available to me at this time suggest that this control was abused. It dismays me that the information required for my return to Canada was withheld for seven months. Only now that the woman for whom you left your family is pregnant, is revised and edited information slowly being released. The reluctance to fully disclose my and our family's information under your control makes one wonder what there is to hide.

The desire to distance myself from you became stronger as the details of your varied sexual adventures entered the mainstream of Montreal cocktail conversation. The obvious next step was to file for divorce which would guarantee me access to financial information and distance me from the growing scandal. The tax plan that was masterminded by you cleverly prevents my filing for divorce, yet allows you to file at your convenience. While remaining married to me and remaining in full control of our marital status, you made the choice to bring another woman, pregnant with your child, to live with you in Montreal. How does one reconcile the vulgarity of these actions with your former positions of Church Warden and of legal Counsel to the Anglican Diocese of Montreal? Your sons, whom you have not seen since July, 1992, remain appalled by your behavior. The failure to confront a difficult situation with honesty, integrity and compassion has left your family with a great sense of disappointment.

Please understand that nothing will be agreed to until we have equal access to unexpurgated financial information and there is nothing more important to me right now than a speedy resolution to this very unpleasant state of affairs. The choice is yours. Either fully disclose all financial information and transfer control of my assets to me or face a prolonged court battle. The confrontation will reveal information that will embarrass and have negative financial

> implications for our sons, Arthur Hailey, Bennett Jones Verchere and those clients with whom you have mixed our family's affairs. My discretion to date, notwithstanding your provocative attitude, shows that a court case is not my first choice, but you may leave me with no option.
>
> Sincerely,
>
> Lynne

Cool, to the point, threatening. What exactly did she mean when she demanded immediate financial information and the transfer of her assets to her control? What did she mean when she said a court battle and a confrontation would "reveal information that will embarrass and have negative financial implications for our sons, Arthur Hailey, Bennett Jones Verchere and those clients with whom you have mixed our family's affairs"? Which clients? There weren't many. Mulroney, for whom he still acted as tax lawyer and trustee? The Swiss Bank Corporation, still a client but also a bank in which the Vercheres themselves had accounts? What exactly was she saying when she stated bluntly that she had shown "discretion to date"? He considered her words carefully. Given that she'd also set up his computer system, she could no doubt access just about anything without much trouble. He understood that she was a powerful enemy and that he would have to proceed with extreme caution. Despite his joy at Diane's arrival in Montreal, a small black knot of fear was growing inside him.

Lynne wanted the divorce as quickly as possible, she told close friends, but Bruce was stalling because he didn't want to give up the financial information she was seeking. "I'm entitled to it and I want it now," she insisted, but he resisted. To Arthur Hailey, she added that she also thought it would be a good idea to divorce quickly so that Bruce could marry Diane before the babies were born. This sounded to Hailey as if she had finally reconciled herself to the idea of her husband's relationship with Diane, that there was no longer animosity on her part and that all she wanted now was a settlement. Nor did she have hard feelings towards Arthur and Sheila, she reassured him; they were all just puppets Bruce had manipulated. "The way he's going," she asked rhetorically, "what's he going to do next?"

It wasn't long before it was clear that Lynne's sweet reasonableness was temporary. Geoff Walker, one of Verchere's partners, wrote a memorandum on March 31 — initialled by Verchere — listing the couple's assets and suggesting a strategy to meet her demand for financial information. She found it almost meaningless. All Walker had done, in what he called "starting points," was suggest that William Mitchell, the firm's accountant, look at events from 1987 on: the Manac sale, the organization of 147626 Canada Inc., the opening balance of their Merrill Lynch arbitrage accounts, the opening balance in 1987 of related accounts, and "all other assets." Mitchell was to study bank account statements, investment account statements, personal tax returns, and company account books to make his calculations; all of this was to run up to December 31, 1992. Walker laid out an informal spreadsheet as a means of breaking down the information as he pulled it together, and gave Mitchell a month to complete the work. Walker stated he would supervise the work and "keep both parties informed." Verchere signed Walker's memorandum and a deadline of April 30 was set.

All of this only upset Lynne further; she concluded Bruce was engaged in an elaborate stalling exercise with his partners' acquiescence. The more he procrastinated on handing over financial information, the more she lashed out at everyone. Hailey listened unhappily. It made him sick to think of his child living with Bruce on Lynne's money, but he was mindful of Diane's firm request to him to let her make her own mistakes. Worse, he decided, as Lynne told him what she'd said in her letter to Bruce, was the possibility of a sensational court battle. It would be lapped up by the press. He felt it was imperative that Bruce and Diane be made to understand the danger they were creating. Oblivious to everyone's happiness but their own, they had no idea what damage Lynne's rage could wreak.

Hailey decided to try to reason with Diane one more time. He asked Lynne if she'd mind if he and Sheila sent a copy of her letter to their daughter. Yes, of course, said Lynne. I'll send it to you and you can pass it on. Maybe then she and Bruce will understand what's at stake. On March 25 Lynne mailed a copy of the letter to the Haileys, along with a note:

> Dear Arthur,
> Bruce's latest actions mean our affairs regretfully are no longer private. I send you this letter to enlist your help in providing what guidance you feel might encourage Bruce to bring a speedy resolution to this very unpleasant situation.
> Best regards,
> Lynne

Given Diane's reaction the last time her father had interfered, Hailey was glad that Sheila was willing to act as messenger. It had taken her several months, but she too was beginning to see that a marriage with Bruce Verchere might not be the best choice for her daughter. If Diane was to go ahead, at least she needed to be alert to the dangers lying in wait. On April 1, Sheila wrote Diane:

> My dear Diane,
> The attached copy of a letter from Lynne to Bruce, with the covering note addressed to Arthur, arrived here yesterday.
>
> I believe you should see both.
>
> Diane, I have to tell you that I think it has the ring of truth — and confirms some gnawing concerns I have about your situation.
>
> As a result of Lynne's letter, Arthur phoned her. He has assured me that, between mid-June and yesterday he deliberately has had no discussion with Lynne concerning you and Bruce. The only exchanges they have had was a brief note he wrote on Lynne's New Year's card, and a phone call (initiated by Lynne) concerning her membership in the Lyford Cay Club.
>
> During Arthur's conversation with Lynne he made notes and she told him:
>
> 1. She wants a divorce as quickly as possible but Bruce is stalling because he will not reveal the financial information about Lynne's money that she is entitled to.

2. She believes the divorce should go through as quickly to make it possible for you to be married before your children are born.
3. She has no antagonism toward you.

That's all — except to say Dad and I are always here whenever you need us.

We love you,

Mom

Diane did not resent her mother's gentle note, but it did not diminish her steadfast commitment to Verchere. She loved him desperately and adored carrying his babies. "We fell in love and we had a wonderful time together," she said simply. "We were blissed out." Bruce, she said, "was very warm, very fair, and very open to changing and growing, remarkably so for someone in his fifties. We were in love so we saw and gave the very best of ourselves to each other." His problems with his wife were regrettable and sad, of course, but Diane was a woman in love and an optimist at heart. She had no doubt that, once the difficulties were sorted out, she and Verchere could start fresh, earn a good income, and live happily with their babies in a delightful new city.

NINETEEN
Full Disclosure

DIANE HAILEY was entangled with a middle-aged man with plenty of baggage — emotional, financial, legal. Verchere had not only left a wife who had made it clear that he was dumping her at his peril, he had also set aside the pleas of his sons, whom he loved, to live with the much younger woman who had once been their nanny. There was no hope of a reasonable relationship with Lynne now, perhaps ever; but Diane and Bruce hoped David and Michael would come around. Verchere could not imagine that his boys wouldn't learn, in time, to love this gentle and open-hearted woman, and to enjoy a relationship with their new half-brothers or half-sisters.

The financial baggage was another matter. Simply put, he was strapped. His income didn't begin to cover his debt payments, the rent on the Outremont apartment, travel, upkeep on the Cessna, sailboat expenses, the fine Burgundies he refused to do without, the expensive restaurant meals that were part of his daily routine. His legal worries were just as real as his financial ones. Each day brought Lynne's threatened lawsuit closer. Clearly she would not settle for anything less than full disclosure of what had happened to every penny from the Manac sale. Verchere was still sorting out his own tax problems, including the old Revenue Quebec case against him for his film tax credits, and the far more serious fight with federal tax investigators over his manipulation of the capital gains taxes paid — or not paid — on the sale of Manac. Finally, there was the Special Risks Holdings case which, after seventeen tedious years in the courts, was near the end of its run. After three years of trying, Dick Pound had been unable to undo the damage. Now, in the spring of 1993, with the case coming before the Supreme Court in the next few months, Fred Melling was almost certain he would lose for good. For Verchere, the case had been a devastating black mark on his reputation.

His own law partners hadn't minded when he withdrew from active involvement with Bennett Jones Verchere, nor even when he cut his workload to the three or four select clients he'd chosen to keep. But they didn't like the stink around the Special Risks file and they didn't like what was happening between one of the senior partners and his wife. It wasn't just the usual hideous divorce among the angry, vengeful rich, the kind of thing they'd seen many times before but had usually hushed up before it hit the newspapers. This one involved the daughter of one of the firm's most interesting and high-profile clients. Bennett Jones Verchere had much wealthier clients and far more powerful ones, but Arthur Hailey's celebrity gave them international cachet. And they liked him personally. Hailey had always been friendly and sociable with the firm's partners; he could easily have moved to another law firm in Canada, as many would have. But Hailey was loyal to Bennett Jones Verchere and to the people who had looked after his family so well for so many years. The Haileys were still Canadian citizens and often came back to Canada to visit friends. They were sentimental about their connections here, and that meant the law partners as well. But Verchere's partners knew they couldn't take Hailey's business for granted any longer. He now did most of his consultations with Janice McCart out of the Toronto office. Bruce Verchere's personal adventures had the potential to blow up, and if the details became public the reverberations would undoubtedly be felt in the law firm.

Verchere tried to remain upbeat. He'd convinced himself that in any divorce settlement he'd be entitled to half the money generated by the Manac sale. Perhaps he and Diane would receive some income from the Haileys. If necessary, he could set up his own tax boutique in Vancouver, where he was still remembered as Justice Verchere's son and a UBC law graduate. Many of his old friends, he knew, such as Royal Smith and Pat Dohm, now a judge himself, would make him feel welcome. In the meantime, he and Diane settled in together in the new apartment and began to circulate. Lynne didn't find out about all these occasions, but she certainly knew when Bruce took Diane, visibly pregnant, to a gala dinner hosted by the Mulroneys at the National Gallery in Ottawa. This was Verchere's defiant coming-out; he introduced Diane as his fiancée and their happiness was obvious to everyone. It was also clear that the Mulroneys had given the couple their blessing. It was more than Lynne could bear, especially when she discovered that Mulroney had also just placed Bruce on the board of Atomic Energy of Canada Limited.

For their part, the Mulroneys must have known how hurt and embarrassed Lynne was; Mulroney made an effort at appeasement, producing a second patronage appointment for her, on April 26 naming her chairman of the

Official Residences Council, a position that recognized her interest and expertise in restoring and furnishing old houses. Although she accepted the position, she was not mollified; the Mulroneys were simply no longer people she cared to know. Like many Canadians, she was outraged by the sleaze that had characterized the Tories' years in office.

More than ever, Lynne was determined to divorce her husband and make him pay dearly for the grief he'd brought on his family. April 30, the deadline she'd set for full financial disclosure, was only a few days away, and she waited eagerly and angrily. A letter arrived on the deadline from Adrian Phillips, one of her husband's law partners in the Toronto office. All Phillips said was that after both Lynne and Bruce had talked to him and to Geoff Walker, the firm had decided it was in a conflict of interest and could no longer advise them — "nor provide legal services on matters that concern you mutually or the companies in which one or the both of you are interested." Both were clients of the firm. Phillips went on to advise each of them to retain their own lawyers. Once they did that, he said, the firm was willing to answer questions or help on relevant matters, but only if Lynne and Bruce agreed to five conditions.

First, Bennett Jones Verchere insisted on written confirmation from their lawyers that each of them — Bruce and Lynne — was to have "full access to all information in or coming into our possession respecting matters on which we have acted for you and your companies in the past." Then, for each request made by either Bruce or Lynne, the firm wanted written instructions from their lawyers "detailing the information to be provided or the things that you both agree we should do."

Phillips also said that while all information about their activities would be confidential outside the inner circle, it would be shared among Bennett Jones Verchere, the couple themselves, and their respective lawyers. Phillips's fourth condition required them to agree that Bennett Jones Verchere's role would be restricted to providing information in response to specific requests and "facilitating the transmission of specific information requested. The firm would not initiate anything nor advise either person about what they should be looking for." And finally, Phillips wanted them to get their lawyers to send him confirmation that they had gone through the whole discussion of client confidentiality and professional conduct and that they both "specifically waive your rights in regard to the function we would perform."

When Lynne read all this, she was livid. She'd expected and been promised a full accounting of what had happened to her money and to the family assets. Instead she'd received another letter that she believed was stuffed full of legalese. Even if the firm had been acting properly, Lynne refused to believe it; her conclusion was that the letter had one simple purpose — to hinder, obstruct, and in every way possible prevent her from obtaining the financial information she needed. She was convinced that her husband's partners were protecting him.

A week later, on May 7, she wrote a curt note to Bruce to say that she recognized his partner's letter for what it was — a stalling tactic — and that it wouldn't work. "Please resolve this impasse," she wrote. "My patience is wearing thin." She attached a copy of the letter she had written to Phillips, telling him she was shocked by his letter. "I don't understand the position now taken by your firm in connection with its express undertaking of March 31, 1993 to provide me with the information. This reversal of your firm's position more than a month after the fact could be very damaging to me." She reminded Phillips that Walker's memorandum had been agreed to by all sides, and she expected the firm to carry out the agreement. And she bristled at being dumped as a client on what she saw as the feeble excuse of conflict of interest. "I see no reason why I should hire an independent counsel to tell your firm what I, your client, instruct you to do."

The letter to Phillips was infused with vitriol. "I will not tolerate any further delays for the reconciliation of the assets," she raged. "Since your firm's input could prove critical to the work presently being done by Bill Mitchell I will hold BJV responsible for any delays and for any loss I may suffer as a result." She demanded that Phillips withdraw his letter of April 30 immediately.

To make sure that Bennett Jones's senior brass knew she meant business, she sent a copy of this letter to Bill Britton in Calgary. Although Britton remained a loyal friend to his old law school buddy, other lawyers in the firm were less understanding. Quietly, among themselves, some of the partners at Bennett Jones Verchere began to talk about asking Verchere to leave the firm.

Steadfastly, Verchere ignored the thunder clouds gathering overhead and behaved as if life were grand. In mid-May, he took Diane to Vancouver to meet his family and friends. Not surprisingly, everyone liked her enormously and made her feel welcome. "Bruce was the happiest I'd seen him in twenty-five years," says Royal Smith. What surprised him and Linda was Bruce's excitement about the babies Diane was carrying; for a father whose children had been largely raised by nannies, he seemed incredibly keen on his new family.

Verchere, for his part, was happy to see how well the Smiths had done. Royal, who had come to UBC from a humble background in Saskatchewan, started as a car dealer after he graduated but moved into real estate development with a group of friends and was the brains behind Kits Point, a chic new community of expensive condominiums in a quiet enclave near the water at the bottom of the Burrard Street Bridge. His own home, along Point Grey Road, was on a property that ran down to the ocean and had one of the best views in town. The glass-walled living room looked out over the harbour past Stanley Park to the mountains above West Vancouver; the deck that ran across the front of the house overlooked a deep and beautifully landscaped garden. A house in Hawaii and another in Arizona were pleasant refuges in Vancouver's rainy seasons. But when he talked about success, it was his old friend Bruce he pointed to, not himself, not a developer who'd happened to do well in Vancouver's golden real estate market. Bruce, the brightest boy in the fraternity, was the one who'd gone east and became a great tax lawyer and hobnobbed with prime ministers; he was the one who'd made a real success of his life. "Not that Bruce ever bragged about the people he knew," Smith added. "He never lorded it over anyone."

Any hurt feelings about the distance that had developed between Smith and his best friend disappeared when Diane arrived in Vancouver. She had restored Bruce to the cheerful, energetic young fellow he'd been, full of plans. During the visit, Bruce's cousin David

Verchere and his wife, Mary, invited the Smiths to a party for Bruce and Diane. Everyone rejoiced in the couple's happiness. Later they heard that the family party for the couple had made Lynne extremely unhappy. "We're just going back to Montreal to clear up things," Bruce told the Smiths before he and Diane left Vancouver. "Then we're coming back to make a home for ourselves here." After Bruce finally pulled himself and Diane away from the comfort of the Smiths' warm embrace, Royal turned to Linda. "Bruce is back," he said quietly to his wife. "Bruce is back."

SOON AFTER BRUCE and Diane left Vancouver, they used the Cessna to fly to the summer place in Southwest Harbor for a week's holiday. They took *Niska* out for a sail on good days, read contentedly, enjoyed each other in peace. Diane was too big with the twins to risk walks along the rocky coastline, but it was like a honeymoon for them; this, after all, was where they'd met again in the summer of 1991, and where he'd fallen desperately in love with her. Here they talked about their future, cocooned from reality; Bruce had no idea what Lynne's team of lawyers and accountants were putting together for his return, and he tried not to think about it.

Lynne's fury over what she saw as stalling by Bruce's partners Geoff Walker and Adrian Phillips, and over the way she believed the other partners were protecting him, had made her as focused as a laser. He could humiliate her with his pregnant mistress, he could offend a valued client like Arthur Hailey, he could forge her name at the bank and steal her money and lie to her; fine. But he wasn't going to get away with it. He would pay dearly for what he'd put her through.

Lynne understood the shock she knew he would feel when he discovered she had enlisted their sons in her legal battle. Lynne had explained to the boys that their father, who was living with another woman he intended to marry, who was planning to start a new family and move to B.C., had complete control of the trust set up to provide an inheritance for them. Their father was stealing their patrimony and nothing could prevent him from giving it to his new family. They could all be left with nothing unless they stopped him. To do so, she needed their help. Perhaps not fully understanding, David and Michael agreed to support her plan.

On June 3 James Macnutt, the lawyer Raynold Langlois had retained in Prince Edward Island, took steps to remove Verchere as the trustee of the Blue Trust. If he could accomplish this, Bruce would no longer control the family's money or property. In a letter to Lynne and the boys, Macnutt listed various legal precedents for removing trustees and concluded that, after studying this case, "it is our opinion that there have been several instances of misadministration of the Blue Trust by the Trustee and that sufficient grounds exist on which an action for breach of trust could be founded and that the additional remedy of the removal of the Trustee would probably succeed."

Macnutt pointed out that while the Blue Trust had been created to abide by the laws of Prince Edward Island, Lynne and her sons needed to go to the courts in Quebec for an interim order to remove Verchere as trustee, because that was where he lived and conducted his law practice. In Montreal, Langlois Robert planned to bring a motion for "interim relief" to restrain Verchere from dealing with any of the Blue Trust's assets until the P.E.I. courts could hear the case. Meanwhile, Macnutt would start the action in the Supreme Court of P.E.I. He would challenge Verchere's administration of the trust and demand his removal from office and the appointment of a new trustee, one who would meet with Lynne's approval and who wouldn't have the same conflicts of interest as Verchere. He would also ask, Macnutt said, for a complete accounting of trust funds by Verchere and for damages and compensation for the money taken from the Blue Trust's assets.

Along with his analysis of the case against Verchere and what steps he was taking in the P.E.I. court, Macnutt attached the statement of claim as part of the lawsuit. Although statements of claim are only allegations and have to be proven in court, they represent the plaintiff's case against the defendant. This one didn't mince words. It said that while Verchere had set up the Blue Trust, he had made no contribution to it; all the money had come from Lynne and she had never received a proper accounting of it. It accused him of converting assets to his own use without paying for them, of buying assets for his own use and maintaining them, all with trust money. It charged him with using trust assets to pay off his personal debts and of illegally depleting other trust assets. Finally, the document said, he was unfit to manage the trust and must be removed because the beneficiaries "have a reasonable apprehension of the continued dissipation of the Trust assets."

Once he'd sent this document off to the court in Charlottetown, Macnutt hurried to Montreal for the next act of this drama; it had to be completed swiftly, before Bruce got wind of it and moved any assets out of reach. They couldn't have chosen a better time to strike; Bruce and Diane were in Maine, and most of his associates and all of Montreal's Tories were preoccupied with the leadership convention scheduled to begin in five days. The talk was all about what Mulroney would do when he stepped down and whether one of his younger cabinet ministers, Jean Charest of Sherbrooke, had a chance of beating the leading candidate, Kim Campbell. Mulroney himself had started to work behind the scenes on the Charest campaign. Tory politics, last-minute rewards, and backroom deals were on everyone's lips; no one was paying any attention to the comings and goings at one of Montreal's prominent Liberal law firms.

The following morning, Friday, June 4, Lynne and David and Michael had their breakfast and dressed carefully. Solemnly, the three Vercheres arrived at the offices of Langlois Robert; Jacques Grandmont also turned up; so did Macnutt. All read the lengthy affidavits that had been prepared for their signatures; once signed, the affidavits would be used to obtain an interim injunction preventing Bruce from touching any of the Blue Trust's assets.

The affidavits told, simply but strikingly, the story of each player. Macnutt's described who he was and why he was hired and what he found; Grandmont's did the same; David and Michael explained how they came to be the beneficiaries of the Blue Trust and how their father had abused his position as trustee. Each asked for his removal. Lynne's affidavit went through the history of the marriage, their careers, and their accumulation of assets. Step by step, year by year, she described what her husband did with the money she made, how he had forged her name to a bank document, and then, in a section titled "Awakening to the Truth," how he had left her for another woman and how he had squandered their money.

Shortly after they signed the affidavits, Justice Bernard Gratton of the Quebec Superior Court issued the injunction they'd sought. Lynne breathed a sigh of relief, though she knew the work was far from finished.

Later that day, Verchere heard someone knock on the door of the summer house in Maine; he and Diane both looked up in surprise — they weren't expecting anyone. Their visitor was a process server, who handed him a copy of the injunction. Bruce did not need to spend more than a minute with it before the colour drained from his face. To Diane he looked suddenly frail and old. Bruce was always silent when deeply troubled, and he said nothing after he put down the document. But he knew he was ruined.

Reading the injunction Lynne had engineered, Verchere realized that the biggest mistake he'd ever made was underestimating his wife. The court order she'd won was sweeping, punitive, and pointed. Justice Luc Parent had frozen his assets for ten days and instructed him to return the Cessna to its hangar at Dorval Airport by 4 p.m. the next afternoon. He was given seventy-two hours to inform all the agents acting for him on various shell companies, lawyers such as Nat Fenton in Bar Harbor and Horacio Alfaro in Panama, not to transfer, sell, or move any of the assets they oversaw or to take any action that would affect their ownership or their value. And within those seventy-two hours he had to provide proof to Lynne's lawyers that he'd sent these instructions to his agents. The judge also ordered him not to take any action with regard to the house on Montrose, the family art collection, the Maine property, the sailboat, or the condo in Telluride. He was ordered not to touch any of the bank accounts or safety deposit boxes he controlled, and just in case his memory had slipped, the injunction listed them. Finally, the judge ordered him to prepare a full accounting of what he had done with every penny from the sale of Manac.

Verchere knew at once what it meant: financial disaster, professional disgrace. But what cut him to the quick, and what Lynne had known would hurt him most, was that David and Michael had joined their mother in this court action. His own boys. His own sons had signed affidavits accusing him of misusing money meant for them and behaving shamefully. Diane, distressed and alarmed to learn the nature of the documents, tried to comfort him. We'll be fine, she reassured him. We'll get through this. Whatever else happens, we have each other. We have our children. We'll be fine.

"That's right," said Verchere, draining his glass of wine. "You're right. We'll be fine."

TWENTY
The Sky Has Fallen

VERCHERE HAD NO CHOICE. To defy any part of the court order would be to risk criminal charges of contempt. He and Diane flew back from Maine to Montreal, returned the plane to its hanger in Dorval, and contacted Claude-Armand Sheppard, one of the city's toughest and shrewdest litigators. As they began to work their way through Lynne's injunction, they realized how thorough she'd been and how much her accountant had uncovered. It wasn't complete, Verchere knew, but Grandmont had come frighteningly close to peeling back all the shells and uncovering all his financial secrets. At first, to those reading the affidavits and statements, the most damaging information appeared to be Grandmont's conclusion that at least $3 million of Lynne's money had disappeared and he had no idea where it had gone. Once he had noted the breathtaking loss, Grandmont went on to list the assets ultimately controlled by the Blue Trust — by Bruce.

It began with the family home on Montrose Avenue. Then came a description of each of their twenty-eight pictures — owned by Mancor Inc. — everything from the 1926 painting by Robert Pilot, *The Maples: Quebec from Lévis*, to a *Still Life* by Goodridge Roberts to *Daisies No. 2* by Molly Lamb Bobak. Next, Grandmont listed any money and other assets deposited in four separate accounts with the CIBC, accounts set up for the Blue

Trust, for 147626 Canada Inc. (which had two accounts), and for Mancor Inc.

Grandmont included the Telluride condominium and the shares held or controlled by the Blue Trust, by 147626 Canada Inc., by Mancor, and by Ride Investors Inc. The four Griffith Island Club debentures worth $20,000, the Hinckley sailboat, the Cessna, the summer place in Maine. Then came the next shock in Grandmont's report: the number of other bank accounts and safety deposit boxes Verchere had tucked away in Montreal, New York, Zermatt and Geneva in Switzerland, and in the village of Southwest Harbor, Maine. Grandmont had found a total of twenty-seven accounts in banks or financial institutions; another one had been noted in Lynne's affidavit. The documents listed each one, noting whether the account was in U.S. dollars, Canadian dollars, or Swiss francs (SF). All the accounts in the United States were in U.S. dollars; so were all the Swiss accounts except the one in Zermatt. Three of the CIBC accounts in Montreal were in U.S. dollars. The remaining accounts were in Canadian dollars.

Account number	Bank, financial institution	Location
89-08214: Blue Trust	CIBC	Montreal
03-96516: 147626	CIBC ($U.S.)	Montreal
70-42213	CIBC	Montreal
59-05818: Mancor	CIBC	Montreal
Safety deposit box	CIBC	Montreal
02-55815	CIBC ($U.S.)	Montreal
58-09118	CIBC	Montreal
03-51016	CIBC	Montreal

16-41239	CIBC	Montreal
03-38214	CIBC ($U.S.)	Montreal
54-08113	CIBC	Montreal
Safety deposit box	Bar Harbor Banking & Trust	Southwest Harbor, Maine
777-509488	Bar Harbor Banking & Trust	Southwest Harbor, Maine
72601084	Bar Harbor Banking & Trust	Southwest Harbor, Maine
77531432	Bar Harbor Banking & Trust	Southwest Harbor, Maine
82506659	Bar Harbor Banking & Trust	Southwest Harbor, Maine
72-601076	Bar Harbor Banking & Trust	Southwest Harbor, Maine
77611177	Bar Harbor Banking & Trust	Southwest Harbor, Maine
82-506640	Bar Harbor Banking & Trust	Southwest Harbor, Maine
Fenton-Trust	Fenton law firm	Southwest Harbor, Maine
130117	Darier Hentsch & Cie ($U.S.)	Geneva, Switzerland
33259	Darier Hentsch & Cie ($U.S.)	Geneva, Switzerland
J.F.K.33.260	Darier Hentsch & Cie ($U.S.)	Geneva, Switzerland
13232236	Swiss Bank Corp. (SF)	Zermatt, Switzerland
452-822-779	Swiss Bank Corp.	New York, NY
822779	Swiss Bank Corp.	New York, NY
85058	Pictet & Cie ($U.S.)	Geneva, Switzerland
9500254611	Bear Stearns	New York, NY

Why did Bruce have nine accounts in Bar Harbor, one of which was a safety deposit box and another a trust account with Nat Fenton's law firm? Why did he have seven CIBC accounts in Montreal, above and beyond the four he and the family used for their business and personal expenses? How much money was stashed away, and whose money was it? It was not surprising that he had three Swiss Bank Corporation accounts, given that he was the bank's Canadian lawyer and a member of the board, and it's probably no more surprising that he held three other accounts in Geneva, one with the Pictet Bank and three with Darier Hentsch. He did business with James Crot at Pictet, after all, and had opened an account there for himself. He and Lynne had put much of the Manac windfall in accounts at Darier Hentsch.

Twenty-eight accounts could perhaps be explained away, though Lynne had implied, in her letter to Verchere, that a court battle would reveal that he had been using personal accounts for other purposes ("and those clients with whom you have mixed our family's affairs").

The threat had been clear, yet Bruce had ignored it. Lynne had shown she was quite prepared to expose his dealings with clients, that he could no longer expect her to be discreet. She made the same point to Arthur Hailey when she called him a few days later to tell him what was going on. "She is concerned that the action in Superior Court," Hailey wrote in his notes of his conversation with her, "might prompt tax investigations of 'other people' — though the meaning of this is unclear." The meaning may have been unclear to Hailey; it was no doubt perfectly clear to Verchere.

While Verchere was still absorbing the implications of the court order, Lynne fired the next volley. On June 7 she arranged for another process server to knock on his door, this time with the papers for a divorce action. When Lynne called Hailey that evening to bring him up to date, she explained that Bruce had backed her into a corner and left her no option but to act aggressively. For nearly a year, she said, she had tried to get the financial details the court was now demanding, but her husband had provided only bits and pieces of information. She'd done "hard work" on the material Bruce had given her, she said, but the material didn't stand up to scrutiny; it was full of "irregularities," "questionable transactions," and "one direct lie."

Both in her affidavit for the injunction (which her lawyers also attached to her divorce action) and in frank conversations with close friends, Lynne described the years of her marriage. Ever since the sale of Manac, she said in the affidavit, Bruce had complete control of her money, even though it was always understood that her assets and his were to be kept separate, "without being blended in any way whatsoever." She went on, "Until the breakup occurred on February 22, 1992, Michael Verchere, David Verchere and I had no apparent reason to distrust Bruce Verchere and had the utmost confidence in his ability to manage our assets and liabilities in view of the fact that he was my husband and the well respected father of my children, and because his professional training and apparent success in his profession made him worthy of trust."

This point she made again and again: she had loved her husband and had trusted him implicitly. Over the years, she said, her husband had given her very limited financial information and was always reluctant to talk about his financial dealings on her behalf. She'd worked hard to make Manac a success, so hard that her health had been affected. As the affidavit stated, "It was my personal knowledge and skills alone that led to the substantial investment developing in Manac." Once they'd made the money from the company's sale, she stated, her husband had insisted they all become non-residents of Canada to avoid capital gains taxes; the hitch was that he didn't join them. "Bruce Verchere constantly delayed his leaving Canada and, ultimately, he never changed his residence or his tax status although he told me he was a non resident: I discovered that in fact, Bruce Verchere secretly continued as a resident of Canada without any interruption and continued to file tax returns in Canada."

Lynne also described her efforts to get a financial reckoning from her husband and all the futile calls and letters to people like Geoff Walker and William Mitchell. She laid out the complicated financial transactions her husband had gone through, the tricky share swaps and interest-free promissory notes and intricate tax shelters — page after page of them. In the section "Awakening to the Truth," she went through details of the bank accounts he had opened in Switzerland and the huge loans he had washed through Niskair and the shopping spree for vacation homes and expensive toys.

Her statement also implied that Bruce had co-opted others to assist him in taking control of her assets. In a lengthy description of everything that had taken place, for example, she told the court that her husband had put all the property in Maine under the control of a company called Blue Wave. And Blue Wave's "director, president and clerk of the company" — Nat Fenton, of course — "is a friend of Bruce Verchere." Yet Fenton claimed he never even met Verchere.

In the days after her successful court action, Lynne worried that Verchere would try to have the injunction quashed. "Bruce is very clever with anything like this," she fretted during a conversation with Hailey. But her lawyer Langlois calmed her down. Langlois didn't think Bruce would succeed and assured her that if her husband didn't comply fully with the judge's order, he'd be in contempt of court. Still, other demons tormented her. I don't know who really owns my house, she'd say to friends. I don't know if there's a mortgage on it, and if there is, I don't know how much it's for. "I've got lawyers coming out of my ears," she told people, but she said she had no choice. Because their assets and activities were in so many different places, she knew she needed every one of the lawyers she'd retained in Ontario, Quebec, Prince Edward Island, and Switzerland.

If there was any good news in this misery, it was that she didn't have to fight Revenue Canada about the capital gains taxes on Manac; to her great relief, Bruce informed her that he'd settled their case. Whether they had to pay millions, or thousands, or nothing, is known only to the Verchere family.

On Wednesday, June 9, five days after Verchere was served the injunction in Maine, Chris Borg, a Toronto process server, arrived at Bennett Jones Verchere in First Canadian Place and served Geoff Walker, who had enraged Lynne, with notice of the injunction she had obtained against Bruce. Now the cat was truly out of the bag: Verchere's partners knew instantly. Around the firm, in its offices in Montreal, Calgary, Edmonton, and Toronto, the corridor chat was subdued and anxious. People were horrified by what had happened and by the potential for damaging publicity for the firm. Fortunately for the firm, other events were drawing everyone's attention at the time. Mulroney was coasting through his last few weeks as Conservative leader and prime minister, and the Tory leadership convention was scheduled to begin on June 11. People talked of little else, and most of the Mulroney cronies Verchere had come to know over the past nine years were in Ottawa working out details of their farewell presents (Senate seats, directorships, Immigration and Refugee Board jobs, Canadian Pension Commission sinecures) or twisting arms for their favourite leadership candidates.

Back in Montreal, Verchere, frightened and angry, refused to talk things through with Diane. Ashamed to be in such trouble, wanting to appear strong and successful, all he could do was try to reassure her that things would work out and that he and Lynne would ultimately settle their financial issues in a civilized way. "After the lawsuit started," she recalled, "he was tending to it all the time. I hardly ever saw him. He was fretful. He became very remote, very closed, hard to reach." Someone close to him at the time put it more succinctly: "He was a wreck." Before the lawsuit, the friend explained, "Bruce was euphoric. He was a middle-aged man in love for the first time in his life. Then his wife not only deprived him of money, but in court her lawyer said he was a thief and a forger. She created a kind of jail for him and his world collapsed."

On June 14, Verchere lost a second court battle when Justice Derek Guthrie agreed to renew the interim injunction for another ten days. Verchere and his lawyers at Robinson Sheppard Shapiro scrambled frantically. Verchere fought off his depression, growing more determined to defeat his wife in court, ordering his lawyers to use every weapon at their disposal. The reason, says one of the people giving him advice at the time, was Diane. "I love Diane," he told his confidant, "and I'll fight Lynne with my last breath."

Diane sought to comfort Bruce and give him courage, but it was not easy; he became increasingly withdrawn. On June 16, she called her mother in London. "Very upset and unsettled," Sheila recorded in her diary. "I called Arthur later in the day to find out what was going on re: B & D. A real mess!"

On June 21, Verchere's lawyers presented their counterattack, filing a motion for particulars, a motion containing fifty-four pages of questions for his wife and her legal team. The thrust of Verchere's defence was simple: Lynne knew of the actions he had taken and had agreed with them. They had built the family business together, and he was entitled to half the proceeds.

Verchere's lawyer, Claude-Armand Sheppard, was a tough and wily practitioner, particularly skilled at handling cases when rifts tore families apart and warring factions wanted to fight it out in court. Short, stocky, and carefully dressed — his round Russian astrakhan hat was his winter trademark — Sheppard acted for one side of the Kruger pulp and paper family during the famous family feud of the late 1980s. With an annual $400 million in sales, Kruger Inc. was one of Canada's largest paper companies, and when both sides of the family were sufficiently bloodied and tired from the battering they had inflicted upon each other, they called in Simon Reisman, renowned for his leading role in negotiating the Canada–U.S. free trade deal, to broker a settlement in 1989.

Sheppard's strategy was usually to dictate the pace of litigation, slowing it to just the right speed for his client so that he could get as much of his client's evidence before the court as possible. He would later represent the federal government, for example, in its defence of Brian Mulroney's $50-million libel suit in the Airbus affair. Many lawyers who knew of Sheppard's reputation expected him to grind it out, forcing the exasperated Mulroney to take a number and wait his turn, spending huge sums while his lawyers' meters ticked away. Mulroney's lawyers, perhaps in anticipation of Sheppard's tactics, made an exceptional request: a fast-track hearing and a judge who was willing to see the litigation come to court in record time. Their request was granted.

The Verchere litigation was cut out for Sheppard's usual style. Lynne was angry, in a hurry; slowing things down might well serve to cool her off and make her understand the damage she was gearing up to inflict on Bruce. Certainly Sheppard tried, infuriating Lynne with some of the clarifications he requested. Lynne had sworn, for instance, that she had worked hard to develop Manac, work that included extensive travelling; Sheppard asked the court to order Lynne to be more specific and explain in her lawsuit, as he put it, "What is the extensive travelling that is referred to?" As if Bruce didn't know that over the years Lynne had often been away on sales trips across Canada and the United States. But all Sheppard was trying to do was get all possible evidence into the record.

Lynne stated in her lawsuit that she had managed the business and financial affairs of Bruce's law firm. Sheppard asked the court to require her to explain, "What were the business and financial affairs that were managed by Lynne Walters for Bruce Verchere's law firm?" Lynne said that Bruce had given her legal advice during the sales negotiations with Gulf + Western; Sheppard wanted to know what advice Bruce had given her, as if Verchere did not know the work he'd done, for which he had charged $300,000. Such nitpicking, tedious questions slowed the process, dragging it out. Sheppard, however, wasn't able to stretch the deadlines as he'd hoped, nor make effective use of the evidence he was pulling out of Lynne, fact by reluctant fact. The judge said his decision on whether to uphold or quash the injunction would be ready in three days, by June 24.

By this time, a small circle of Montreal's elite had a fair idea of what was going on in Bruce Verchere's life. One such person was Mulroney. He wanted to help his friend and turned to the most effective method he knew, the one he had used with great success for nine years: patronage. Verchere was promoted from being a mere director of AECL, who had so far been able to attend only two meetings, to the chairmanship. Mulroney barely got the appointment through; the next day he resigned as prime minister of Canada and Kim Campbell was sworn in. But on June 24, he rammed through a few last-minute appointments for some people who mattered to him. Ottawa lawyer Stu Hendin, a backroom pol and former fundraiser, went to the board of VIA Rail; Marty Wakim, the wife of one of Mulroney's cronies from student days at St. Francis Xavier University, went to the

Immigration and Refugee Board. Those close to Verchere believed Mulroney was extending a lifeline to his loyal trustee. The chairmanship came with prestige and power, the thinking went, and would boost his self-confidence and burnish his reputation. What it wouldn't do was pay him enough to live on; the job wasn't worth more than $10,000 a year.

The new honour was the only bright spot in a terrible day. Late on June 23, Justice Derek Guthrie had extended the injunction for an excruciating ten weeks, until September 6, at which time Verchere was to turn up with a full accounting of what he had done with the Manac sale money and all their other assets.

Guthrie's decision was released, as promised, on June 24, the same day Verchere's appointment as AECL chairman was announced. Verchere paid little attention to the AECL appointment; it wouldn't help him. He wasn't sure if anything could help him.

He and Diane spent the rest of the day talking about their future, about what to do next. At first Verchere tried to see what his way out could be. He knew he had no choice but to make a reckoning with Lynne on September 6. All that could happen, he told himself, was that he'd lose everything. It would be a terrible blow, certainly, one he could hardly bear thinking about. But with everything else gone, he'd still have Diane. They'd still have each other. We'll be fine, she assured him. We won't starve. I can make money, you can make money. Perhaps the AECL chairmanship would lead to other things.

Verchere tried to see things from her point of view. Diane was right, of course — they did have each other, and their babies, and that was what really mattered.

Perhaps, perhaps — things aren't quite as wretched as they seem. We'll manage.

The following morning Hailey was working at home when the phone rang. It was Diane.

"Dad, I'm in trouble."

AFTER A SLEEPLESS NIGHT and despite Diane's reassurances, Verchere had seen before him nothing but failure and disgrace, and he'd made up his mind. He could not have been clearer. He told Diane she had to leave Montreal right away. He had nothing to offer her, no hope at all, and he had pleaded with her to accept his decision. He was a foundering ship, he said despairingly, and she'd go down with him if she stayed. "The only hope," he had told Diane, "is for you to get away." Diane disagreed. She was determined to be with him during this terrible time.

"It's over between us," he insisted bleakly. "I'm going back to Lynne. You have to go right away."

Horrified, disbelieving, Diane pressed him for reasons. Why was he sending her away? He wouldn't tell her. She suspected there had been some kind of confrontation with Lynne she knew nothing about, but he wouldn't explain his decision. Why had he broken his vow to her? How could he abandon her now, she asked in tears, when she was so close to delivering their babies? How could she suddenly mean nothing to him, when a few hours earlier she had meant so much? Bruce, despondent, withdrawn, refused to answer. He told her only that he was powerless to change anything and that she had to leave Montreal at once. Her intention was to stay right where she was.

When she called her father, she didn't know where else to turn. Her mother was still in England and Diane couldn't reach her. It couldn't have been easy to call her father after all the anger and hurt that had come between them for so long, but she had known all along that he loved her and would do anything for her. When he heard her words, "Dad, I'm in trouble," his defences collapsed. All he wanted was to listen and to help. He started to make some plans.

When Diane finally reached Sheila later that day, the call came into her hotel room and she grabbed a notepad from her bag to scrawl notes. "The sky has fallen," Diane told her mother. "Everything else has fallen." She explained to her mother how catastrophic Guthrie's decision was to her future with Bruce. "This is big — and difficult," Diane said. "It's potentially unwinnable. Bruce is facing bankruptcy." She also told her mother that she had already talked to her father. If Hailey still harboured any anger towards Diane, it had completely melted away by the time he'd finished speaking to her; all he could feel was grief for her distress. "Dad was wonderful," Diane said to her mother. "He started to cry."

In spite of everything, Diane did not allow herself to indulge in self-pity. She explained to her mother that Verchere, though filled with remorse for what he had put her through, had to fight for his own survival. Now she had to plan for her own as well — and that of the babies.

Sheila was appalled by the news. "Bruce and Diane were a great couple," recalled Sheila. "They were good together. I couldn't believe he'd do this." But being practical souls, Arthur and Sheila were on the phone to each other for the rest of the day trying to sort out a way to help Diane.

After talking through the options, all agreed it made sense for Diane to stay in Canada until after the twins were born; she'd get excellent medical care, the babies would have Canadian citizenship, and if Bruce came around, as Diane hoped, they could be reunited again quickly. She wasn't willing to leave him altogether and return to the States. Lyford Cay was an obvious possibility and, as a mother, Sheila longed for her youngest daughter to be with her. But when there were serious medical problems in the Bahamas, most residents went to Florida for care. Here was Diane, under terrible stress, carrying two babies; they couldn't take chances.

The most persuasive argument came from Jane in Vancouver. As a pediatrician, she could find her sister a good obstetrician and make all the necessary arrangements. Diane should come to Vancouver right away, she said. She can stay with me until the babies are born and then I'll find her a nice apartment at a residential hotel until she decides what to do. I'll look after her here; she'll be fine.

In Lyford Cay, a few hours after hearing from Diane, Hailey got another call. It was Lynne, elated by her victory in Quebec Superior Court. "I've had strong success," she announced. She told Hailey about the court hearing, saying her husband looked "totally devastated" and "very old." Seeming to forget that Hailey was, after all, the father of her hated rival, she exulted over Bruce's defeat. He'd been totally surprised by her actions, Lynne reported. "He didn't believe I'd do it."

While she chatted happily to Hailey — without any inkling of what he, Sheila, and Jane had been going through with Diane — she dropped some interesting information. Because she prepared her husband's tax returns, she said, she knew he hadn't worked for two years back in the late 1980s. Nor, she claimed, had Mulroney ever been required to pay him for all Verchere's work when Mulroney was prime minister. Verchere was content to do the work for the prestige. "Mulroney never paid," she confided to Hailey. "In fact, doing work for him actually cost Bruce money."

While Lynne revelled in the court's treatment of her husband, Bruce and Diane sat down together on Saturday and drew up a statement. Whatever happened now, they wanted to be sure no one could ever question the paternity of the twins.

> We, Diane Hailey and Bruce Verchere, hereby confirm that the two children presently being carried by Diane Hailey and who are expected to be born in September of 1993 are the children of Diane Hailey and Bruce Verchere.
>
> Signed at the city of Montreal on the 26th day of June, 1993.
>
> Diane Hailey
> Bruce Verchere

Diane sent a copy to her father with a note: "Dad: This is a copy for your files. The original is in the thin (unsealed) envelope in the fireproof safe."

Signing the statement, Verchere realized with pleasant surprise, had buoyed his spirits. Lynne wouldn't like it, of course, but he was proud to state he was the father of the children Diane was carrying. Nothing could take that away from him.

TWENTY-ONE
Strictly Personal and Confidential

An ultimatum can be delivered any number of ways. No one, except those directly involved, knows exactly what transpired, or even when. It's unclear whether the exchange was wildly volatile or cool and businesslike. All that's known for certain is that sometime before he told Diane it was over between them, Bruce Verchere had a long talk with his wife.

On June 29 Diane was on a plane to Vancouver, her future shattered. Even as she left the apartment on Côte Sainte-Catherine they'd shared for three months, Verchere refused to tell her why he'd changed his mind. He offered no explanation, no word of comfort, no hope. Equally puzzling and hurtful, he offered no financial help. Since her move to Montreal, he had been supporting her, and now she had only enough money for an economy ticket to Vancouver. When Hailey heard about this, he could hardly contain himself. A woman in her condition, weeks away from delivering twins, flying coach? He arranged to upgrade her to business class.

For weeks now Hailey had longed for a way to win back his daughter's affections. He wanted her forgiveness for the harsh things he'd said. At the same time, he couldn't let go of his belief that the true victim here was Lynne, and he didn't want to turn his back on an old friend who had been deeply wronged and who counted on him for friendship and advice. As long as Hailey felt this way, Diane — not surprisingly — found it difficult to resume a comfortable relationship with him. Now, despite their reconciliation, her father had hardened his heart against Verchere more than ever.

The man is a total fraud, thought Hailey contemptuously. He despised Verchere and was ready to wage war. His first priority, though, was Diane; she had to be comfortable and safe. Find a good lawyer, he instructed Jane by phone. We're not going to let Bruce get away with treating Diane like this. He's going to take responsibility for what he's done.

By July 3 Jane was able to report some progress. She'd not only made arrangements for Diane's medical care for the remainder of her pregnancy, and for the delivery of the twins, but she'd also tracked down an excellent lawyer, Hugh Stark, on West Georgia Street. Stark had a good reputation as a family law expert.

Diane, who still had no idea why Bruce had abruptly broken off with her, accepted the need for legal advice. She didn't have a problem with letting her father talk to Stark, but she was determined to remain in charge of any legal action against Bruce. Stark would be away until July 19, Jane told her parents, but they could call him after that.

Arthur balked at Diane's demand to control Stark's actions on her behalf. He agreed to wait until after July 19 to talk to him, but warned his daughters that he wasn't going to hold anything back. "I'm going to speak freely to him," he told Jane, "and I'm going to pass on all the information I've collected concerning Bruce." He reminded them that Verchere had been his lawyer for almost a quarter-century, and that entitled him to collect whatever information he could about him, especially since Arthur himself had been named in Lynne's injunction before the Quebec Superior Court as the person who had opened the Blue Trust by serving as settlor. Apparently Verchere had used the Blue Trust illegally, as a conduit for money, he told Jane and Sheila. And Lynne had told Hailey that her lawyers might want to question him about the way the Blue Trust was formed. "I'll never in my life again," Hailey said, "sign any legal document without knowing exactly what it is."

As the Haileys talked things over, their main concern, of course, remained Diane's well-being. Jane told her parents about the talks they'd had since Diane's arrival in Vancouver. Bruce was "increasingly unstable," Diane had told her sister; he was full of remorse and guilt. "I've been watching him deteriorate," she'd said. "He's been grey and ashen."

This cut no ice with Hailey. "Bruce's condition will not inhibit me at all," he told Jane bluntly. "While Bruce is certainly in deep trouble, it's of his own making. My objective is to do the best possible for Diane and her children, irrespective of what happens to Bruce." Concerned about her father's apparent intransigence, Jane told him that Diane didn't want a vendetta against Bruce. "I'm not seeking a vendetta," her father replied. "If Bruce comes through with a proper settlement for Diane, that could be the end of it."

Determined as he was, Hailey also recognized reality; he knew that Bruce might well have no money after Lynne was finished with her lawsuit. And if the court decided Verchere had misused trust funds under his control, which seemed probable, there was a good chance he would no longer be allowed to practise law. Perhaps he would even face criminal charges. "Therefore a lump sum settlement, if possible, and soon," noted Hailey, "might be better than some promised future support, though this would need to be reviewed and advised on by Diane's lawyer."

Hailey reminded his wife and daughter that it was important not to antagonize Lynne. Her continued friendship was valuable to them, he suggested prudently, because Bruce might not be able to honour any commitment once Lynne's lawsuit was over. As long as Arthur and Lynne could still talk freely, he pointed out, the Haileys would be able to influence decisions Lynne might make.

While the Haileys looked for solutions in Vancouver, Verchere was doing the same in Montreal. His situation was grim. Rumours were rife in the legal world, and the embarrassment was almost unendurable. So far he'd been relatively lucky; not only were people disappearing on summer holidays, but there hadn't been a squeak of publicity. It would be terrible if a court reporter stumbled across the file and blew it open in the *Gazette*. Verchere was also mindful of the professional repercussions if the details of his wife's legal action against him leaked into the legal community and the salons of Westmount, where his marital indiscretions had already drawn disapproving clucks.

Verchere sought to put a lid on his wife's potentially devastating proceedings against him. He asked for an order that the case be argued in camera to avoid the possibility of a nosy reporter or a loose-lipped lawyer wandering into the courtroom. The privacy of all the Vercheres, he maintained, required that the courtroom doors be locked to all but themselves, their lawyers, and the judge. This was a family affair, Sheppard argued in his motion on Verchere's behalf, and it included a divorce action. It was necessary to protect the private lives of the parties so that the defendant's professional life as a lawyer would not be harmed. "The maintenance of public order, the efficient administration of justice, the protection of the family and of their private lives and professional secrets are the reasons which should justify withholding public access to the files," stated Sheppard. He also argued for lawyer-client confidentiality: because Verchere had acted as the lawyer to his wife and sons, there was a lawyer-client relationship the court had to protect. The request was presented to Justice Bernard Gratton in his chambers.

On this issue, Lynne agreed. Neither of them wanted their nasty litigation to become public. Gratton gave his blessing to their request on July 5. It was the first good news Verchere had had for many weeks, but it wasn't enough to cheer him up for long. He sank deeper and deeper into depression. Eventually he got so low that he went to a psychiatrist, something quite against his nature. Twice in the past, when he'd been forced to go to marriage counselling, he'd loathed the experience; a psychiatrist felt like more of the same. Yet he knew he was drowning and needed help. Soon he was seeing the psychiatrist every day and taking powerful anti-depressants. "He was a broken man," someone close to him at the time said later. Besides the psychiatrist, Andrew Hutchison, the Anglican bishop of Montreal, tried to give him advice; so did Verchere's lawyers, who recognized his desperation.

"You have to tell us everything," the lawyers insisted. "We can't help you if you don't." Verchere stalled. Then one day, wild with grief, he broke down and told someone close to him, someone who'd been giving him advice, what had happened just before he'd broken off with Diane. "My wife gave me an ultimatum," he said. "She said I had to give up my opposition to the injunction and I had to leave Diane. I had to return to her and the boys. If I didn't, she said she'd go to my law partners and the police with the details of what she knows about my business. That's why I told Diane to get out of Montreal right away. That's why I told her I was going back to my wife." Verchere's disclosure brought him no relief; if anything, his confidant's reaction made him realize just how hopeless his situation was.

In this period, when Lynne and Bruce were both distraught and angry with each other, there occurred an accident that mystified the confidants to whom she later reported it. She and Bruce were together in a car. With Bruce at the wheel, the vehicle suddenly sped up and crashed into a stone embankment. The passenger side caved in. Lynne was not seriously injured, though she was, said a friend, "black and blue." She told a few close friends that she believed Bruce had tried to kill her, that she was frightened out of her mind. Then she seemed to calm herself and tried to laugh it off, telling her horrified listeners it was nothing.

Over the next few days, still in the apartment he'd shared so happily with Diane, Verchere imagined the life ahead of him and tried to reconcile himself to it. September 6 was the next big hurdle, the day he had to produce a full accounting of the assets under the Blue Trust. Overtaken by lassitude, despondent, he could barely think about it. After that would come the birth of the twins. What would it feel like then, disgraced and bereft, a new father 3,000 miles from his lover and their children?

Verchere stirred himself and called his lawyers. On July 12 he and Lynne arranged to direct the Blue Trust to sell her the house on Montrose Avenue for $1. Putting the house back in her name alone was one of the ways he could placate her for all the damage he'd done to her financially. There might be liens against it, but she could afford to pay them off. Now, at least, no one could take the house from her.

In an odd irony, Lynne, desperate to avoid publicity about her personal life, was dodging reporters pestering her about a different scandal. As the new chairman of the Official Residences Council, she was the logical person for reporters to call when the story broke that, before the Mulroneys left Ottawa for good in early July, Mila had sold some furnishings and china to the government for $150,000. The deal had been negotiated in great secrecy with bureaucratic allies on the National Capital Commission before being passed in even greater secrecy by the Treasury Board. There was "spontaneous support among council members for the furniture purchase when the deal was first presented," confirmed Montreal architect Roger Desmarais, a generous Tory donor, a member of the Official Residences Council, and one of the architects who had shared a $4.2-million contract to design a new prison in Mulroney's riding.

A public uproar swept across the country when people heard about the furniture deal; by this time the Mulroneys were widely disliked for their greed and lavish spending on the government tab. No one in the government could find any paper trail for these goods to show who had paid for them in the first place; the head of the National Capital Commission, Marcel Beaudry, feebly admitted that no one at the NCC could find any original receipts.

The press began hounding Lynne for answers. She simply refused to take their calls. When April Lindgren, an *Ottawa Citizen* reporter, called her on July 12, the same day she and Bruce were working out the deal to sell back the house for $1, "a man answering the telephone at her house insisted the caller had the wrong number," the paper reported, "and then turned on the answering machine."

ARTHUR HAILEY HAD BEEN waiting impatiently in Lyford Cay for Hugh Stark to return from holidays. On July 19, the appointed day, he phoned Stark to talk about strategy, and he later faxed the Vancouver lawyer background information on the relationship between Diane and Bruce, as well as the history of Lynne's success with Manac.

"One thing I did not say on the phone," Hailey said in his fax, "and that is my wife Sheila and I are totally supportive of Diane and will do anything necessary to help her and her children. Incidentally, Sheila will be flying to Vancouver to be with Diane immediately after the children are born, and I may be there soon after. Meanwhile, if there is any more information you need please let me know. For my part I will keep you informed of anything I hear about developments in Montreal."

Hugh Stark didn't waste time. Two days after talking to Hailey, he couriered a letter to Verchere, marked STRICTLY PERSONAL AND CONFIDENTIAL.

STRICTLY PERSONAL AND CONFIDENTIAL

July 21, 1993

Bennett Jones Verchere
Montreal, Quebec
Attention: Mr. Bruce Verchere

Dear Sir:
Re: Diane Hailey.
We have, as you may know, been retained by Ms. Diane Hailey to negotiate an agreement with you for the maintenance of Ms. Hailey and the twin children she is bearing. Her desire is to raise the children in an environment that they would have enjoyed had you and she been able to cohabit together and marry. We say that, not that such a relationship is necessarily possible, but so that you will understand her needs and desires in relation to raising your children.

We, therefore, would ask you to provide us with an insight into the present legal proceedings between you and your wife and how, if at all, that affects your asset position and your income flow. We further would appreciate receiving copies of your last three years income tax returns, a statement from the Chairman of the executive of your law firm as to your present and expected income with the firm and a list of your assets and liabilities so that we may discuss the implications of your financial position on the availability of money for the maintenance of this new family unit with Ms. Hailey.

> As you can well imagine anyone in Ms. Hailey's position would be concerned about her future and the future of her children. She does wish to reach therefore an amicable and expeditious settlement with you, which will not impede your relationship with her and the children but will protect her and your children in the future.
>
> We await your earliest reply and thank you in advance for your anticipated cooperation.
>
> Yours very truly,
> Hugh G. Stark

Verchere was stunned to receive such a tough letter. How could Diane do this to him? Didn't she love him? Didn't she understand that he'd had his reasons — overwhelming reasons — for doing what he'd done? Didn't she know that he adored her, that he'd never have ended the relationship if he hadn't been forced to?

Verchere's failure to explain himself had left Diane feeling devastated, vulnerable, and alone. Instead of trying to understand her plight, however, all he could see was his own oppressive problems and the insulting commands of a stranger to share legal information about his battle with Lynne and to explain how this might affect his own financial situation. The very idea of having to send income tax statements to some unknown lawyer in Vancouver — or, worse, of having to ask his old friend Bill Britton in Calgary, now the firm's managing partner, for an income statement, and, worse still, of having to supply a list of his assets and liabilities — it was all repellent and horrible.

A week later, Claude-Armand Sheppard answered Stark's letter to Verchere, buying time.

> July 27, 1993
>
> Mr. Hugh G. Stark
> Stark and Maclise
> Vancouver, BC
>
> Re: Diane Hailey
> Dear Sirs:
> We represent Mr. Bruce Verchere who has asked us to acknowledge on his behalf your letter of July 21st, relating to the above-mentioned subject.
>
> We are reviewing the matter with Mr. Verchere and will communicate with you in due time.
>
> Yours truly,
> Claude-Armand Sheppard

Lynne, meanwhile, had got wind of the fact that Diane had hired a lawyer and was going after Bruce for support. For Lynne, this raised the ugly spectre of a public brawl with her husband's mistress, something she wanted to avoid now that she'd obtained the injunction. Her lawyers worked closely with her husband's to see if they could resolve their dispute peaceably. At last, on August 3, her lawyers at Langlois Robert and his at Robinson Sheppard Shapiro signed an out-of-court settlement. It meant that Verchere would not have to appear in court on September 6 with a detailed accounting of his spending after all; but it also meant that his defence had collapsed. As part of the settlement, Lynne was awarded ownership of everything; whatever Bruce would have thereafter would be given at her discretion. He had been reduced to little more than Lynne's own charity case.

Other major issues were still on the table. The divorce action she'd launched, for example, remained in place. She intended to see it through. And an even more important matter was settled during these weeks, again with the help of the lawyers. When Lynne had delivered her ultimatum to Bruce, the agreement they reached — with the help of lawyers and other advisors — was that Bruce would drop his fight over assets and would end his relationship with Diane. In return, Lynne would turn over certain documents to an agreed-upon intermediary. These documents were indeed tendered; whether Lynne kept copies for herself is known only to her.

Lynne now took an active interest in the settlement being worked out between Bruce and Diane. Three days after she and Bruce reached their out-of-court settlement, on August 6, Sheppard wrote to Stark once again. He told Stark that his advice to Verchere was simply to ask Diane about her needs, and those of the twins after their birth. If Diane would send them "a detailed claim based on need," he said, the matter "could be resolved amicably without need for complex financial analysis or litigation." As for Stark's request for information about the legal situation between Lynne and Bruce, and for income tax statements and other documents, said Sheppard, "It is our view that the material requested is not necessary for a resolution of the problem." He did not mention that the case in

Montreal had been settled, with his client having caved in completely to his wife's demands.

While the lawyers fenced, Diane was enduring as sad a time in Vancouver as Bruce was in Montreal. It was still midsummer, and she was uncomfortable as her delivery date grew near. She'd always been athletic and appeared healthy and strong, but she was worn down by the tense battle between the two men she loved so dearly — her father, who was still talking constantly to Lynne, and Bruce, who she still hoped would end her bad dream and join her.

During this excruciating time Diane was again touched by the kindness of Bruce's family and friends in Vancouver. David and Mary Verchere called and visited and became almost surrogate parents. David was Bruce's first cousin and had been so fond of him that he and Mary had named their own son after him. From the start they had let Diane know they would be her friends, and during Diane's lonely wait they followed through on that promise. She was a young woman involved in a tragic relationship and, except for a devoted sister, very much alone as she awaited the birth of her babies; while they did not know exactly what was going on, they knew it was serious and they tried to let her know they were there for her no matter what. Two others who became close to her at this time were Royal and Linda Smith. They dropped in and gave her moral support.

The days ground by. She and Bruce spoke on the phone about half a dozen times during these weeks, but their conversations were brief and difficult. No letter arrived. No money came. No plans for the future. No talk of the children. Diane could only let the lawyers fight it out. The battle escalated dramatically on August 12, when Stark sent a long letter to Sheppard. One word in Sheppard's letter of August 6 had sent Stark into a fury, and his response was icy and unyielding.

> Your use of the word "claim" is particularly offensive in that it was our client's understanding that she and your client, albeit working through lawyers, would plan the future of the children both financially and socially.
>
> Before my client was asked to leave Montreal by your client, it is our understanding that both of our respective clients planned a lifestyle for themselves and their children that consisted of mother not working and being home with the children, au pair assistance, travel and homes both in Montreal and possibly in Maine. She now finds herself at thirty-five years of age expecting twins within the next three or four weeks and having no means of supporting herself, let alone her children.
>
> This of course, is a drastic change from the lifestyle contemplated with your client and as well a significant change in lifestyle to that which she enjoyed prior to becoming pregnant, leaving her career at Universal Studios, L.A. and moving to Montreal at the invitation of your client.
>
> Your client, although having lived and continuing to live an affluent lifestyle, has not paid any money to our client to assist her in defraying even normal living costs since he

> asked her to leave Montreal. In addition to these normal living costs, she is faced with medical costs in excess of the coverage offered to her by the Quebec Insurance Plan of which she was a party.

Stark said that Diane, without knowing Verchere's finances, had prepared a plan to protect her and the children in future and to allow her a "reasonable standard of living, but one which falls far short of that which she had expected for her children had the relationship with your client continued."

In Montreal, aghast, Sheppard and Verchere (and, no doubt, Lynne) examined Diane's financial requirements. No wonder Stark had a good reputation; he'd thought of everything, and he and Diane had put together a wish list that stunned Verchere. Under the heading "Capital Expenditures," Diane asked for a three-bedroom house in West Vancouver. The estimated cost was $725,000. Next was $40,000 to furnish the house, and $30,000 for a car. There was a demand for $24,000 to cover her expenses to date; these included $1,030 for her last-minute airfare to Vancouver; anticipated baby supplies; medical expenses including $7,500 for a day and a night nurse for a month after the babies' birth, and a nanny for two months after that; and rent for a two-bedroom apartment for her and the babies for three months.

On top of this, Diane asked for $12,000 a month for her and the children. She arrived at this figure by adding up maintenance and utilities on the house, car expenses, household costs for such things as food, cleaning, cable, and telephone, and medical expenses. Other lists included clothing, entertainment, and birthday expenses for herself and the children.

Stark ended the letter with Diane's commitment to giving Bruce generous access to the children because she wanted them to see their father frequently, "which should not be too difficult for him (bearing in mind his present lifestyle which includes ownership of a plane)." Did Stark not know that Lynne's injunction had forced Verchere to return the Cessna to Dorval Airport? Was he just being malevolent? Perhaps he'd concluded that, once Verchere returned to Lynne, she'd allow him to fly his beloved plane again.

And return to Lynne he did. Maybe it was Stark's jolting letter. Maybe it was the fact that Lynne's lawsuit had been settled. Maybe Bruce had simply run out of money and had nowhere else to go. Maybe he was honouring his agreement. Whatever his reasons, he cleared out of the apartment on Côte Sainte-Catherine and moved back into Lynne's perfect, showplace house on Montrose Avenue.

TWENTY-TWO
The Honourable Thing

FRIENDS WHO RAN INTO Verchere that August were shocked. This was a shell of the man they'd known. Although his thick hair had been white for years, he was usually tanned, summer and winter, thanks to holidays in the Bahamas; and he had always been fit and energetic. By the time he went back to live with Lynne he was gaunt and drawn and pasty-faced. His drive, his sense of fun, his interest in other people — the qualities that had made him such a compelling and seductive person — were gone, replaced by sadness and an overwhelming depression. He'd turned into an old man.

All Verchere could think about was what he'd lost when he sent Diane away, how he had messed up his own life and those of the people around him. He knew his partners were talking about him, about how the firm should deal with this tragic fiasco. He knew that Lynne would be an integral part of the legal decision-making between himself and Diane.

During this period, Gary Fountain, the real estate salesman in Mount Desert, was on a holiday in Nantucket when his phone rang one morning. "I asked my wife, 'Who the hell knows I'm here?' I picked it up and it was Bruce. He said, 'I've got to sell Pretty Marsh.'" Fountain was stunned. After five years, he'd come to know Verchere well and they were good friends. "When he bought that camp," Fountain said, "he told people he would absolutely never sell it. I knew something was up. He would never have sold that place for love or money." When he returned to Mount Desert, Fountain did as Verchere asked and listed the property for sale. Around August 20 Verchere went down to Maine to stay at the camp and talk to Fountain about the sale. Fountain, too, was upset by his friend's appearance. "He looked worn and tired."

Lynne, meanwhile, having won everything she was after — including her husband's forced return — found herself with renewed energy, although her appearance, too, showed the strain of the last two years. She'd lost weight; she was fragile and jittery and often close to tears. "She was a bundle of nerves," said one friend. The legal thumping she'd given Bruce was just punishment, she believed, for his deception of her. Almost every day she called Hailey to update him, but she was smart enough to know that Hailey's ultimate loyalty was to his own family. She told Hailey that she was encouraging Bruce's lawyers to make an offer to Diane so that Diane would have financial support for herself and the twins.

The Haileys found these machinations, discussions, and worries debilitating. Frequently during these weeks, the last entries in Arthur's diary said much the same sort of thing: "A long talk w/S; both exhausted," or "An exhausting day." His main therapy was his new novel, although even here there had been setbacks. Doubleday, his publisher for thirty-seven years, had rejected his idea for the novel without explaining why or even inviting him for a discussion. Although Hailey's agent, Nancy Stauffer, had quickly arranged a contract with Crown

Publishers, a Random House subsidiary, which was delighted to have Hailey on its list, he found it a painful surprise to be turned down so coldly by the publisher that had made so much money from his previous books.

At least the work was going well. He was writing steadily, there were long research talks with Steve Vinson, his retired detective friend in Miami, and frequent conversations with Sam Vaughan, his editor at Random House, and Janice McCart at Bennett Jones Verchere in Toronto, about contractual matters. By mid-August Hailey had some chapters ready to send to Vaughan. For a man of seventy-three, the hours were long and tiring, but at least the discipline of turning out chapters and working with Vinson kept his mind off family problems for a few hours each day.

On August 23 the Haileys learned that Bruce had returned to live with Lynne at the house on Montrose Avenue. Exactly when he went back, no one was sure. For Diane, it was hard to believe; she was terribly hurt and phoned her mother for solace. Every day she waited for him to explain or to comfort her, but that call never came.

But her father got on the phone to offer his ideas on what to do. The situation was almost as frustrating for him as it was for his daughter. This was a smart, strong-willed father and a wealthy writer who, for many years, had been able to control most aspects of his life; now, his lawyer and old friend was destroying his happiness. Worn out and cross as he was, though, the conversation with Diane brought enormous happiness and relief. This tragic crisis, with all the tears, had finally broken down the barrier between Diane and her father that had so often forced Sheila to act as a go-between. He and Diane finally cleared the air, apologizing to each other for their stubbornness and for the hurtful things they'd said to each other over the past year. "No recriminations," wrote Hailey on a scrap of paper from their boat, the *Sheila III*; "no more discussions. No arguments. Wipe clean." At the end of their conversation he'd told her, "We'd like you to come and live here with your children in Lyford Cay, for as long as you want."

The next morning Diane faxed him a note with some information he'd requested. She ended with a plea for understanding:

> Yesterday you made a generous gesture to put our troubles from the past year and a half behind us and start afresh. My hesitancy was not due to any lack of desire but rather to a sense that these kind of emotional difficulties are only superficially resolved with the sweep of a hand. However, I've thought about it a great deal and cannot see any point in rehashing all that has transpired, complete with explanations and recriminations. Life is short, as you say, and given all the present and complicated circumstances, I think it is for the best to move forward and resume a relationship based on love & trust.
> Diane

With this thistle pulled from his heart, Hailey felt he could tackle anything. Briskly, first thing next morning, August 24, he called Janice McCart. If Diane's negotiations with Verchere weren't complete by August 27, he told her, he would reluctantly withdraw as a client of the firm.

McCart, who was fond of the Haileys, was concerned and sympathetic and said she'd call him back. She knew that Hailey didn't want to leave Bennett Jones Verchere, but given that Bruce was a partner he might be forced to do so.

Later that day, after winning Diane's agreement, Hailey had a long discussion with Hugh Stark to plot strategy and to tell him that the senior partners at Bennett Jones Verchere now knew what was going on.

IN MONTREAL, in the house on Montrose Avenue, the mood was gloomy. Lynne told close friends she and Bruce were trying to reconcile. The strain was exacerbated because Michael and David had both been living there, too, for several months; the effort to make things seem normal in front of them was exhausting. A sour undercurrent of betrayal ran through the household; Bruce had betrayed Lynne, and she, he felt, had betrayed him by convincing the boys to join in her injunction. The boys, who now understood that their father had been devastated by their participation, were full of remorse for hurting him so deeply.

What made the atmosphere even more tense was that David had invited his lover, Gregory Williams, a McGill rowing star, to stay at the house. There couldn't have been a worse time to have an outsider in the home. But one of Lynne's friends pointed out that it was fortunate the young men were all there when Bruce came back; Lynne was still deeply disturbed by her husband's rage and the potentially fatal car "accident." Having David, Michael, and Greg in the house made her feel safer, and over the months he lived with the Vercheres,

Greg became very close to Lynne and she grew to depend on him.

Was reconciliation possible between such tormented people? Lynne would get on the phone to her closest confidants and rhyme off the ways Bruce had failed as a husband, a lawyer, and a father. The only money we have, she'd say, is what I made, and there's still $3 million he can't account for. It's gone. Every single asset we have, I paid for. Bruce has nothing except his position in the law firm and now that's up in the air; his partners will probably get rid of him. He no longer has any credibility. And we both have horrendous legal bills, which are all his fault. As for his philandering, there were other women before Diane. He and Diane went through a tremendous amount of money, Lynne told Hailey, even adding nastily that if Bruce were to go back to Diane, he'd be living on handouts from Arthur and Sheila.

The same day Lynne fired this shot at Hailey, Janice McCart called Hailey back, with Ross Eddy on the speakerphone. After thinking it through at their end, they'd decided that the firm could find itself in a conflict of interest given the possible lawsuit between Diane and Bruce. If Arthur wanted to take his business to Stikeman's, they said, there would be no hard feelings; in fact, it might be best for all concerned. They'd do everything they could to make it simple. Hailey thanked them and said he'd let them know where to send his files.

After talking it over with Diane, Arthur had another discussion with Hugh Stark. Now that he was no longer a Bennett Jones Verchere client, he said, he'd decided on a strategy to force Verchere's hand. This is what I'd like to do, said Hailey. When you file this lawsuit for Diane against Bruce, I want to hold a press conference in your office. I'll be there. Can you do this? It was an extraordinary notion, Stark realized, but, sure, he'd be quite prepared to do so.

By the end of the day, Hailey had talked to his friend Jim Cockwell, a banker in the Bahamas, for advice on finding a new law firm. He was told that Stikeman's was still a great place; Heward Stikeman's son-in-law, Brian Rose, was a good man, said Cockwell. That was all Hailey needed to hear; he was soon on the phone to Stikeman, telling him the whole story. Shocked, Stikeman confessed to Hailey that he'd thrown Verchere out of the firm many years earlier; until then Hailey, like almost everyone else, had thought Verchere had chosen to leave. "We'd be delighted to have you as a client," Stikeman added graciously.

Arthur called Diane to bring her up to date, then briefed Stark one last time. It had been a long day and he looked forward to a quiet dinner with Sheila and an early bedtime, but at 8:50 p.m. Diane called to say her water had broken. The Haileys spent the rest of the evening in great excitement and anxiety; this was a month before Diane's due date. Finally, at 2:30 a.m. their time, they were wakened by the phone. It was Diane, calling to say she'd given birth to two splendid, red-haired babies, a boy and a girl. Both were normal and healthy. They were to be called Paul and Emma Jane.

Now that the children had actually arrived, Hailey redoubled his efforts to get their support settled. He faxed Hugh Stark with the news, and soon afterwards he got a phone call from Lynne, who had learned of the birth of the twins. She'd also heard of Hailey's plan to hold a press conference the next day in Stark's office and was agitated; hold off, she begged. "If you do this, Bruce will not only lose his partnership, he'll be unemployable." Hailey's position was that this was not his problem.

Once Lynne understood how intractable Hailey was, she moved quickly. Before long Hugh Stark called Lyford Cay to tell Sheila and Arthur he'd heard from Verchere's lawyers with a financial offer for Diane. Bruce (in other words, Lynne) could manage $3,000 a month. Stark's response was concise — "Ridiculous" — and the Haileys agreed. But now at least the Vercheres understood that Hailey meant business and were addressing the issue of support. Hailey would postpone his trip to Vancouver, and the press conference, until the Vercheres had run out of offers. "Long talk w/S about day's events," Hailey wrote in his diary before going to bed. "Both exhausted."

Diane had made another call from the hospital that day. She called Bruce in Montreal. It seemed a long while since they'd spoken, and this conversation was emotional and painful beyond words. They thought of all the plans they'd had for a life together, for marriage, for the suddenly real family they had started with such high hopes. How they had loved each other! Verchere was sick with remorse for letting her down, for what he'd lost. "We have two beautiful children," she told him gently. "And they're well. We're all well." Verchere broke down and hung up the phone.

The next morning, Friday, August 27, life began to return to normal for everybody. Sheila arranged to leave Nassau immediately and fly to Toronto; from there she would fly to Vancouver the next day. Arthur planned to join her there as soon as he'd tidied up a few commitments at home. In the meantime, Diane was doing well;

not only was Jane there to make sure she was looked after, but her brother, Steven, called to say he was flying up from Menlo Park in California and would be there by Sunday. David and Mary Verchere and Royal and Linda Smith already felt like family.

In Montreal, Bruce too was trying to return to some sort of normalcy. This was an important day for him; he was scheduled to chair his first board meeting at Atomic Energy of Canada. It was to be held in Ottawa at AECL's headquarters at 344 Slater Street. His old friend Bruce Howe, another Vancouverite who had moved to the public service in Ottawa, would be attending his first meeting as president. It was scheduled to start early, at 8:30. Ordinarily Verchere would have zipped up in his Cessna, a flight that took no more than forty-five minutes. This time he had to drive, and it made him miserable.

When he opened the meeting, few would have known he was under stress. "He did all the gracious things at the beginning," recalled Marnie Paikin, a long-time board member from Hamilton. "He talked about how pleased he was to be appointed and thanked me for being acting chair and others there for filling in until a new president and a new chair had been appointed. He was always charming. None of us knew anything about any personal problem he might be having."

One board member, Peter Harris, didn't know anything was wrong, hadn't even heard any rumours. He was himself a tax lawyer, a partner at McCarthy Tétreault in Toronto, and he'd known Verchere well for many years; like Verchere, he'd begun his career at Revenue Canada, and Verchere had once tried to hire him. This was Harris's last board meeting — Mulroney had replaced him with a Tory fundraiser, Ralph Lean — but he certainly bore Verchere no ill will for being dumped and looked forward to a chat. "Our relationship was always cordial and friendly," said Harris. "We were always running into each other in the course of our practices, and we even saw each other socially a few times. I had a respect for him and I think it was a mutual respect."

But Harris was horrified at Verchere's appearance. "I noticed just how thin he had become." Verchere, he said, looked much older, and very tired. Harris later heard about a tax case that had gone badly, Special Risks, and wondered if this was why his old friend looked so beleaguered. At 12:30 Verchere adjourned the meeting. The members, eager to get home for the last summer weekend of August, hurried out of the room. The only person who knew about his relationship with Diane was another board member, Louise Vaillancourt of Montreal, one of Quebec's best-known businesswomen and a member of several high-profile boards. As far as she knew, Bruce and Diane were still a couple and planning to marry. In a private moment, as the others were saying their goodbyes, Vaillancourt asked him if the babies had been born yet. She was startled by his stiff reply: "There's a problem, and I don't want to talk about it."

As he was leaving, Verchere paused to speak to AECL's corporate secretary. He pulled out his wallet, took a few $100 bills from it, and handed them over to the surprised official. "I made some overseas calls, personal calls, on my AECL phone card," he explained. "I'd like to make sure I pay for them now." Leaving the official gawking at the money, he made his way out of the building, got in his car, and began the two-hour drive back to Montreal.

IN LYFORD CAY, Arthur Hailey was beginning to feel the storm clouds lift. The joy of the babies' birth was working its magic on the family and it seemed the worst might be over. Sheila was on her way to Vancouver via Toronto, where she would stay overnight, and he bustled around the house, trying to get all his chores done over the next few days before joining her. When Lynne called, she was friendly and positive, a far cry from her usual litany of miseries; clearly she didn't want to alienate Hailey further. She was terrified he would make good his threat to hold a press conference. She was going to be supervising the exchanges between Bruce's lawyers and Diane's, she announced cheerfully, to make sure there was good communication. The best news, she added, was that the Bennett Jones Verchere partners had decided they didn't want to lose Arthur as a client after all; Bill Britton himself had changed his mind and the others agreed. Hailey was pleased with this loyalty from partners he had come to like so much and relieved not to have to go to a new firm. He called Heward Stikeman immediately to tell him the news, leaving a message with his secretary.

The only person who wasn't happy with the way things were progressing was Diane. As far as she was concerned, Lynne should have been using her money to support her and the twins Verchere had fathered. Hailey, as he put it, "disabused her of the idea." The arrangement should be between Bruce and Diane alone, he believed; Bruce was responsible for the support of Diane and the children, not Lynne. When Diane also told her father she thought it would be a mistake to stick with Bennett Jones Verchere, despite the partners' decision, Hailey told his daughter bluntly she was very "self-oriented."

Later that day, Hailey faxed a note to Hugh Stark to tell him about another call he'd just had from Lynne.

> Dear Mr. Stark:
> Continuing to keep you informed …
>
> At 08:50 EDT today I received a phone call (the second in two days) from Mrs. Lynne Verchere. The call was positive and friendly. At the same time, Lynne sounded strong, appearing to be in command of the current situation while representing — at least for the time being, and in their dealings with me — both the law firm, Bennett Jones Verchere, and Bruce Verchere personally.
>
> Lynne informed me:
>
> #1 — She will personally deal with Bruce Verchere's lawyers, Robinson Sheppard Shapiro, making sure that back-and-forth communication with Diane's lawyer is handled expeditiously. I did tell Lynne that yesterday you received a call from a woman lawyer at the firm, but when Lynne asked if I knew details (obviously she didn't), I told her it would be improper for me to discuss this, except you conveyed to me that a sum of money mentioned was absurdly inadequate, or words to that effect.
>
> Lynne dropped the information that R-S-S were the lawyers Bruce used during Lynne's own lawsuit against him (which she won) and

my fine tuning told me she has a distaste for having to deal with them, but she will. In all of this and what follows, as already mentioned, Lynne was forthright and strong.

I did tell Lynne categorically that, Hugh Stark is Diane's representative and in charge of all decisions concerning her case. Of course, I am keeping in touch and am informed, but any action on my part would only be on Hugh Stark's advice or instructions.

#2 — Bennett Jones Verchere, Lynne reported, does not after all wish me to leave them as a client, and Lynne said she was conveying that message directly from Bill Britton, the managing partner. She said there had been a misunderstanding in that B-J-V believed I was contemplating suing the firm. I told Lynne that was ridiculous; I had never considered the possibility, nor could I see any reason why I should. (It's interesting, though, that you mentioned this possibility during our talk yesterday.) Lynne also conveyed a guarantee from B-J-V that Bruce Verchere would be excluded from any knowledge of, or participation in, Arthur and Sheila Hailey's legal affairs.

I told Lynne that while there would be some embarrassment in explaining this to Heward Stikeman, who had agreed to take on our legal file, I would stay with B-J-V. Actually, Heward is a friend and fellow Club member and I know he'll be understanding; he's on vacation, but I've already talked with his secretary.

Anyway I'm relieved at not having to make a change which would have created a lot of time and trouble for me, and probably expense; also I have good confidence in Janice McCart, the lawyer at B-J-V with whom we have dealt for the past several years.

By this time Lynne and I were talking pretty casually and she also made the comment that my decision to return to the B-J-V fold would help Bruce keep his job and give him some income to support Diane. So from that I believe we can conclude there has been quite a bit of decision making going on, in which Lynne has participated, all of which causes me to wonder if Lynne has some leverage we don't know about — or need to. Hope some of this is of interest, but felt I should report it to you.

Cordially,
Arthur Hailey

Hailey's suspicion that Lynne had "some leverage we don't know about" was especially astute. He knew nothing of her threat to her husband to reveal information that would "embarrass and have negative financial implications" for "the clients with whom you have mixed our family's affairs"; nor was Hailey aware of the negotiations then under way to get those documents out of her hands. He did not know that Bruce had agreed to leave Diane and return assets to Lynne. Yet he smelled something; his nose told him Lynne had a card that would trump any hand.

By the time Verchere got back to Montreal that evening, he was weary and silent. He went into his study and sat at his desk for a while; later he and Lynne went out for dinner at the Hillside Tennis Club. They weren't sure if the boys were all home by the time they came back; they just turned off most of the lights and went to bed.

In Vancouver, three hours behind Montreal time, Royal Smith was worried. He talked to Pat Dohm, who decided to come over. Dohm arrived at the Smiths' on Point Grey Road at a quarter to nine that evening. "Something's happening," Smith told Dohm. "Diane's here without Bruce. She's just had twins." Smith told Dohm how depressed Bruce had been when Diane had called him in Montreal with the news.

There's got to be a way out, Smith thought. If it's money he needs, we can find some money to get him through this. After Dohm left, Smith chewed it over for a few more minutes, anxiety rising, then decided to talk to Bruce. It was after 9:30; almost one in the morning in Montreal. Too late, he thought, I'll call in the morning. Get him to come out here, help him sort things out. See Diane and the kids. We've got to let him know there's a way out of all this.

On Saturday morning in Lyford Cay, Arthur Hailey rose early; after his usual two-and-a-half-mile walk, he planned to deal with a couple of repairmen and was looking forward to a cocktail party and buffet supper that evening at the home of Bill and Catharina Birchall, their near neighbours. Sheila called from Toronto; her trip had been long and frustrating, and on one of the legs between the Bahamas, Miami, and Toronto her luggage had disappeared. Hailey told her about scolding Diane the night before, and the two parents chuckled, agreeing, as Hailey put it, that "her perspective needs adjusting."

While Arthur and Sheila were chatting on the phone, Bruce and Lynne had wakened in Montreal. They went downstairs, made a pot of coffee, and brought a tray back to bed with the morning newspapers. About 10 a.m. Bruce finally got up. He padded naked down the hall towards his own bathroom, beside his study.

David was up, too, and soon afterwards he wandered into his parents' bedroom. He looked around. "Where's Dad?" he asked Lynne. Before she could answer, a gunshot boomed nearby, then another. The air reverberated and sang in their ears and everything grew still.

Lynne scrambled out of bed and she and David ran down the hall to Bruce's bathroom. The door was locked. They couldn't hear a sound beyond the pounding of their hearts. "Phone 911!" Lynne screamed. A police operator answered the emergency call at 10:15 a.m. The call had gone downtown to headquarters, which immediately rerouted it to the station in Westmount. "We just heard gunshots in the bathroom and the door is locked," David cried, the words falling out too fast to be understood. The operator asked for more information. "There's been a shot," he yelled again, "and the person is in the bathroom off his office, the door is locked." Finally, the operator got an address and calmly promised that help was on its way.

Michael, who hadn't come in until 5 a.m., was still sound asleep; he finally woke up when he heard the commotion and hurried in to see what was wrong; terrified, he looked around his parents' room. "Where's Dad?" he said, panic rising in his voice. "Where's Dad?"

Within seconds six or seven police cars from Station 23, the Westmount detachment, and Station 25, the central station at De Maisonneuve and Saint-Mathieu, were racing towards Montrose Avenue; an ambulance sped right behind them.

In Pierre Grégoire's house next door, his sister-in-law had just arrived to put on her wedding dress. She hurried; the photographer was waiting to take the pictures and they were due at the ceremony soon. With their windows open, they heard the screams and the shouting, the sirens, the frantic screeching of tires and more shouting. Blue and white lights flashed from police cars; red strobed from the fire truck that came racing down the street. As the cars slammed to a stop along the curb and the police, fire, and ambulance workers hurried to the front door, anxious neighbours had already started to gather in hushed groups while the dog walkers in the park stood around awkwardly in fascination.

Inside 4481 Montrose, while David stood back, Michael, Lynne, and Greg Williams were desperately trying to open the locked bathroom door. Williams grabbed a *pioche* — a kind of crowbar — and tried to force the lock; when that didn't work, he ran at the door, smashing it in.

Bruce was lying on the floor between the toilet and the sink, his head against the shower door, a rifle in his left hand. Two empty cartridges had fallen beside his head. The floor of the bathroom was covered with blood. One of his sons grabbed the gun and shouted at his father's still figure, desperately, but there was no response. Frantically, Williams tried to shield the body from Lynne and her sons.

By 10:30 the house was swarming with police and medical people. Lynne was screaming in anguish as the police raced into the house. Eventually they were able to calm her enough to take a statement.

Dr. Mohammed Taalat, the medical examiner, arrived within minutes and went upstairs to the bathroom to examine the body; at 10:40 he formally pronounced the death. He needed a family member to identify the body and Michael agreed to do it; he went to the bathroom, glanced at his father, and nodded in pain. Lynne stayed downstairs, numb with shock, while two policemen, a detective sergeant from downtown and a sergeant from Westmount, began questioning her. Two other uniformed officers stood guard inside to protect the scene so that nothing would be disturbed until the investigation was finished. Another officer did an overview of the whole scene, what police call a "surveillance."

The investigative work took most of the day, although the officers were certain they knew what had happened within minutes of entering the house. The way Lynne, distraught with guilt and grief, told the story, their marriage had been in terrible trouble. Her husband, she told the policemen, was having a relationship with a young woman who was now pregnant. "The father of the young girl threatened Mr. Verchere that he would make public his daughter being made pregnant — if no compensation was made," an officer stated later. "Everything was going to crumble around him — his career, his family. He decided to commit suicide."

When the police questioned David, Michael, and Greg Williams, they got much the same story. According to these interviews, "there was a threat of a lawsuit from Arthur Hailey. Diane Hailey was in Vancouver right now." The three told the police that Verchere had been a partner at Bennett Jones Verchere in Place Ville Marie and that the firm had offices in Calgary and Toronto. Verchere, they told the officers, "had neglected his work for which his partners had reproached him." David told the police that the family had talked things over and that he and his brother were worried about their father's stability. A few days earlier, he said, "I told my dad I loved him and not to do anything stupid." Williams told the police that "Mr. Verchere had left home a year before and had been back for about a month. He was an emotionally destroyed man." (Williams's estimate of a month was not confirmed by others; most people believed he had been home only ten days or so.)

About half an hour later, the detective sergeant on the scene, who was required to make sure the death had not been a murder, returned to Lynne to ask her more questions. Her answers confirmed what Williams had told him. "She was hurt by his behavior with the other girl," he reported, "but they were trying to get back together. A Dr. Ellman, a psychiatrist, was treating him."

Lynne explained that she and her husband had gone out for dinner the night before. Then, over a bottle of wine, they'd talked "a good part of the night about these events and the malaise that he had caused, as well as a long discussion concerning the other woman," reported the police. The conversation lasted until about 1 a.m. "We fell asleep in each other's arms," Lynne told the police. Then, said one officer, "they woke up about 10 a.m. and were reading the papers and having coffee. The husband gets up and goes to the bathroom."

Verchere left the bedroom, the police concluded, made his way down to the basement where he kept his guns, selected a Sturm, Ruger semi-automatic hunting rifle, chambered two .22-calibre bullets, and quietly climbed back up the stairs to his bathroom. He went in, locked the door, and, still standing, brought the gun up to his face; he stuck the barrel in his mouth, and, using his thumb, pulled the trigger. The rifle's sharp recoil caused his thumb to hit the trigger again instantly and the second shot was fired. The burning gas of the propellant, exploding at 27 to 37 pounds of pressure in his mouth, would have blown his face apart, killing him before the bullets destroyed most of the bones in his face and his skull. Strangely, with such a devastating round of ammunition, there was no exit wound. The gun's bullets are designed so their thin copper tips shred on impact, sending the bullet tumbling around inside the skull before breaking up.

Sometimes the witnesses' stories and the timing of events were a little confused, but that was to be expected. Besides, the police had what they considered definitive evidence of suicide. Bruce had left a letter in his study. There were two sheets of paper. It appeared he had written them the day before, after returning from the AECL board meeting in Ottawa. Whether he wrote the letter in the afternoon, or before they went out for dinner, or after they got home, no one knows. But there they were, on his desk.

One sheet of paper, which he'd numbered "2," was a kind of macabre shopping list — a list of reasons to kill himself:

Transfer of file to S&E
Diane has lawyer
AH is anticipating a court case — extremely unhappy
Clearing[?] Wants to make a case against me
The possession of info from Lynne
He explained D's lawsuit to Janice
Lynne told him everything
I am to know that he has a letter from Lynne to Bruce, 31 March 92 [sic] that he will use only if he has to
He wants to settle
He has the ability to make things public
Lawsuit is a family lawsuit
It's going to be complicated.

The other page, which he'd numbered "1," was a letter to his wife:

27 August

Dear Lynne,
I have made such a mess of my life and caused you so much pain that I cannot bear it any longer. There seems to be no end to the burdens I create for you and the disgrace I bring down upon myself.

It is a hard thing to do but I have decided to end my life. I do this believing it is the right and, in the end, also the honorable thing to do.

Please tell David & Michael that I love them & ask for their forgiveness.

As for you, dear Lynne, please believe this is for the best. I regret so very much all the misery and devastation I have caused to you. I beg for your forgiveness and understanding.

I love you and I always did.

Bruce

TWENTY-THREE
Free From Every Bond

DEATH ARRIVES WITH its own grim bureaucratic chores in any household, even when the circumstances are as wretched and horrifying as these. The police had to do their investigation and their interviews. A doctor had to examine Bruce's body. Ambulance attendants had to remove it from the bathroom, enclose it in a body bag, place it on a stretcher, cover it, and carry it out to a waiting ambulance. In any violent death, the law requires an autopsy. Greg Williams took it upon himself to show the police six other guns Bruce had stored in the basement, and to ask them to take them away, permanently.

Neighbours, strangers, gawkers in the park all hung around, waiting for news of what had happened. Slowly bits and pieces of information began to spread. A silent intake of breath, a widening of eyes, when people saw the men carrying the stretcher to the ambulance. Suicides are not unusual in that area of Montreal; the police see about one a month.

But a violent death like this one, in a huge house on Montrose Avenue, in a neighbourhood where millionaires like Stephen Jarislowsky and Brian Mulroney and Sophie Desmarais were near neighbours, was handled with extreme care and sensitivity. Now, as the police wound up their interviews and the ambulance rolled down the street with the body, and the spectators finally drifted away, it was time for the Vercheres to begin making calls. The job fell to David, who began by phoning close friends. Michael, the quiet one but nonetheless the apple of his father's eye, wept alone in the back yard.

═══

SHEILA HAILEY HAD spent the night at the Airport Hilton in Toronto; her Air Canada flight to Vancouver left at 1:05 p.m. Toronto time. Later on Saturday David Verchere phoned Arthur Hailey to tell him his father had shot himself. Hailey immediately phoned Vancouver and left urgent messages for Jane and Sheila to call; then he was able to get through to Air Canada headquarters in Montreal. The airline sent a message to the flight deck of Sheila's plane asking her to call home as soon as she landed. "I knew it was serious," she said. "He wouldn't have done it otherwise. So I learned from Arthur that Bruce had shot himself." Hailey recorded David's call and the news of the death in his diary, and then — still stunned and disconcerted — found a sheet of writing paper with the letterhead of the Lyford Cay Club, dated it, and wrote: "Today Bruce Verchere committed suicide." He put the paper away among his files.

Sheila, anxious to get to her daughters, asked Arthur to call Janet and Pierre Berton, close friends who knew something of what was going on, to tell them. Jane's husband met Sheila at the airport in Vancouver and drove her to the hospital. "Jane was already there," said Sheila. "They had all heard the news." One of Bruce's Vancouver relatives had telephoned Jane, who broke the news to Diane. Sheila called Arthur from the hospital room to tell him Diane and the twins were well, though it was, of course, a terribly difficult time for her.

That afternoon Pat Dohm was working in his yard when his wife, Barbara, ran outside to tell him what had happened. Immediately she went to the hospital to comfort Diane. It was a long, dreadful day, and that night Sheila slept in the hospital room with her daughter, then spent all the next day with her. When Steven arrived from Menlo Park at 9:30, he took over, staying with Diane while Sheila went back to Jane's house to rest. The Verchere cousins, the Dohms, and the Smiths did everything they could to help.

Very quickly, the news was everywhere. David called Brian Mulroney, who called back at least twice that day; he spoke to David because Lynne refused to talk to him. Ann Bodnarchuk, now suffering from a recurrence of her cancer, arrived to comfort Lynne; the man who looked after the Cessna at Dorval dropped by to pay his respects.

That evening another visitor knocked and asked for Lynne. When she came to the door she found Mila Mulroney standing on the threshold, hoping to come in for a private word of condolence. Lynne stared at her in disbelief and shrieked at her to go away. Then she slammed the door in Mila's face.

THE NEXT MORNING Hailey's first task was to write Lynne, and he thought hard as he poured his writer's talent into composing a letter to console her. The sentiments in the letter were genuine, but Hailey knew exactly what else he was doing: removing the possibility that, later on, any claim could be made against Lynne

Verchere for financial support of Diane, Emma, and Paul. The letter would be Lynne's insurance policy against any such action, which Hailey believed she did not deserve. At the same time, he also realized, he was shouldering that financial responsibility himself.

> August 29, 1993
>
> My dearest Lynne,
> There is so little that can usefully be said and I will not attempt to define with words the tumult that is in all our minds.
>
> I simply wanted you to know that I am thinking about you, and caring, and remembering that in all that has happened during this past year and a half, you are the one who has suffered most, and paid unsought, unjust penalties both mentally and in material ways.
>
> As far as I can, I am taking steps to ensure that you are not bothered any more with concerns over matters which were never, either morally or legally, your responsibility and should not be yours now. Please get in touch with me if there is anything of this nature which happens and should be stopped.
>
> Finally, I trust that later, when time has passed, our friendship will continue; and further, that when you, David and Michael are at Lyford Cay Club, a connection which I hope you will keep, you will all visit the Haileys — Sheila, me, Diane, Emma and Paul — in our home.

With sadness and affection.
Arthur

The time for anger and discord was done. It was time for healing. What mattered to Hailey was that his new grandchildren maintain a relationship with their half-brothers, David and Michael, and with Lynne, too. It may have been an unrealistic hope, but that's what he wanted and that's why he extended the invitation to Lynne.

As the day wore on, Hailey continued to reach out to friends to share this appalling news. One of them was Heward Stikeman. During their talk, Hailey told Stikeman he'd decided to stay with Bennett Jones Verchere after all; Stikeman graciously brushed aside Hailey's apologies. "Friends are friends," he told Hailey. Tired, sad, lonely without Sheila there to share his thoughts, Hailey ate a solitary meal and watched a favourite old movie, *Twelve O'clock High*, before finally turning in. It had been a dreadful, gruelling day.

In Montreal, the horror continued for the Vercheres at Montrose Avenue. Technicians arrived back at the house to look at the bathroom again; Pierre Grégoire, looking out a window from his house next door, saw them leaving by a back entrance, carrying the broken, splintered door.

The following day, Monday, August 30, Montreal coroner Claude Paquin conducted his autopsy. Except for the lack of explanation of the second shot, the report was straightforward. Verchere had been depressed for a long time, wrote Paquin, and had been under psychiatric care. There were no drugs or alcohol found in his system, but his depression may have made him decide to kill himself. There was no evidence to suggest any other person was involved in the death and Paquin's verdict was unequivocal: suicide. (Paquin was in no hurry to record his decision formally; it took him until November 11, nearly two and a half months later, to write his two-page report.) He did not ask, as a few people did, why, if Verchere was known to be so depressed and if he was under psychiatric care, no one had removed the cache of weapons from his basement.

Verchere's family described his suicide note as "a love letter"; that's all that was said to close friends. No one except his wife and the Haileys would have understood it. The four brief paragraphs in which Bruce told Lynne he had decided to take his life were straightforward. His vision was clear: he was the architect of his own misfortune and was responsible for all the pain his wife had suffered. Along with the emotional wreckage he had created, there was the public and professional disgrace he now faced. He asked her to tell Michael and David that he loved them. And, almost as if reassuring himself that the disgrace was real and unavoidable, he listed it all. His brief notes were a clear guide to what was going through his mind that day before he died.

Transfer of file to S&E:
The Haileys planned to move their business to Stikeman Elliott, the very firm that had fired Verchere back in 1973 when he overstepped himself and tried to wrest control of the firm from Heward Stikeman. Wouldn't they gloat at Stikeman's to see that business come their way.

Diane has lawyer:
Not only had he hurt the woman he adored, but he hadn't been able to explain why he had done so. Hearing

she'd hired a lawyer to fight him compounded his guilt and depression.

AH is anticipating a court case – extremely unhappy:
Once Diane's father entered the fray, Verchere knew he had taken on a formidable enemy. If he had found it impossible to tell Diane the truth, how could he face telling Hailey, a much tougher person who, since February 1992, had been his opponent and his wife's ally?

Clearing[?] Wants to make a case against me:
Although the first word of this line was almost unintelligible — was it a name or was he scrawling the word "Clearly"? — the import was obvious. Hailey was building a powerful case against him.

The possession of info from Lynne:
Possibly a reference to material Lynne may have given to Hailey or to others, in case Bruce returned to Diane or resisted the court order to disclose exactly what he did with her money. Was it possible she had kept copies of the material she gave him as part of the conditions of their settlement, the material she was prepared to show to others unless he told Diane to leave Montreal? Or was he simply referring to the documents she had gathered from Jacques Grandmont? Only Lynne Verchere herself could answer these questions.

He explained D's lawsuit to Janice:
Hailey had outlined the gist of Diane's lawsuit to Janice McCart at Bennett Jones Verchere in Toronto. This meant that his partners knew all the sordid details of

their affair, including his abandonment of his pregnant mistress.

Lynne told him everything:
Bruce knew that his wife had kept no family secrets from Hailey, not even about his past indiscretions with other women.

I am to know that he has a letter from Lynne to Bruce 31 March 92 that he will use only if he has to:
This was the long, angry letter Lynne sent to Bruce dated March 19, 1993 (which Hailey received on March 31). This was the letter in which she threatened her husband with court action that would reveal how he had mixed his family's financial affairs with those of unnamed clients.

He wants to settle:
Verchere knew that Hailey, angry as he was, had no wish to put his daughter or, indeed, Lynne through any more grief than they had suffered already. He wanted justice, but he was willing to let the lawyers work out a decent arrangement.

He has the ability to make things public:
Hailey's fame and credibility ensured that if he did hold a press conference, the whole affair would explode in public. Verchere would become a national cad, humiliated, snickered at by former colleagues, pitied by those who still cared for him. Unendurable.

Lawsuit is a family lawsuit:
This could have referred to any of three lawsuits, each one

of them soul-destroying. The first was the injunction into which his boys had been dragged. Even though he knew by now that they were remorseful about their roles, it had been a body blow. Or the line could connect to Lynne's divorce action; her statement of claim laid out his transgressions against the trust which had been set up for his sons. Most probably, however, he was thinking of the lawsuit Hugh Stark was preparing to launch, with Hailey's support, if a settlement wasn't reached for Diane and the babies.

It's going to be complicated:
Weary, sick at heart, guilty, Verchere gave up. Complicated was a word that had once delighted him. He'd made a career of structuring complicated tax deals and hiding money so it could not be traced. He'd kept complicated secrets — from his wife, his mistresses, his partners. Now he evidently no longer had a taste for complication. Let's make it simple. As simple as it gets. He put down his pen, set his notes neatly on his desk, and walked out of the room.

THAT SAME DAY, the business community began to hear the news. One of Verchere's partners phoned the corporate secretary at AECL, who in turn called Marnie Paikin. "Bruce [Howe] then called me," Paikin remembered, "and said, 'I am going to need you to stand by.' Over the next day or two the corporate secretary called people on the board to tell us what was happening and when Bruce's funeral was."

Hailey himself had business to attend to on the Monday. The first thing he did was send Hugh Stark a copy of the fax he'd sent Lynne, with instructions to wind up all the files.

August 30, 1993

Mr. Hugh Stark
Stark and Maclise
Vancouver, BC

Dear Hugh Stark:
Following this page is a copy of a letter I sent yesterday to Ms. Lynne Walters (Verchere).
From September 9 through 16 I will be in Vancouver and at that time will accept responsibility for your account concerning Diane.
Thank you for all that you have done.
Most sincerely,
Arthur Hailey

The proposed lawsuit was cancelled; Diane would no longer be asking for any support from the Vercheres. She paid Stark herself. Arthur and Sheila were giving her a home in the Bahamas, and they would take care of her and the children.

And life went on. That evening there was a supper party at the home of Christiane and Harry Oakes; the next day Hailey flew to Miami for a couple of days for errands and shopping and a lengthy research meeting with Steve Vinson about the new novel. He finished off his day with a new movie, *The Fugitive* ("mostly action, not v/cerebral," he complained in his diary that night), and a lonely dinner at the 15th Street Fisheries

Restaurant ("Think place overrated. Dinner not outstanding").

In Montreal, people were talking about Verchere's sudden death; a notice had appeared in the *Gazette* that morning.

> VERCHERE, Bruce. On Saturday, August 28, 1993 at home. Survived by his dear wife, Lynne and by his sons, Michael and David. The service will be held at Christ Church Cathedral (Phillips Square) on Thursday, September 2 at 3 p.m. with visitation during the hour preceding the service. In lieu of flowers, donations may be made to the Bruce Verchere Memorial Fund for Choral Music c/o the Rt. Rev. Andrew Hutchison, Bishop of Montreal, 1444 Union, Montreal, Quebec, H3A 2S4.

Perhaps not surprisingly, Lynne had failed to mention that Verchere was also survived by two other children, Paul and Emma Hailey.

═══

BY TUESDAY MORNING, August 31, Diane was able to leave the hospital. Steven and Sheila picked her up, and the little family moved into a furnished apartment in the Rosellen Suites on Barclay Street, their home for the next month, until the twins — who had weighed only four and a half pounds each at birth — had gained enough weight for their pediatrician to give the okay for the flight to the Bahamas. "Steven and I went out for a big grocery shop," remembered Sheila, "then he left for the airport to go home to Menlo Park in California. I noted in my daybook we settled down to look after Paul and Emma and work out a plan. After a supper of barbecued chicken, Diane and I went to bed at 10 o'clock and had our first good night's sleep."

As soon as he could track her down, Brian Mulroney called Diane to tell her how sorry he was to hear about Verchere's death and ask her how she was doing; their conversation was brief and emotional.

"I stayed with Diane in the apartment for the whole month," said Sheila. "We looked after the babies together, night and day — a reason I feel so closely bonded with them."

A picture taken by Royal and Linda Smith soon after Diane left the hospital showed the new mother, her slumbering children bundled cosily in their little blankets, her face wan and tired, trying to smile but staring into the camera with haunted eyes.

ON THURSDAY, SEPTEMBER 2, Lynne and her sons prepared for the funeral service. This was not going to be an ordinary funeral, she had vowed. They weren't going to have a mean little service, something to be done quickly and furtively. Bruce would not be "the deceased." He was going to be buried in a style that befitted their station in life. She and the boys were going to hold their heads high; they were going to be proud and gracious. Montreal would never forget this funeral.

She chose the pallbearers with care. Their sons, of course, Michael and David, and David's friend Greg Williams. Two of his law partners, those closest to him

— Bill Britton and Geoffrey Walker. The sixth? Perhaps Royal Smith or Pat Dohm? No. Brian Mulroney.

By this time, Lynne's contempt for the Mulroneys was well known. That they'd condoned — even celebrated — Bruce's liaison with Diane by including her in the invitation to the gala dinner at the National Gallery was unforgivable. Mulroney and his Tory cronies had corrupted Bruce, she told her closest friends. Bruce had been a fine person until these people came into his life to use his talents and turn him into someone else.

So why ask him to be a pallbearer? She knew he could not, in all conscience, refuse. Perhaps the rank of office still impressed her; it would show people just how powerful her husband had been. Maybe she just wanted Mulroney to squirm, to see the end of this sorry business. If she'd known he had called Diane to comfort her, Lynne might have changed her mind.

People still talked years later about the Verchere funeral. His law firm published a funeral notice extending its sympathy to Verchere's family and announcing that the firm's offices in Montreal, Ottawa and Toronto would close at noon that day out of respect for his memory, and so that colleagues from all three cities could attend the service at the cathedral. "It was out of this world," said one of Lynne's close friends. "It was surreal," said a colleague of Bruce. Just transporting the body to Christ Church Cathedral in the heart of Montreal's business centre involved a whole service in itself; mourners were guided by a three-page church bulletin with the sombre heading, "The Reception of the Body of the Late Bruce Verchere at Christ Church Cathedral Montreal." An Anglican priest met the coffin at the door of the church with a brief prayer and a few moments of silence, followed by a second prayer. "Deliver your servant, Bruce, O Sovereign Lord Christ," intoned the priest, "from all evil, and set him free from every bond; that he may rest with all your saints in the eternal habitations; where with the Father and the Holy Spirit you live and reign, one God, for ever and ever."

The Twenty-third Psalm followed; then a responsive prayer with the mourners. "Receive, O Lord, your servant for he returns to you. Wash him in the heavenly font of everlasting life, and clothe him in his heavenly wedding garment. May he hear your words of invitation, 'Come, you blessed of my Father.' May he gaze upon you, Lord, face to face, and taste the blessedness of perfect rest. May angels surround him, and saints welcome him in peace."

When Mulroney arrived, it was in a motorcade with RCMP cars ahead of and behind his limousine. At 2 p.m., people began filing in to pay their respects to Lynne, Michael, and David, who received them near the altar. "There was a solemnity about it," remembered someone who went forward to offer condolences. "The wife and children seemed . . . well, almost noble." Each mourner received another bulletin, ten pages long, titled "Requiem Eucharist for Bruce Verchere September 22, 1936 — August 28, 1993." As Lynne had planned, there were no half-measures about this service. It was led by the Right Reverend Andrew Hutchison, the Anglican Lord Bishop of Montreal, but three other Anglican priests took part: the Reverend Michael Pitts, the dean of Montreal, the Reverend Canon Jan Dijkman, and the Reverend Joan Shanks. Alex Kuihlman served as crucifer, the person who leads the procession down the aisle, carrying the tall crucifix. Gerald Wheeler, the cathedral's director of music, assisted by Michael Capon and the Reverend Stephen Crisp, conducted the combined choirs of the cathedral and of St. Matthias, Westmount. Mourners noted that the family had asked for memorial donations to go to a new fund in Bruce Verchere's name to encourage choral music throughout the Diocese of Montreal.

The choirs performed an introit by William Croft, "Kyrie Eleison," Psalm 121 ("I will lift up mine eyes unto the hills, from whence cometh my help"), "Agnus Dei," and three pieces during the communion service: "Rise, Heart; the Lord Is Risen," "Five Mystical Songs" by Vaughan Williams, and John Gardner's classic, "Tomorrow Shall Be My Dancing Day." The mournful Russian "Kontakion of the Departed" ended the choral presentations. During the service, the congregation joined in the singing of four of the great hymns of the Christian church: "Thou Whose Almighty Word," "I Heard the Voice of Jesus Say," "The Strife Is O'er, the Battle Done," and finally, as the recessional hymn, the mighty "For All the Saints."

When Michael Verchere rose to read the first scripture lesson from St. Paul's letter to the Corinthians, giving Paul's famous sermon on charity and love, the congregation were moved to reflect on their own failings and weaknesses. "Though I speak with the tongues of men and angels," he began, "and have not charity, I am become as sounding brass, or a tinkling cymbal." Brian Mulroney listened carefully, looking stricken and worn. Michael continued, "Charity suffereth long, and is kind; charity envieth not; charity vaunteth not itself, it is not puffed up; doth not behave itself unseemly, seeketh not her own, is not easily provoked, thinketh no evil; rejoiceth not in iniquity, but rejoiceth in the truth."

When it was David's turn to read, he chose Revelation, chapter 21, the wonderful passage we so often associate with William Blake's hymn "Jerusalem." "And I saw a new heaven and a new earth," David read, "for the first heaven and the first earth were passed away; and there was no more sea. And I John saw the holy city, new Jerusalem, coming down from God out of heaven, prepared as a bride adorned for her husband. And God shall wipe away all tears from their eyes: and there shall be no more death, neither sorrow, nor crying, neither shall there be any more pain: for the former things are passed away."

Again and again through this service, the music and scriptures and prayers seemed to have been written especially for the deeply troubled man who had flown so high, consorted with prime ministers and presidents, tasted riches, enjoyed so many pleasures. The congregation wept openly at the tragedy of his wasted life.

In his generous homily, in which he called Bruce "the boy from Kamloops," Bishop Hutchison did not try to gloss over what had happened. "We find ourselves with feelings of guilt and helplessness," he said. "Is there something I could have done to rescue him from the melancholy and despair which rendered him unreachable at a level we could not know, or understand? If we could have an answer it would probably be no; for as responsible as we are for one another in love, there remain mysteries which we understand neither in ourselves or in others."

Hutchison did not know Bruce as well as the previous bishop, but he had met him a few times and he was close to Lynne. In his homily, he spoke of the relationship he had had with this tormented man: "Bruce reached out to me in his time of distress as he did to some of you, so I share with you some of your feelings," he said. Still, Hutchison seemed to know little of the real story behind the terrible last few months. People squirmed when he followed a glowing tribute to Verchere's professional success with a view of his private life. Commenting on Paul's belief about the nature of love — that success counts for nothing "if it is not enlightened by love" — Hutchison added, "It is only how we have loved that will be of life-giving value to us and to those who follow us. Bruce did not do badly on that score. He was a family man who preferred an evening at home with his wife and family to an evening out." The silence in the cathedral was awkward; it seemed to last an eternity.

Hutchison continued, this time to praise his relationship with his sons. "Michael and David speak of the tremendous commitment of time and support for his sons in every situation. 'He was always there just looking on — never obtrusive, demanding or judgmental — just always there with a soft smile and some good advice.' Michael adds, 'He used to joke that we were lucky not to have to pay for his advice.' Speaking of the rich variety of experience his father shared with the boys, travelling, skiing, hunting, fishing, just being with them, he concludes, 'You could not ask for a better father.' A year ago David had said to me, 'He is my best friend.' What better tribute could a father receive?"

Hutchison also seemed unaware of the dreadful irony when he exhorted, "Be there for your families! It is the one legacy worth leaving them, for it echoes a love which gives life and courage."

The coffin, carried by Michael, David, Williams, Walker, Britton, and Mulroney, left the church; the hearse, followed by many mourners, took it to the Mount Royal Crematorium for cremation and the final committal. After that the family drove to the University Club, where they held a reception. Mulroney didn't attend the reception, but he had the last word on the day, one that the people who heard him will never forget. Turning to Bill Britton, Mulroney tried to inject a little levity by cracking a joke. "You know what we Irish say about funerals," he grinned. "The bigger the guilt, the bigger the funeral."

TWENTY-FOUR
Ties of Blood

TWO DAYS AFTER the funeral, Arthur Hailey called Lynne to offer his sympathy. She seemed glad of the chance to talk openly to someone from whom she had no secrets. They spoke twice that day. "Not surprisingly," he wrote in his diary, "she was very emotional." What did surprise him was her new attitude to her husband. Hailey was a realist, blunt and tough. Although he grieved for both Lynne and his own daughter, he was surprised to hear Lynne "converting Bruce to sainthood."

The legal thrashing Lynne had given her husband had backfired in the most brutal way possible — with his destroyed body, cradled by his own son, lying in a blood-splashed bathroom in her own house. His revenge could not have been more complete. David and Michael were as wretched as she was; they tore themselves apart for having signed affidavits against their father. Even Lynne's lawyer Raynold Langlois, who'd done his best for a client who had been deeply wronged, was devastated. "He felt as if he had pulled the trigger himself," said one of his colleagues.

Everyone who'd been close to Verchere claimed some part of the blame. "If only I'd called him that last night," mourned Royal Smith, eyes welling with tears, "I could have talked him out of it, offered him some help, some money. Linda and I would have done anything." Some of

Verchere's law partners and a few of his new board colleagues at AECL blamed themselves, too; their sins, they believed, were in not recognizing the signs of a desperate man at the end of his courage and his hope.

Arthur Hailey would not speak ill of the dead but could not share these sentiments. To Hailey, Verchere was a man who had betrayed his wife, stolen her fortune, and lied to her; who had ordered his pregnant lover out of Montreal with no place to go, no money, and no word of comfort to sustain her. What he had done was despicable, and no amount of post-funeral sanctimony could make the facts more acceptable. Hailey's view was more along the lines of those who thought that the calculated act of killing oneself in one's own home, for family to discover and deal with, violated the unwritten code among gentlemen. It was unforgivable.

On September 13, little more than a week after the funeral, Lynne's lawyers discreetly filed a document in a Montreal courtroom withdrawing her divorce action and closing that file. Another was opened: Verchere's will, which had not been changed since it was drawn up in 1982. It left everything he owned to Lynne, David, and Michael. There was no last-minute provision for Paul and Emma, nor any remembrance for Diane; even if he had wanted to find a way to leave them something, of course, by the end he'd had nothing left to give. Among the papers in his home were clients' files, including a thick one labelled "Mulroney." Lynne gave it to him.

Arthur and Sheila arranged for Diane to move into a new townhouse on a canal just a few blocks from their own place in Lyford Cay. Large, sunny, and comfortable, the house, painted in Lyford Cay's ubiquitous shell pink, gave Diane her independence and a place to raise the children on her own, while allowing her to be close enough to rebuild a relationship with her father that had been so difficult for nearly two years.

Just as Hailey made it easy for his daughter to adjust to her new circumstances, he made it easy for Lynne to stop worrying about a possible lawsuit from his side. In early fall, while he and Sheila were making final arrangements for Diane and the children to move to the Bahamas, he wrote to her in Montreal.

September 22, 1993

Dear Lynne —
I do not wish to intrude either on your privacy or your grief, and if you do not wish to respond to this note I shall understand and will not bother you again.

My reason for writing now is simply to let you know I have not changed my opinion that, during this past sad and finally tragic year, you are the one who has suffered most in every way.

For a while you and I were able to be mutually supportive, even though only by telephone, and though it seems so long ago, I valued those exchanges and you made it clear that you did too.

And even now, although changes, sadness, and complexities exist which neither of us ever dreamed would happen . . . if at any time you wish to talk or unburden yourself to this former friend who would like to remain a friend, I am available — not to debate, nor argue, or disagree about blame, some of which, alas, attaches to all of us, including me — but simply to be a listener to anything you may wish to say, which at times of grief and trouble can sometimes be of help.

I am alone, at home, for the time being until September 30, though I may go briefly to New York in the intervening time. In the daytime I am not taking phone calls, but if you tell whoever answers it is Lynne, they will immediately put you through.

As I said to begin, this is my last communication if you wish it thus.

But whether it is, or isn't, this message comes to you with my affection and fond remembrance.

Arthur

Aside from his pity and fondness for Lynne, Hailey took the long view. For twenty-four years he had been connected to the Vercheres as Bruce's client and as a friend to them both. What was different now was the ties of blood that would always bind them together. Paul and Emma were half-brother and half-sister to David and Michael, and this, in Hailey's eyes, was a precious relationship. Forget everything that had happened; let these wonderful young people get to know each other, become friends. Whatever he and Sheila could do to keep this family tie between the children strong, they would. And one sure way to encourage it, he imagined, was to release Lynne from any sense of obligation. Lynne never responded to his letters, nor to his suggestion that someday she and the boys visit the Haileys in Lyford Cay. Few could blame her, including Hailey himself, though he had hoped for the sake of the children that someday she might yield.

AUTUMN THAT YEAR was beautiful, but most Canadians barely noticed; they were engrossed — watching television, talking over back fences and on open-line radio shows — in the campaign for the federal election that Prime Minister Kim Campbell had called ten days after Verchere's suicide. The election was set for October 25, and the six weeks leading up to it became an unmitigated, historic disaster for the Conservatives. Campbell herself had not won an easy victory in June; at the last minute there was a determined effort by Mulroney and a number of his closest allies to derail her leadership campaign and ensure victory for Sherbrooke MP Jean Charest.

Though she took the leadership, it was a squeaker, and many Tories faded away, unwilling to get involved in an election campaign which the polls were predicting would end in a Liberal majority. Leading the flight to safety were a group of senior cabinet ministers who'd decided to move to better-paying havens in the private sector and who declined even to campaign. Infighting and serious mistakes in campaign strategy eroded the energy of those who remained; large corporate donations dried up halfway through the campaign; and when the party finally had to yank negative television advertisements which pointed out Liberal leader Jean Chrétien's facial paralysis — ads that appalled the Canadian electorate — the Tories knew they were doomed.

No one could have predicted how bad it would be. By the end of election night, the Liberals had taken 178 seats, the separatist Bloc Québécois had become the official opposition with 54 seats, and Preston Manning's western-based Reform Party had come in third with 52 seats. The New Democratic Party lost ground, limping in with only nine seats, but it was the Tories who were utterly demolished. Having begun the campaign with 154 seats, they struggled in with exactly two: one in New Brunswick, belonging to Elsie Wayne, and the other, Jean Charest's seat in Sherbrooke. And they wound up more than $7 million in debt — this in a party which had refined fundraising to a high art, setting records for the cash they'd hauled in over the previous nine years.

The stunning reversal focused Canadians' attention on federal politics that fall and, amid scandalous disclosures of sleaze and greed during the Tory years, few people gave a second thought to the minor player on Mulroney's team who had disappeared so abruptly and so tragically.

═══

FOR LYNNE THERE SEEMED no end of things to do in the wake of her husband's suicide. One of the least pleasant tasks was having to deal with Bruce's lawyer, Claude-Armand Sheppard, who sent her the bills for all the work he'd done defending Bruce against her injunction. She paid, but found it impossible to be friendly to him. She also set about getting rid of the properties and playthings, which were draining her resources. She sold the camp in Pretty Marsh for $925,000 (U.S.), said Gary Fountain, a good price and well over the $685,000 they had paid for it. *Niska*, Verchere's beloved sailboat, was also sold, though the price was undisclosed. Lynne sold the Cessna and the float plane; again, the prices are not known. She did less well on the sale of the condominium in Telluride; it went for about $590,000 (U.S.), still a slight gain over the $550,000 purchase price.

In Lyford Cay, meanwhile, the Haileys settled into a comforting routine. Through the winter of 1993 and into 1994, Arthur was hard at work on his new novel. The story of an ex-priest who had lost his faith, become a cop, hunted down depraved killers, and damaged his own police career by standing up for what he believed in, it absorbed him completely. Hailey's plot was intricate and daring, pulling the reader into layered subplots and flashbacks that could have made the book impossibly complicated. As he wrote, he found he had a new reader to please: Diane. Not long after she moved to Lyford Cay, she began using her experience as a script editor in Los Angeles to work with her father on the novel. Both found this partnership productive and enjoyable. It gave them a new professional relationship, something positive to build on after two years of sadness and anger.

What really helped to heal the bitterness, though, was the deep love the Haileys felt, right from the start, for Paul and Emma. These two, with their red hair and startling resemblance to their father, were a joy to their grandparents.

The Haileys' delight in the children shows clearly in the New Year's card they sent in January 1994. An annual tradition, the card sported a new family picture each year; that year the photo showed off the beaming grandparents and mother, holding two plump and healthy babies. Inside, Sheila wrote:

> Wow! I waited a long time to be a grandmother — but this is truly amazing.
>
> In July 1992 little Charlotte came into our lives — the beautiful daughter of Steven and his wife Susan.
>
> Then on August 25, 1993 Diane gave birth to twins, Paul and Emma Hailey — each weighing four-and-a-half pounds — at Grace Hospital, Vancouver. Dr Jane Hailey, our pediatrician daughter, was present at the birth.
>
> Diane is now living nearby in Lyford Cay and, to our great delight, Arthur and I have become involved, hands-on grandparents.

Tactfully, the Haileys did not send the card to Lynne. In recent months, in fact, Hailey had lost touch with her. She hadn't responded to his September letter, when he'd left it up to her to decide if she wanted to remain friends. It was not until May, eight months later, that she finally phoned. She talked about how she was coping and what had been going on in her life. One positive step had been her work setting up the Athena Foundation, an organization to assist well-to-do women with their finances, women who in many cases had little self-confidence and little idea how to manage their money. Here, meeting in Lynne's living room, women could get investment advice and educate themselves. The group became the talk of Montreal's wealthy classes. "It wasn't like other investment clubs," said a friend of both women. "This one would get people from Lazard Frères or Warburgs to advise the women on their investments."

Despite Lynne's Tory background, Prime Minister Chrétien had kept her on as chairman of the Official

Residences Council. One memorable visit she made in her official capacity was to the Citadel in Quebec City, one of the governor general's residences; her sons went with her. She had also agreed to help develop a computer system to make charities more efficient, she told Hailey, and was doing some work with an American foundation. Still, as she admitted to Hailey, coping wasn't easy, and one of the ways she managed was simply to cocoon — staying close to home with friends and family.

Hailey listened with interest and affection, feeling deeply sorry for her, not just because of what she'd been through but because she seemed detached from reality. For the first twenty-seven years she and Bruce had had a good marriage, she insisted. Bruce spent all his time with her and the boys, and wanted to shelter her from the world. At the end, she said, their dream had been to grow old together. She said she wanted to forget the last two years.

Dealing with the detritus of Bruce's life had been grim; she'd had to clean up all his office files and sort out their business affairs. Bruce had been very sick, she told Hailey, and again she spoke of the money he'd squandered. Finances were still a mess, she confided. The yacht had been a big investment, and there was still a lot of cash missing. Tax had been paid twice on some of their income. On a personal level things hadn't been any better; Bruce, she admitted, hadn't even seen their sons in the year before he came home. Still, she insisted, the boys hadn't been hurt.

She told Hailey she thought Bruce's decline had started when he stopped practising law at Bennett Jones Verchere. He became obsessed with his toys, and in his last year, she said, he'd become mean to her. "He had no one else to be mad at," she explained. "I regret I didn't see this." Diane's pregnancy, she suggested, had made her husband feel trapped and embarrassed. He'd grown horribly depressed and had lost weight.

Recalling past injuries, Lynne became more and more upset. "Contempt is close to hate," she commented solemnly. "Bruce wasn't blameless."

Her conversation turned to complaints against Hailey's wife and daughter. The world didn't understand how Dianc and Sheila could have behaved the way they did, she insisted. "I don't respect them," she told Hailey. "I don't want anything to do with them. I'm terrified I will be hurt again. I want to protect my two children."

By the end of the call, Lynne was despondent. As far as she was concerned, she said in her parting shot, Bruce was simply a sperm donor for Diane. Hailey flinched and hung up.

At 7:30 the next morning the phone rang. It was Lynne again. This time, she said firmly, she wanted to speak to both him and Sheila. Sheila moved to another extension, and Lynne began by referring to earlier conversations with Arthur, when he'd tried to help and comfort her. Then, assured they were both listening, Lynne read out a list of three demands. The first was that Arthur, Sheila, and Diane stop referring to Bruce as the father of Diane's children. "Specifically," wrote Hailey in the notes he made while she spoke, "we should say that Diane was impregnated at a sperm bank." (Lynne may not have known that Bruce had left a signed document certifying that he was the father of the children.) "We should refuse to discuss with anyone, including our friends, the subject of the children's parentage."

Someone had evidently shown Lynne the Haileys' New Year's card, because it triggered her second demand. "We should not send out anything similar to the Haileys' New Year's card featuring the children. (Note — this card did not refer to Bruce V. at all)," Hailey wrote. The third demand was that "Sheila and Diane should send a letter to Lynne stating that at no time in the future will they make any financial claim against Lynne concerning Diane's children."

This demand especially infuriated Hailey, who had twice taken pains to let Lynne know that she would never receive a claim. "Note," Hailey stated in his diaries, "no such claim has been made, nor will one ever be made. Further, immediately after the children's birth, A.H. sent a letter to Lynne making the above clear and it is accepted by the Haileys that Lynne has no financial responsibility whatever so far as the children are concerned."

Just as upsetting as Lynne's demands was her attitude. "Lynne accompanied the above demands with derogatory statements concerning Diane and Sheila," Hailey noted. "Lynne further states that failure by A., S. & Diane to agree with the foregoing would cause her to take 'fighting steps' against the Haileys, including publicity, particularly against Diane, based on documents she holds."

Hailey, finally, had run out of sympathy. "Under no circumstances will Sheila or I respond to threats," he told Lynne angrily, "and specifically we will not comply with your ridiculous demands." As for her threat to take "further action," Hailey didn't budge. "Go ahead," he said. "Do anything you want. You need to see a psychiatrist, Lynne. You're sick."

Epilogue

ARTHUR AND SHEILA HAILEY sent out their annual New Year's card in January 1996 with a picture of themselves on the beach with Charlotte, Paul, and Emma. "Ever tried to take a photo of three squirming grandchildren?" Sheila wrote. "Ain't easy. Here's the best of 55 attempts on New Year's Day. Two-year-old twins, Paul and Emma, continue to delight us every day, while the annual visit of three-year-old Charlotte from California is an added bonus. Arthur is marvellous. Almost 76, he exercises for 15 minutes, then walks for 40 minutes every morning, seven days a week. A tad compulsive, maybe, but look at the result! He's still slowly producing the concluding chapters of his new novel, which he plans to finish by May. Expect publication late '96 or early '97." In turn, Hailey wrote his own note: "Sheila ages gracefully, don't you think? She's still a tennis buff, also a computer whiz — she produced this card on her faithful Compaq."

The only hint of trouble was that Hailey's book was coming slowly. His work had been delayed by the terrible news that his good friend and researcher, Steve Vinson, had died in Florida of a heart attack. Hailey's eleventh novel, *Detective*, finally appeared in the summer of 1997. Well before its North American publication, nineteen foreign publishers had bought rights to the book — in Germany, Brazil, Spain, France, Hungary, and Russia, for starters — with more to come. Reviewers were surprised by the rich plotting and character development; the usual meticulous research was still there, but this time there was more. "I'm sure I'm not the only mystery reader who assumed Hailey was in his dotage, living out retirement in sunny splendor in the Bahamas," wrote Jaimie Hubbard in the *Financial Post*. "While he may be doing that he must still have his faculties because with this newest novel he has written an intriguing, coherent mystery. It's his best work since the early successes with *Hotel* and *Airport*."

In early September 1997, Hailey was scheduled to sail with Sheila on the *Queen Elizabeth II* for England to do a lecture tour and book signings for nine days before going on to Munich for the German launch of the novel. Just before he was due to leave the Bahamas, he felt tightness in his chest during his morning walk. A checkup at a Florida clinic showed he needed a triple heart bypass. At first he demurred, saying he'd had a great life and would settle for angioplasty, a much less complicated procedure. In a letter to a friend, Sheila described what happened next. "When Diane heard about this, she exploded: 'That's nuts — like committing suicide! It's a selfish decision and all your family loves you and wants you around for a while.' Arthur gallantly did a complete about-face. So Diane is the heroine of the family right now — bless her!" Hailey recovered well from this second bypass operation and has enjoyed seeing *Detective* sell more than a million copies around the world. It's his last novel, he insists; from now on, except for a small history of Lyford Cay he's working on, he's through writing books.

Only the people closest to Hailey, and to Lynne Verchere, would have understood a scene in *Detective* in which he made use of recent events in his own life. The scene revolves around a wealthy businessman who has found out that his much younger, thirty-three-year-old mistress is pregnant. When Malcolm Ainslie, Hailey's detective, visits the woman, she tells him she is expecting twins and that she has met with a lawyer for her lover's family, who has offered her a deal. On condition that she never use his family's name for her babies, the businessman would support her. But there was an extra safeguard to ensure that his family's name would never be associated with the children: she "would have to certify under oath, in a legal document, that her pregnancy resulted from fertilization in a sperm bank, with an anonymous donor. Documentation would then be obtained from a genuine sperm bank to confirm the arrangement." In the novel, the woman agrees to the offer. Her lover not only has a mistress pregnant with twins, but he owes gambling debts to Florida mobsters who are threatening him. Early one morning, to avoid a public scandal, he shoots himself at his desk.

AFTER BRUCE'S DEATH, Lynne Verchere steadfastly maintained that her late husband was a good man corrupted by his association with Mulroney's Conservatives. In the 1995 by-election in the riding of St. Henri–Westmount, she worked as a volunteer for the Liberal candidate, Lucienne Robillard, who won the election.

Slowly, Lynne returned to a more public life, taking part in several charity galas, escorted by some old, trusted male friends. On June 21, 1996, she sold the

Montrose Avenue house for $960,000 to Andrew Howick, a wealthy manufacturer of jeans and children's wear, and moved to an apartment in the Château, a fashionable old apartment building on Sherbrooke Street in Montreal. Before she left her house, in the fall of 1996, she held a farewell party, hiring well-known Montreal caterer René Pankalla to prepare the food. She also took trips to Europe with groups of friends, often to study architectural sites, sometimes with Phyllis Lambert, the founder of the Canadian Centre for Architecture in Montreal, as their guide. Not long ago, she moved to New York, where she lives in a large apartment on East 75th Street on the city's Upper East Side overlooking Central Park, one of the best addresses in New York. She's been working with David to help him develop his advertising business. "Lynne is lonely," says one good friend. "She's still basically devastated," says another.

BRUCE VERCHERE is all but forgotten these days. All the hunting gear and fishing tackle, the clothes and boots and odds and ends he kept stowed at the Griffith Island Club are still there. So far, despite reminders from the club, no one has come to get them. It makes the staff sad to see them; they liked Bruce and they believe his kids, someday, might like to have these things.

Verchere's paper empire of shell companies and offshore accounts has evaporated — almost. There's still one bank account left at Bar Harbor Banking & Trust in Southwest Harbor, Maine, where the camp and the boat were sold. Just one account — the other seven were closed years ago. It's account number 777-509488, the account for Niska Inc., the company that owned Verchere's Hinckley sailboat. Niska is still controlled by Thunder Investments Inc., and Thunder is still controlled by the Geneva bank Darier Hentsch & Cie. Nat Fenton, Verchere's lawyer in Maine, still has the signing authority on the account. Earlier this year there was about $40,000 in the account. Whose money is it? Why was it left there?

Bruce Verchere always did like a secret.

DIANE, PAUL, AND EMMA HAILEY no longer live in Lyford Cay; Diane believes they are better off living near their cousins in the United States and attending a regular school. She and her parents are in touch every day.

David Verchere lives in New York where he runs his own small advertising company, the Verchere Group.

Michael Verchere lives and works in Halifax.

Greg Williams is a lobbyist in Ottawa.

Martha O'Brien is happily married.

Marc Noël is a judge in the appeals division of the Federal Court of Canada.

Ross Eddy has retired from Bennett Jones Verchere and lives in Cobourg, on the shores of Lake Ontario.

Bill Britton has retired as chairman and managing partner of Bennett Jones Verchere.

Heward Stikeman, at eighty-five, remains a force in Montreal's legal community and spends the winter months in Florida and Lyford Cay. His only concession to age is that he no longer flies his Cessna.

Arthur Campeau spent several years as Canada's ambassador on the environment. Today he does international environmental consulting and lives in Montreal.

Peter Tolnai lives in Toronto, where he runs his own investment company, Orchard Capital.

Larry Smith, after serving as commissioner of the Canadian Football League, is now the head of his old team, the Montreal Alouettes.

Manac Solutions continues to sell legal software systems to law firms out of its offices in Place Ville Marie.

Brian Mulroney is a partner at Ogilvy Renault in Montreal and lives on Forden Crescent in Westmount, around the corner from Montrose Avenue. In the summer of 1998 he was appointed a Companion of the Order of Canada.

Bennett Jones Verchere closed its Montreal office in the spring of 1998; later that year they dropped the name "Verchere" from the firm's letterhead.

Index

INDEX

ALSO BY STEVIE CAMERON

ON THE TAKE: Crime, Corruption and Greed in the Mulroney Years

Stevie Cameron's stunning exposé of greed and crime in the Mulroney era is a Canadian publishing phenomenon. The widespread corruption the public suspected during Brian Mulroney's regime is confirmed and detailed in this meticulous journalistic account. *On the Take* is compelling, gossipy, required reading for all Canadians.

Seal Books/ISBN: 0-7704-2708-1